THE GURU
OF
JERUSALEM.

IN THE SHADOW OF JAMES K BAXTER

DOUG McPHILLIPS

Guru of Jerusalem: In the shadow of James K Baxter.

Also by Doug McPhillips

Novels:

From Darkness to Light.

The Sword of Discernment.

Santiago Traveller.

I, Prophet.

Masters at my Table.

Biography.

We is me Upside Down.

Travel guide:

Camino Guide book.

Albums.

Country Camino.

Santiago Traveller.

C: Doug McPhillips 2021.

Apart from any fair dealing for purpose of private study, research, criticism or review, as permitted under Copyright. No party may be reproduced by any process whatsoever without the editors written permission. this book is a work of fact and fiction giving rise to research herein.

ISBN 978-163649005-2.

The National Library of Australian Catalogue -in publication data:

Autobiography of James K.Baxter: A Portrait W.H. Oliver 1987. Life of James K Baxter. Frank McKay.1990. Alcoholics Anonymous Big Book references. The Oxford History of New Zealand Literature. Notes referenced throughout this book detailed in acknowledgments.

Introduction.

James K Baxter was born in Dunedin, New Zealand on 26th June 1926 of strong Scottish hardy parents of altogether different backgrounds. In order to gain an insight into the character of this unique and largely unknown poet of the twentieth century, one needs to search the spirit of his ancestors to get a real glimpse into the poetic boy genius who grew to become a man of many contradictions- sullen youth overtly brooding on sex, religion and death; wild man who grieved his imperfections and was draped in them, family man, prayerful and unqualified academic lecturer, poet, long haired drop-out founder of a community of the casualties of society, raging alcoholic and deviate. It is essential to this work to follow the shadow of the man for it parallels the life of another, that is essentially me. It is by looking into the shadow land of another of poetic persuasion that I may indeed get a glimpse into my own defects of character, my craving for an inner spiritual acceptance with my Lord and my God, whilst struggling with my inner demons namely my alcoholism; attempting to work on the death of my ego to be somewhat born again.

Baxter is the genius and I am but a shadow of his ability; a hack writer, would-be poet, composer of songs and musical rhyme. So in drawing back the curtain on his ancestors, his genius of spirit, not just his poetic genius, I may align my real self with his shadow to see and learn benefits of what makes us tick as creatives. It may uncover more truth about the relationship of the linear logical conscious mind with that of the imagination and how the two merge or are opposed to each other. To do this I have taken the liberty of taking a leaf out of the works, books and information provided by the genius and for whom I give full acknowledgement in my table of contents as source material. For to delve a little into the spirit of the man and find the logic of his egocentricity and mine, my cause here is.

So much has been written by literal geniuses, poetic critics and those who have the gift of journalism on Baxter that I see no reason to go down that path. For me I would rather focus on Baxter the human being and to some extent go back in time to evaluate his family tree, to uncover the where and why of him in the land of the long white cloud. That is to consider how much he achieved and did not of his own grievous fault, of his foibles, fantasies and cult like leadership for those less fortunate than himself. The clues lie in his poetry and his lifestyle. Here I take the liberty to delve into the suffering of one who lived on the same knife edge of those he ultimately sought to help. I should state from the outset that I take the liberty throughout this little work to sometimes call the poet James or Baxter or JKB, dependent upon my viewpoint of the man at any given point of writing. From time to time I may have an opinion of him that may resonate in me personal feelings of respect, dismay, amazement or disgust depending upon the facts of which I write. You need not be privy to why I have done this, for I have my own personal reasoning for doing so which has really nothing to do with the content of the facts herein. Accept it as my indulgence if you will and forgive me for doing so. Baxter's journey from atheist to a follower of the way of Christ's cross are clues only to the dying of his ego and his untimely death at the age of only forty six years, it left much unfinished business.

This little work is devoted to no particular person, but may have more appeal to those like me who are looking to a way forward through their own psychological difficulties. To put ones boat of personality upon a new river of life, trim the sail and follow the current to wherever and whatever it brings is a new beginning. All it takes is just a small touch of the rudder every now and then to stay on course. James K Baxter found this towards his end. We who admire the man for his genius may somehow now realise that most of his life he lived in his ego, and had major defects of character as I and most humans do. The kink in his armour to some degree parallels mine, in a sense of inferiority and low self esteem. The wake up call to move from abandonment to acceptance, from alcoholism to sober manhood, childhood to adult in considerations of others before ones self is my own objective. My efforts here I trust I have achieved what I set out to do. Thus, I can move out of the shadow land of my own disillusion and out of that of Baxter as this book is complete..

JKB's last poem, expresses disillusionment with bourgeois Christianity, with the educational and cultural institutions of city life. It is the poem 'Ode to Auckland' that depicts Auckland as a loathsome place lacking in humanity. It was written as a kind of a joke voiced by a humanist and pacifist with a Christian bent, in his search for the inner Christ. JKB had met at universities many youthful followers of a materialistic classical Christ of the version he had satirised in his 'The Holy neighbours' poem of 1971. He had glossed over that poem in his reading at the University of Canterbury in July that year. 'If you live in a Church you're a Church member, you'll always find some of the Pharisees around, you may love them but you don't want actually to be associated with them. This is a distressing fact if you yourself are a humanist.' I might add, for if you do they will ultimately kill your spirit too. In my own lifetime, I have experienced these types in the political sphere, in corporate life, in the Church, in society at large, but to a lesser degree within Alcoholics Anonymous. Suffice to say that in AA more of the followers of the programme live the steps and traditions of the founding fathers, for they have a genuine interest in the human spirit and less interest in the individualism of ego maniacs. The old slogan 'Judge not, less you yourself be judged' rings true for the masses of men and women whom I have grown to love in AA. I have been sober for a considerable time now and keen to hear fellow alcoholic's stories, what happened to them, what changed and what it's like now. It's the lessons I hear and learn from the depth of their hearts that keeps me coming back. I dare say, James K. Baxter, a dyed in the wool alcoholic like me, came to believe in that Higher Power in a moment of complete powerlessness like I myself had done. So in the spirit of of letting go to the slow work of God i trust you gain in the miracle of the fateful tale I tell here.

Table of Contents.

Introduction	Page	3.
Chapter 1. A New Jerusalem.	Page	7.
Chapter 2. Spirits of the Ancestors.	Page	15.
Chapter 3. Fond Farewells & New Horizons.	Page	27.
Chapter 4. The Power of the Written Word.	Page	39.
Chapter 5. Days of Wine and Roses.	Page	49.
Chapter 6. From Apathy to Empathy.	Page	65.
Chapter 7. The Way to Orthodoxy.	Page	73.
Chapter 8. A Geographical to Asia.	Page	81.
Chapter 9. A Man of Letters.	Page	91.
Chapter 10. The Calling of the Pacifist.	Page	101.
Chapter 11. A Vision for Junkies.	Page	109.
Chapter 12. The Guru of Jerusalem.	Page	119.
Chapter 13. The Dying of the Light.	Page	129.
Chapter 14. Poets of a Common Denominator.	Page	139.
Chapter 15. Acknowledgments.	Page	159.

A thing or two worthy of comment regarding AA and my shadow self. "I made it to AA through a recommendation of a fellow Alcoholic in rehabilitation after a fall down the hole of depression, confusion and anxiety of which the mental turmoil seemed to be only quenchable by another drink. The band-aid of being in the grip of the grape worked for a while but then, whilst under the influence one night, I finally cracked into a screaming mess. To be fair it was not all to do with the grog, for I had in that year had a multitude of personal tragic events that beset me and the course of my alcoholism increased at a level that could only result in a massive breakdown of all that I thought my life was about. My mind was a wall of pain and suffering and my heart was torn apart. I had lost my way. I was falling deep into a hole, into the dragon's mouth of hell on earth and misery. It was a calamity I could see no way out of and I crashed. My ego self lost all meaning for existence and I was on the edge of suicide more than once. My cry for help came with the guidance of a fellow patient who suggested AA. It was there I came to realise that I was powerless; came to believe in a power greater than self and thus began my journey of handing over to that power whom I choose to call God. It was whilst I was still in the depressed state that I overcame the desire for alcohol in my first six months of the AA programme, but it took another couple of stays in rehab before I could see my way clear to begin to really let go. It was learning to free-fall into the dragons mouth with no expectations but to let go my fears that the change began to happened. The miracle of my journey inward first began as I walked the Camino de Santiago, that famous pilgrim's pathway in the north of Spain. I had entered the dragon's mouth and it turned into a lotus flower of creative ideas. By chance I had written a poem about my grandfather and it was from this that a song emerged and a miracle happened and is still unfolding. For in a new way of living I am learning to accept my shadow self, my alcoholism and a new found spiritual consciousness in creative expression. It is in this regard that I view the life of another of similar disposition, with me as the shadow self of of one, James K. Baxter. "

Doug McPhillips,

Autumn 2021. (author of this story herein,)

CHAPTER 1.

A NEW JERUSALEM

The Sisters of Our Lady of Compassion were in Wellington to search for one of their own who had gone missing from the nursing home where she resided. We shall call her Sister Clair to protect her anonymity for that is how she would have liked it had she lived long enough to read this story. This humble Nun had known James Baxter during his spiritual struggle for conversion to Catholicism, his pain filled steps to recovery from Alcoholism, his escape from the clutches of his ego as an honoured poet and his Guru like stance in establishing a commune for lost souls at Jerusalem, a small Maori settlement beside the Wanganui River, some sixty six kilometres from Whanganui and a further hundred and twenty clicks north of Wellington.

Sister Claire had been missing for four days and nights in Wellington where the local police, volunteers, nursing home staff and her godly companions of the Sisters of Compassion helped in a desperate search for her whereabouts. The police suspected fowl play as did the age care nursing home staff, but the Sisters of Compassion would have none of it, for they trusted in the power of God to work a miracle and see the good sister back safely. As it turns out she did return, for Sister Clair was found wandering in a back street of Wellington city dressed in her pyjamas. When found the poor Nun was bewildered and with amnesia and with no recall as to the events of the past week. Her bright blue eyes had a mystic brightness about them and the smile on her lips was a replica of the Mona Lisa. Apart from the memory lapse she appeared to be in good health and her pyjamas were still relatively clean despite living on the street for four days and nights. The only comical thing about the whole event was the cardboard sign that hung from her neck when she was found. It read: " I am cracked, that's how the light get's in."

Jerusalem, the little Maori settlement at a narrow bend upstream on the Wanganui River is the location of the Sisters of Compassion mission established in1883 to teach devotion to Jesus for the Maori. It was Sister Clair's last location before she ultimately passed away in a Wellington Nursing home. It was on my visit to Jerusalem that I first heard the history of the Order of the Sisters of Compassion and was introduced to James Baxter's poetry, learnt about his life and the commune he had founded nearby for the misfits of society.

I had been tramping the slopes of Mount Tongariro on one of the three active volcanoes of the central plateau, with Kiwi friends Tony and Lorraine Freeman, when I had a fall. It was the first day out with back pack full of supplies for our four day trek. We were 1740 metres up the volcano and coming down a slope when I lost my footing and tumbled head first, the weight of my backpack thrusting me forward like a rocket. Luckily I had not landed on my head; my right arm being severely torn from wrist to elbow on the rocky shale surface as on instinct I held it out to save my head from the likely impact. My body now pinned underneath the heavy backpack, I was lying head toe tow with legs in the splits position. I had the presence of mind to take in my predicament. The right arm was half buried in shale and the only limb I could move was my left arm which was still clutching a walking pole. Luckily my head resting on a rock which was a saving grace as it relieved the strain on my neck.

Tony had looked up from the ledge below me at the precise moment he heard the falling rock caused by my accidental loss of footing. He was no more than 100 metres below me and quickly climbed back up to relieve me of the burden of my pack. After returning to my feet and finding the shock had not yet hit me, I made my way down the slope close behind Tony who insisted on carrying my heavy burden. There were only two other mountain climbers on the ridge that day, and as luck would have it one arrived on the scene with a can of artificial skin spray to seal my wounds so that I could soldier on. Soon we were on our way again up to 1700 metres, down to 1500 metres and clambering back up tp 1600 before crossing a crevice and dropping to 1100 metres. We finished that day staying in a hut 1540 meters on the side of a slope. All in all I had three falls that day and Tony had but one. Seated around the camp fire that night we all agreed that it was the hardest days tramping we had ever done. Walking on an active volcano is not such a good idea at the best of times. I was reminded of a climber who lost both legs two years previously on that self same route up the mountain. At the end of day four three weary warriors made our way to a village below the mountain where our transport to the main route back to civilisation via the river was awaiting us. Tony took the driving task and we followed a dirt track along the Whanganui River edge to the settlement of Jerusalem were we had planned to stay nearby overnight in an almost abandoned Maori commune, before returning downstream to Whanganui and on to Wellington the following day. It was upon arrival at Jerusalem later that afternoon that we took time out to take in the sights of the settlement.

The settlement of Jerusalem visible to the Wanganui River has in the courtyard of its Maori meeting house a dozen houses, Catholic Church, convent and presbytery. We made our way up to the entry of the church and finding no presence of nun nor priest, we took the liberty of entering an old but well maintained timber building. The vestibule had a small table with prayer leaflets for the taking, a vase of brightly coloured flowers that stood in front of a timber framed painting of Our Lady of Compassion, hanging on the wall. Entering the little church which would house no more than a couple of dozen people, I was taken in by a quiet sense of peace and sacredness. The whole place smelt solitude and harmony, leaving the mind with a quietness reminiscent of the feeling one gets in meditation.

Tony and Lorraine had wondered off in search of some other site. I made my way up the stairs at the back of the Church. There I found a dormitory with freshly made beds seemingly ready in anticipation of someone to lay on them. I later discovered that pilgrims often stayed there for a time in search of some spiritual harmony in their lives or just an escape from the madness of the world beyond. A way took me to a private hall set up as a family retreat. There I came across a young nun appearing to be counselling a young couple with small children who were playing at their feet. The good Sister suggested I visit the grotto near the convent were I would find a walkway with plaques telling of the history of Jerusalem and the church. The Sisters of Compassion pointed the way to the Stations of the Cross, suggesting that I may wish to avail myself of spiritual benefits I had not yet discovered.

The suggestion intrigued me as my mood was melancholy and I was in need of rest and recuperation from the ordeal of our tramping the mountain and crossing great ravines. I wandered down the pathway and read the history of how the settlement come to be, of the pioneering spirit of the mission, of Sister Mary Aubert, founder of the Sisters of Compassion and her remarkable charity of good works. The plaques also told of the early history of the settlement and of New Zealand. I wandered down the pathway and revised much of the story of the Rosary which happened to be the only stable strength and resource to call upon in my own childhood and early abandonment.

On my way out I met the nun who had given me the warm smile earlier outside the church door. She told me the story of the life of Suzanne Auburn who had left her native home in Lyon France in 1860 to follow a spiritual way of life in New Zealand.

Suzanne Auburn was just 25 at the time when she accepted an invitation to join a mission in the Catholic Auckland diocese. Initially working at a boarding school for Maori girls, Suzanne left to work at the Marist mission station in Hawke's Bay with the Third Order of Mary. She became well known in the area for her ministering to all religious denominations without compromising her own belief. The catch cry was her tolerance and friendship for her mission in life which she carried with willingness in tending the sick day and night and in which she later became famous all along the Wanganui River. Her mentor was piety which she derived from the famous Cur'e of Arles, John Vianney, French priest who was famously known fro his priestly duty and pastoral care in the parish of Arles, France. It was the radical spiritual transformation of the community attributed to his works that he is remembered for and is venerated as a saint in the Catholic church.

In 1874 Susanne Auburn, with the support of newly appointed Bishop Redwood of Wellington, and an invitation from the Maori from the Whanganui River area, began to revive the mission at Jerusalem. It is here that Sister Susanne become the founder of a new home-grown congregation - the Daughters of Our lady of Compassion was born. She made the Maori village the cradle of the first institution for the Maori and the first claim to the love of the sisters. A new church was built in 1885 and burnt down three years later. So Susanne Auburn set forth on a mission throughout the whole of New Zealand to raise funds to rebuild and returned in 1893 with enough funds to rebuild both church and convent. During her tour she became acutely aware of the challenges of the poor and especially the unmarried mothers, taking their babies into her care. Jerusalem was too isolated for medical services, so she set her sights on Wellington, arriving unannounced with two fellow Sisters and immediately started to work with Wellington's suffering and destitute planning a much needed home. They set up a soup kitchen which still operates today and a creche for children of working parents. Land was purchased in Island Bay in 1907 and the Our Lady's Home of Compassion was opened. Susanne never stopped still as her reputation spread far and wide, she rose to the challenge. After visiting Rome in 1913 she made a plea to the Pope and four years later, Pope Benedict XV granted the Degree of Praise to the Daughters of Our Lady of Compassion.

11.

The Decree changed everything, protecting all the works she had started, widening Susanne's scope of healthcare, protecting her resolution that the Sisters work would be everywhere and it recognised her interpretation of New Zealand society and spirituality. It was early in 1920 that the triumphant Susanne returned home to Island Bay were the Sisters in her absence remained true to her cause. On her return she arranged for the extension of the surgical section of the home and began nursing training for a new hospital. At the age of 91on the 1st October 1926 Susanne died in the presence of her Sisters. As word spread of her death crowds gathered to pay their respects to her. Wellington streets and roof tops were packed with people silently watching the hearse pass by. It was reported in the Auckland Weekly News as the greatest funeral accorded to a women in New Zealand. I said farewell to the little friendly Nun who related the story of Sister Susanne and the comical event that surrounds the days of Sister Clair's escape from the nursing home. No mention of James K Baxter had been related to me by the Nun, for she had been so busy telling me of her saintly hero, Sister Suzanne Aubert for him to be mentioned. Nor was I aware at the time of his nearby grave in the Maori section of the local cemetery. It was on my journey in the car with my friends Tony and Lorraine after our visit to Jerusalem that Baxter come up in conversation. It was just a passing comment by Tony that Jerusalem is the last resting place of New Zealand's most famous modern poet.

We made our way following the Whanganui River on the same dirt road we had been on prior to our Jerusalem stop over, finally arriving at the drop off point for our two night stay at the old abandoned Maori village, some twenty minutes drive from Jerusalem up river. Tony carefully drove in low gear along a bush track coming to a clearing where we could ride no further, with no choice but to travel on foot through jungle like conditions to our destination. We left the vehicle half hidden in the bush, where an old vehicle hardly road worthy parked nearby. It had current registration plates and was half hidden under some shrubs. Nearby was another car of late vintage which must have been considered more valuable by its owner, for it was covered with a tarpaulin. We made our way a short distance into the bush until we come to an opening with a long cliff face drop to the rapids below. Nearby there was a flying fox line across the river with a box like cable car too easily accommodate us and our packs as we readied ourselves for the journey. Outside was a cabin and hanging on the platform near the car was a large gong with padded Chou gong stick to ring it. The instrument vibrated loudly across the river as we each rang it for the experience and a voice answered a welcome from the far side through an amplifier nearby.

The operator of our mode of transport assured us of safe passage across but warned us to stay seated. So began our brief journey to our tiny living quarters on the once commercial orchard and Maori settlement. We were greeted warmly by our hosts Kelly and Jane who had turned what was a run down old settlement into an alternate holiday location.

We sampled a typical home cooked meal in a make shift dining area near the kitchen and after eating Kelly walked us to our hut with a bedroom, kitchen and open fire place for communal living. After saying good night to Tony and Lorraine, I climbed the stairs to a small attic which was more like an artists garret than a bedroom. The single bed was comfortable enough despite the dampness of the room. I figured it had not had anyone sleep in there for many a long day. It was a God send though this overnight stays in the old orchard accomodation, for it was there I found a treasure that ultimately resulted in the writing of this book. I had come across a small collection of old books and one was a worn and yellowed book of poems. It contained of the early works of one James K Baxter and I read some of his brilliance before ultimately falling asleep. It set up an idea in my head- writing of his life and times.

The next day we went exploring, leading eventually to the discovery of the old ruins of a hut and old post office, reminders of a by gone age when ghosts seemed real, The myth of the 'te taiko,' the bush demon that keeps the local Maori in fear, is present still. They keep their lights burning all night outside their houses just in case it invades through the darkness of the night. We returned through a dense bushland and although I was aware of the safety of the bush without poisonous snakes, deadly spiders and all kinds of creepy crawlies to consider. I breathed a sigh of relief when we emerged from the jungle like conditions to our place of abode for one more day and night. Open ground and the prospects of wild boar appearing from out of the undergrowth was no longer a threat.

On the journey back to Wellington with my tramping companions, I drifted into my imagination of the life of James K Baxter. The Freeman's were busy in the front of their little red car in typical a husband wife conversation as we meandered the dirt road, still following the course of the river.

My mind rest on the life of the poet who started his commune for the dregs of society at that place . The dark and tragic in-depth feeling of his poetry in that little volume of works I had found in the hut library had haunted me somewhat. I wrote poetry which to a great degree was a relief of mind of the images that I managed to articulate in wordy rhyme but that I could not articulate in conversation. His poetry expressed his passion, activism, and anger so eloquently. How brave was the poet, drawn apparently randomly to the little settlement of Jerusalem.

The little settlement of Jerusalem, (Hiruharama to the Maori) on that fertile evergreen patch of land nestled in the bend of the river was now embedded in my imagination as was Baxter the poet. The man who suffered the slings and arrows of outrageous fortune in his pains of expression of life and death in his poetry and letters to friends. The man of intellectual greatness who rejected academia, the adventurer who travelled far and wide, the atlas eater with a jaw for news as once expressed by JKBs hero Dylan Thomas. The misfit, the loner, the apparent rapist, the alcoholic, the man who travelled the spiritual journey from atheist to christianity. This somewhat derelict character who let go of all that world deemed important. He was a wounded soul who was letting go of some of his earlier egotism and embraced the way of the cross though his new recently founded Catholic faith. The now sober alcoholic, drawn randomly to set up a commune in the place of the Maori and its culture.

Back in Wellington with a day to kill before my flight to Australia, I had time enough to frequent some of the haunts of the poet , from university to library, from museums to the back streets were the lost and bewildered still hung out tonguing for a drink, or the needle to take them once more to never never land. Baxter, had been there too, as an alcoholic but ultimately as a friend and as a do good evangelist, who cared and lived the steps of the alcoholic: "Having had a spiritual awakening as a result of these steps, we tried to carry this message to alcoholics and to practice these principles in all our affairs."

Baxter had carried the message all-right and took it a step further in setting up a commune for the suffering, the lost and desolate. He did not judge them for their defects of character, just as he did not in an intellectual sense judge himself, but suffered much in handing over his soul to the God of his own understanding. It may have been his new found faith that drew him to saintly purpose helped by the influence of Susanne Auburn of the first mission at Jerusalem. She was the catalyst that drew James Baxter to his cause at that location. Susanne Aubert, was the spiritually inclined immigrant founder of the order of The Sisters of Compassion who in 1892 at the tiny church of St Joseph, the convent and the Presbytery which overlooks the houses inhabited now by descendants of the then Maori tribe established the mission at Jerusalem.

Seated in a cafe in Wellington I was picturing how strong and sturdy rowers of the canoe travelled up stream against the tide must have been. The little nun, seated in the canoe taking in the river and its surrounds for the very first time. Her religious zeal beating in her heart as they travelled towards the sacred sight of those first settlers, establishing a religious order there. seeing to it for the rebuilding of the Church of St. Joseph. Her later soup kitchen in Wellington for the poor and hungry of streets of Wellington, the creche for children of working people and the home of compassion built in Island Bay would have no doubt crossed the mind of the poet as he made his way to Jerusalem for the very first time. Yes, I fell sure James Baxter was much influenced by the good Sister Auburn in his efforts to establish a commune for the misfits of society of which he was the best example.

The restlessness expressed in the little of the poems of Baxter's I had briefly become acquainted with on my journey of February 2018 and the experience of visiting the village of Jerusalem has been embedded in my subconscious ever since. My trek with my New Zealand friends on Mt. Tongariro, the active volcano and the hardships encountered there still linger to a small degree. However, the life of the poet Guru from Jerusalem never left me and I somehow knew I would eventually write his story as it interrelates to my own life. Here I must confess that I have drawn my conclusions of Baxter from the diligent works of far great minds than my own. For he to the greater part is the hero of the Kiwi academics and writers and much more well know there than here in Australia or for that matter the rest of the globe. Those that are granted a mention in the knowledge of Baxter herein I have give full acknowledgement, for they did the hard work and I just narrated to a lessor degree the outcomes. It is those academics and writers I refer as to the knowledge of the poet personally or from research looked into the complicated character of Baxter and galvanised it into prospective. I am not an ardent reader of his poetry and nor should I be, for it is much too introspective and deeply truthfully defining. I do enough of that delving herein in my own character and apparent defects too, as you the reader will see.

Historically I have flown across the ditch to New Zealand thirteen times to tramp the wilderness with Australian friends. It was on one of those journeys I met Tony and Lorraine Freeman and they have kindly invited me to join them in their quest to cover the North and South Islands tramps of New Zealand even since. Due to the pandemic of Covid-19 in 2020 this was not possible because of boarder closures. So during the isolation of Covid, I found time to write my sixth book, an autobiographical insight into my former life's journey. Still in the vain of introspection, I found my way back to Baxter, and so began this autumn of 2021 the writing of the life of James K Baxter and to a greater or lesser degree, depending on your viewpoint, my own shadow self.

CHAPTER 2.

THE SPIRIT OF OUR ANCESTORS

The Baxter clan like the Macmillan Brown's were fellow immigrants who hailed from the Scottish Highlands and were dirt poor on their arrival in Otago in January 1861. After much hardship leaving Scotland, James' grandfather, John Baxter soon fell on his feet finding steady employment and good wages in New Zealand. The first decade there was one of extraordinary prosperity, following the discovery of Gold in Otago. The surrounding country had initially given good fortune with wheat growing being the first of export crops to Sydney, long before any farmer considered wheat as a crop to grow in Australia. My countryAustralia then rode on the sheep's backend had not considered cropping the land. New Zealand's Dunedin become the first city in the NZ colony to be both industrially and commercial successful. It's Harbour Port back in its infancy was always bustling and busy with cargo loading for export and imports and work hungry immigrants moving there to make a living in an expanding colony. Meanwhile Otago grew to six times its size during that first decade of the new Scottish immigrant's arrival. John Baxter, the grandfather, a peasant of the Western Highlands of Scotland became the clan Gaelic- speaking farmers of Otago, like so many of his fellow countrymen. The Otago Baxter's and their fellow settlers of the Western Highland of the Free Church of Scotland were patriarchal Christians whose reliance on the word of God, took pride in their doctrine of faith and morals according to the Bible teachings. The first settlers were a close knit bunch sternly admonished in their congregation, maintaining the importance of family values and righteous behaviour content to work hard to make a living off the land. Grandfather John was a physically strong man of solid build who was used to the riggers of hard work and tough climatic conditions. He didn't have the capital to initially buy his land but with a keen eye for business set up a cook house at Harper's Pass to cater for fortune hunting gold diggers eager to make their fortune on the West Coast goldfields.

John Baxter did ultimately strike gold and quietly slipped out of New Zealand returning to Glasgow with the money he made to invest in a line of small steamers at Clyde and then returned to New Zealand. He was always on the lookout for opportunity and only relaxed when he played the bagpipes or when he took an early morning swim which he did religiously irrespective of climatic conditions. James's great grand parents were Archibald and Margaret McColl from Glenrevan, who arrived in New Zealand with their seven children in 1859. Whilst many children died on that long voyage, Mary who become James's grandmother survived. The family, like the Baxter's left Scotland because of economic reasons and partly because one of their sons John, who was a keen poacher was reportedly a violent young man. He become a farmer In Otago and those who knew him could not believe such a gentle person deserved his former reputation.but in James' later mythology, he was the type of ancestor deprived of legitimate hunting rights by the landed gentry. So it came to pass that daughter, Mary McColl married John Baxter before the registrar at Winton on 16 August 1879.

Mary had been born at Glencrevan, Ballachulish, Lochaber in the Scottish Highlands in 1858. When John, who was a heavy drinker, asked for her hand in marriage her father spoke to his new intended son in-law: " I have nothing against you personally, but the drink. if you can remain sober, off the drink for six months you can marry my daughter." That was well beyond him but they married all the same. He was twenty two and she was just twenty one when they settled in Brighton were the first son John was born. Their second son, Archibald McColl Baxter, the poet's father, was born on 13th December 1881, and six more children followed. Margaret was a hard working mum who could put her hand to any task and do more than her fair share of domestic duties. John was an excellent worker, but could not hold down a job, spent money like water and become intoxicated after only a few drinks. He was soon to be considered an alcoholic. James Baxter was much like his grandfather and embodied his life style and in particular his moral convictions and his alcoholism.

Grandfather, John Baxter was to all intents a religious man. When the Plymouth Brethren drifted into Brighton one Sunday morning, John Baxter went to hear them. He had an enlightening powerful experience much like that of the cofounder of Alcoholics Anonymous , Bill Wilson whose appearance in this story will later influence James Baxter. Meanwhile John Baxter, the grandfather was effected to the point that he gave up alcohol. His drinking was cured for a time , but not his spend thrift ways, and the large family lived on the smell of an oily rag, as he could not provide adequately for them. Archie was forced to leave school before his teens and go to work. He proved a diligent worker, saved his money and bought his mother a cow, which was a godsend for such a big family. So the cream and milk flowed and butter was made too. All the sons reached manhood skills early in life and as soon as they were considered men, moved up country as labourers on farms, rabbiting, shearing and fencing.

Archie soon become head plowman because of his exceptional skill with horses at Sir John Robert's 'Gladbrook' station , some eighty kilometres from Brighton. The sons always returned to the family home, which had become a popular meeting place for both the Baxters and the McColl families. Mary was especially skilful at entertaining and kept the clans united. John always felt that if he had his own land all their problems would be solved. As luck would have it Archie won a parcel of land in a lottery on Scrolls Hill, Brighton. He stocked it with cattle, sheep, pigs and fowl and handed it over to John, his father. John Baxter was no manager and soon was in debt again bringing the bailiff to the door and the whole place was sold off. When news reached Archie, he came home, bought the farm back and began to work it himself. It soon became profitable. Of the whole Baxter clan Archie was the most successful with money. John Baxter began to hit the drink hard again and then go on the wagon for a few months or even for a long stretch sometimes. To help him stay sober he used to hang biblical texts around the house. He was a typical emotional alcoholic and it was related that when driving back to Brighton via Saddle Hill one time, near to where he had his farm, he burst into tears.

Despite the drink John was a lot of fun to be with and he liked playing the bagpipes and entertaining in local competitions. On the day of a competition he would be up and ready at three in the morning. As a man he was absolutely fearless and Archie often observed, his father was the last one to be silenced by threats. John lived until he was eighty six and his wife Mary died in 1932, seven years earlier. Archie, upon visiting him in his final hours said his father unconscious just before he died, swears he saw an old man laying there beside him on the bed, whom he took for being one of his ancestors. (I can relate to that for I have had my own mother visit me as a ghost like image just days after she died. I had related to her that I was alright and with a final sad stern look in her eyes she faded from view.

Whilst the Baxter brothers due to economic circumstance had to go to work before they received much formal education, they all loved to read and Archie, with an exceptional memory, livened up many a gathering with poetry and the verse he wrote. There was also an unpublished novel which survives in library archives. It is a fictional account of Archie's Gaelic speaking ancestors after their arrival at Gabriel's Gull from Scotland. It is a visionary insight into the time. It is often noted that the distinguishing mark of a poet is technical accomplishment, while vision is often undervalued. Archie in his lifetime was an observer of prominence even though he didn't write well he had a deeper and more delicate insight into what is human experience than many a writer does. He was considered in the district as a quiet dignified man who never expressed violent opinions. He was a natural born leader whose counsel was greatly valued inside and outside the family, but he was to fall victim to the barbarous age of WW1. When the war broke out, Archie already had views based on religious grounds that ran fowl of the Government of his time. Whilst he didn't belong to any organised religion, he used the Christ's common 'Thou shalt not kill and love thy neighbour as thy-self.' Conscription was passed in Parliament and many a young man were sentenced for refusing to serve. The anti-militarist received strong support from protests by the Labour Party which stood for the ideal of universal brotherhood and peace. But up in Brighton Archie felt he stood alone, both in his pacifism and socialist views. Gradually his family began to share his pacifism and Archie inevitably attracted the attention of the military. A conscription bill was passed on 31st May 1916 with little resistance apart from protests the Labour Party. Archie's farm had prospered, but he realised that with the coming of conscription he would no longer be allowed to work it. In the summer of 1916-17 he took to shearing so as to leave behind as large a cheque as possible for his family. He had not even received a draft notice to serve in the army when he and his two brothers were apprehended.

The Baxter brothers were jailed and there began a long process of mental cruelty, physical abuse and flouting of ordinary human decencies. After being confined to jail in Wellington Archie, Jack and Sandy Baxter, together with eleven other conscientious objectors were forcibly sent by ship to England on 14th July 1917. Huge protest meetings in Wellington were held and at other places demanding the return of the men, but it was to no avail. After a term of three and half months in South Africa, they were allowed considerable freedom, and ultimately rejoiced a ship , arriving at Plymouth on Boxing Day. There they were transferred to Sling Camp on the Salisbury Plains and one month later shipped to France. From the initial arrest in New Zealand they were forcibly dressed in military uniform, but Archie always tore his off and accepted corporal punishment for his efforts. During the voyage to France he was saddled with a heavy backpack and kept handcuffed so he could not rid himself of the uniform. Ultimately Archie ended up in a base camp in Belgium from January 1918 to August where his life became a virtual hell on earth. Archie was often tied to two willow poles. The New Zealand Military torturer was expert at his job, knowing how to pull Archie's hands tight with twine making them turn black wth congested blood. They were also tied behind the pole together and pulled up high and tight to strain and cramp muscles into an unnatural position. He was left in hanging position, so that both hands and feet could not grip on the pole or the ground.

The torture continued but the field punishment failed to break Archie, so they sent him to the front station in the ammunition dump within range of German artillery in the hope that he would be shot. Despite the storm of belching artillery fire and flying fragments, Archie miraculously survived. Finding Archie's spirit indomitable, the authorities had him confined to a mental hospital were he was certified by a British Doctor as mentally deranged. Then by September 1919 he was back in Wellington. His case was well known through the press, particularly in the New Zealand Truth which back then was sympathetic to pacifists. To silence public criticism, the Minister of Defence issued an official document in October 1918 on the fourteen pacifists who had been deported to Europe during the war. It also declared that Archie was not insane, and did not require to be sent to a hospital, mental or otherwise. The Government had no intention of allowing conscientious objectors to return quietly to civilian life. In the euphoria that followed the end of the war the return ed soldiers well published courage and heroism left him and his fellow pacifists misrepresented in most news articles. In the years that followed the war, the Baxter brothers still met with a good deal of hostility. Besides their unacceptable views on war, they were political non-conformist and radically independent. It didn't bother the Baxter men as their attitude to work was different from most of the community at Brighton.

The Baxter's were seasonal workers who took on the menial tasks of hard work in shearing, fencing and road work. They were a happy go lucky bunch settling back into life at Brighton not interested in acquiring property or amassing great wealth. When it was fishing season, they just downed tools and set-up camp in Brighton Bay and took time out to go hunting. After making money with their hard work they thought nothing of taking a few months off to enjoy the fruits of their labour. They had learnt the hard way the lessons of excess in drink from their own father's downfall in that regard, so they were not drinkers. Except for Archie, the brothers' weakness was gambling on the horses and they were keen racegoers. None belonged to a Church and Archie was a humanist, though he believed in God and prayed by himself.

The community still reckoned them a shifty breed, who couldn't settle down. Archie was quite capable of doing that and wished to return to farming, but he had to make up for the war years and build up badly needed capital. So he returned to rabbiting in Otago for quick returns. On his father's side, James Baxter's immediate ancestors were of pioneering stock. They took their chances in the uncertain world of Otago settlement, without economic, social or educational advantage. They established themselves in good times and bad with hard physical labour. The ancestors on his mothers side, the Macmillan Browns; one could not compare, for they were prosperous, loaded with large cash reserves, conventionally educated without the flare; most unlike the Baxters. James great grandfather on his mother side was a sea captain and merchant who owned his ship, was a trader, away for period of time in the South China Sea, China or the West Coast of America. The shipmaster had several children, one of whom was John Macmillan Brown who is important to this story. He was born in Irvine in Ayrshire in 1846 and initially in his youth had visions to become a Presbyterian preacher. However, just as he was about to enter university, his father lost his ship and cargo in Belfast. He was not insured and financial support from his parents was out of the question.

He had to make his way by use of his intelligence and industry and went on to Edinburgh University and supported himself by giving private lessons. Between 1865-1869 James grandfather John moved to Glasgow University awarded First Class honours in Mental Science, philosophy and psychology. He also won the coveted Snell execution for Classics and Philosophy allowing him to go to Oxford for five years.

In New Zealand, the founding fathers planned a University as near similar to Oxford and Cambridge and in1873, the government decide to act, and the following year the first professor of Chemistry was chosen to take up the Chair. When the Chair of Classes and English at the newly constituted Canterbury University came up in 1874, Macmillan Browns was appointed. He met a young lady who was the first women student at Canterbury University and matriculated in 1876. Three years later when she was nineteen they become engaged and so began a seven year engagement. When newly married she took Honours in Latin and English and become the first women graduate of a British University.

It was in 1882, at the age of twenty three, she become Principal of Christchurch Girls High school. John Macmillan Brown and Helen Connor married in a simple ceremony in 1886. They had two children after multiple miscarriages. Millicent was destined to a lifestyle she had not expected, when at age 15 her mother contracted diphtheria and suddenly died. With his wife death, Macmillan Brown was heartbroken and Millicent, in a rare moment of revelation, admitted she had little emotional warmth from her mother and regretted it. Whilst her father was busy with university duties, he decide to take her education in hand. He coached her intensively for New Zealand junior Scholarship examination and also for Sydney Senior, but she failed both. Millicent was then sent to attend Presbyterian Ladies College in Croydon, Sydney for one year in 1905, where she did much better. In her final year, Millicent passed Latin 111, German 111 and French 111. She was intelligent, not brilliant and resentful.

During the Otogo University Jubilee celebrations the Professor of English fell dead during a lecture, and at the time John Macmillan Brown was Vice - Chancellor of the University of New Zealand. He generously offered his services, until a replacement could be found. He insisted that daughter Millicent accompany him to Dunedin. They lived in a boarding house at St. Kilda and as she had plenty of time on hand, she continued to read widely. The move to Dunedin gave Millicent the chance to see the person whom she had wanted to meet for a long time, one Archie Baxter. By chance she was handed a letter by a friend. Archie had written of his difficulties at the front, his courage under much personal cruelty and his physical condition. He had wanted to pre-warn his parents of his physical condition before he set sail for home at the end of the war. The reading of this letter change Millicent's life. She had been active in the Red Cross and held a conventional attitude to the war and now she developed strong pacifist views. Whilst she held some guilt for a change of heart, she never the less carried the letter in her handbag and looked forward to the day she could meet her new hero.

When she went to Brighton to meet Archie he was away but she was received well by his family. After a number of visits to the Baxter family property, Millicent at last met Archie. He was not as she had envisaged. She with her well educated way of the elite world, with a cultured English speaking voice, bright blue eyes and radiant complexion caused quite a stir in Archie. She did not find him good looking, but his whole personality and manner matched her own. She knew he was the man for her despite his financially poor status and lack of education. He on the other hand found that her ease of expression matched his own. He liked her common sense approach to life and having similar pacifists views. Neither parents agreed on their marriage. John Macmillian Brown had other plans for his highly educated daughter and he felt that Archie's background and limited financial resources would limit the chance of the marriage surviving. The Baxter clan felt Millicent was not suitable for Archie, being that she was not of the working class, they felt she was not a good match. This did not bother either Archie or Millicent and they went ahead and married anyway. Archie and Millicent had no wedding reception but instead spent a week having picnic's on the Brighton river. Archie then went off rabbiting then back to the farm at Hyde. By spring of 1921 he had enough money to buy a small farm at Kuri Bush south of Brighton. They had no running water and used a tank at the rear of their little four bedroom cottage. The fuel stove was well stacked by Archie with wood kept at the back of the property. She cooked, did the washing in a zine tub on an outside bench using water heated from the stove. The kerosene lamp was the only lighting at night. Despite limited conditions they were very happy there. Archie had purchased a very run down property but it wasn't long before he had stocked it with cattle, sheep and pigs and a few horses for plowing for wheat, despite the fact that the land being close to the sea was sandy and not ideal for farming. It wasn't long before he started to grow fowls for their own consumption.

Because of his pacifist stance during WW1, the authorities found reason to make Archie's life difficult for him. Untrue objections were made to frame him for receiving stolen goods. Strangers turned up to the door to offer him a way out of situations illegally. Archie was too cunning and experienced to fall for such traps. Not all locals were unfriendly though. Many came to lend a hand in harvesting and chaff cutting and all who became friends enjoyed dining at the Baxter's table. First son Terrence was born 23rd May 1922 and Millicent embraced her new role as mother wth great enthusiasm. Terrence grew up a contented child and he often spoke of his childhood as growing up in the 'Garden of Eden." Whilst bullied by his cousins on visits to their property, in the main he had a dream run as a boy. Archie and Millicent wanted another child and after several miscarriages, Millicent conceived again.The baby was born five weeks early on 29th June 1926 at Nurse Roos maternity home in Dunedin. The baby weighed only five pounds four ounces, and ironically was nice named   Jumbo the Elephant, and 'Jam' remained his name with family friends and relatives. He was not Christened but always got James by his parents as they named him after the famous Scottish socialist and British labour founder James Keir Hardie. The newborn bundle was thus registered at birth, James Keir Baxter. Contrary to medical opinion at the time, it was thought that premature babies wouldn't live long, but 'Jumbo James' thrived and survived.

Millicent, could not boil and egg when she was first married but being a determined woman she soon learnt the skills and became an excellent cook. Likewise she learnt to use a sewing machine and until the boys were seven- she made all their shirts out of old cloth. Archie and Millicent greatly enjoyed each other's company. They both had a similar sense of humour and never listen to music much, preferring to sit and read by the fire at night. They were both well read in English and Scottish history. Millicent took a great interest in Archie's family tree. If she had not, then much of what she recorded would have been lost for all time. The house itself was always untidy with books and papers everywhere. It bugged Archie, as he had always been tidy but his protests fell on deaf ears. His wife was always late for an appointment, was no housekeeper. When they had guests for dinner, nobody knew when the meal would be ready but when it arrived it was ample and well prepared. They never had any music on those occasions as they preferred conversion.

Despite this 'everyone relied on Millicent's good sense which was the opposite to Archies anxious approach. She never misplaced a thing, paid all the bills on time and kept good records of expenditure. She had inherited the frugal nature of her father who had instilled in her from a young age the value of money. Archie did not have the domestic skills in the home, but he came into his own in the garden, supplying enough vegetables to feed the family and he had a skill with growing flowers too. He was strong, dependable, gentle with an unassuming natured. He was a skilled talker, and had a reputation as a raconteur. With the wisdom of suffering much in the war years, he was in great demand as a counsellor. He had a warm personality, touched people easily and was comforting with embracing strangers.

Millicent was the opposite in that she did not like to be embraced, which sometimes causes much discomfort to both Archie and the boys. My own mother was of a similar nature and disposition. She was born of cruel French stock on my grandfather' side with wild but sad eyed Irish on my Grandmothers. She died when Mum was only around seven years of age. Mum being one of thirteen children was number four of seven girls and apart from one brother the other five brothers were all older. It must have been tough for my grandad, but I could never warm to him as a child. I sometimes wondered if my Mum may have been sexually abused as a child because she seemed to lack empathy and like Baxter's mum didn't like to be embraced either. Added to that she never complained much and went about her domestic duties as a dutiful wife, was a regular church attendee and doted on my Father like he was king of the roost, and he was just that to me as well.

James was often asked to read by strangers who came to visit. He was a serious child with straight golden hair and the brightest of blue eyes which he inherited from his mother. He was a typical extrovert with a cheerful disposition, being both open and direct with people. Both he and Terrance got on well together but sometimes James in his devilment would often provoke his brother in his overt sense of duty.

Archie remained loyal to his pacifist years; still attended Labour Party conferences, and entered local council politics but he was not elected. The powers that be in Dunedin put pay to that as his war record had not been forgotten. Unrepentant, he and Millicent campaigned against compulsory military training in schools and founded a branch in Dunedin of the "No more war movement." These were the years of the Depression and Brighton felt its effects. Two of Archie's brothers who suffered with poor health were on the dole. Concern for those less fortunate was considered by many to be the character of the Baxters. Their war time experience enabled them to embrace with the suffering of the unemployed and indeed the outcasts of society. Neighbours questioned how the Baxter's managed to support themselves. Archie, whilst then retired seemed to get a hold on jobs and it was also thought that Millicent's father may have sent them money. Millicent, being the fugal one, may well have been saving for a goodly time before the Depression really hit hard. James was to follow his parent's thinking and actions in helping those less fortune than himself, when in his own latter years, he set up a commune at Jerusalem for the street people, alcoholics and drug addicts. James at the age of five attended Brighton primary school, where the headmaster and an assistant taught fifty pupils between them. To prepare her boys for the next phase for their life, Millicent taught them the basics facts of life about puberty and sex. James blabbed about it with his classmates. Before the first day of school he could already read. This contributed to him being lazy because he could do what the teachers taught without effort. James took little interest in what was being taught and scored near the lowest marks in his class. The headmaster mistakenly interpreted his laziness as lack of intelligence. James though excelled at the school plays, but he was uncoordinated at sport, so he didn't excel at Rugby, a must as a New Zealander, even back then. Long before he went to school, Archie use to sit him on his knees and read him Yeats, Shelley and Byron. This substitute for nursery rhyme made him precocious. The little boy's first experience with poetry proved he had natural ability for rhyme.

With Archie's encouragement both boys began to write verse but James motivation to write poetry gained him much approved from his father. He wrote his first poem at the age of seven. From then onward he carried a note book in his pocket with pencil ready for writing. A good deal of his writing was done on impulse and he would often leave whatever he was doing and go off to some quiet place to write. He was, like his parents, an avid reader consuming everything his mother had read in her lifetime housed in a well kept library of books.

James Baxter became steeped in the classic myths of Ireland and Scandinavia, that proved to be indispensable in his later education. The Scandinavian legends appeared most perhaps because they were so close to those of his Scottish Highlands ancestry. When someone considered something or someone ugly he resorted to myth, for here he seemed to make sense of it. Millicent often read stories if the Bible to the boys. Thus, James become familiar with the rhythms, enriching his memory with images and stories. As they grew older both boys could readily commit whole poems to memory and quote passages from the Bible. Time proved James to be more trouble to his parents and he did not fulfil his parents expectations. He seemed to think, and perhaps rightly so, that his brother was the family favourite and he the outcast. Terence later confirmed that this was not so. For he was the sensitive introspective first child and James that of the relaxed more outgoing of the two brothers. They were different in build too as James was thick set and was inclined to amble about, was easygoing and for the most part of good temperament. Terence was the glum, tense and moody one according to himself.

James had his own names for rocks along the coastline: Black Rock, The Big Rock, The Phoenix Head , the Lions Head and on the bend in the river: Devil's Elbow, and Giant's Grave. They were used as reference points said in general terms like 'above the Black Bridge' or ' near Duffy's Orchard.' There was a deep part of the river just a couple of hundred metres from the family home which James named 'A black bottomless hole' and he and Terence often padded a canoe slowly over that mysterious hole. Behind the ridge of nearby McColls' farm there are limestone caves where the boys often searched for fossils. James became quite knowledgeable in the geological period of fossils, even when in primary school.

An old coal cave on McColl's property was also another fascination for James to explore. He later drew on the experiences in his ' The Cave' poem. He was averse to the danger of natures risks which he would rush into without thinking. Don McKenzie was a local old fisherman, the son of a first immigrant from the Highlands of Scotland. He lived up river from the Baxters in an old shack and knew a great deal about the history of Scottish Highland clans and the Baxter family. On the verandah of the old shack by the river, he told the boys many a story. James was more than delighted to find a new piece of history of early immigrants and has own family on his frequent visits. The changing nature of the river McKenzie was also able to be detailed. How the river was cleared before the weed spread and how trout was introduced to the stream where it once had groper and blue cod. Another fellow was old Duffy who owned an orchard near Black Bridge. It was hard to reach, set in a valley surrounded by thick scrub. Duffy had some strange expressions that fascinated James.

These characters appeared in Baxter's late poem: 'The Waves,' which depicts events such as when Mckenzie blasted a channel in the rock between Barney's Island and the shore, to allow his boat to go behind the line of breakers in the Bay.

Further notations on the shadow self of my journey into the unknown. In my very make up, from my earliest memories, I have always been extroverted. Like Baxter, I loved to embrace nature and have impulsively jumped into life's risky situations without fear or favour. In doing so, I wrote poems and stories of my experiences as a child. Escaping into the imagination of expression of my soul searching to overcoming loneliness, I even question my reason for being on this earth at all. Always I felt that somehow I was different to others. life experience and my days of active alcoholism coupled with many adventures in my getting of wisdom all proved this to be true. I had first to find acceptance of the inner core of being a loner and an outsider. Of being numerically designed to belong to the 2-3% of the population. Of not belonging to the masses of mankind who live in the bubbled existence.

This has been an enormous discovery, for over the passage of time I learnt to trust, to accept myself as a born outsider. Coming to terms with the fact that I am genetically blue printed to be as I am. This, coupled with my writings brings peace and hope for the future for me. Whilst I enjoyed time with my childhood mates, birds nesting for another rare egg for my collection or killing lizards for the sport of it, I also enjoyed being alone on the beach or catching waves. Contrary to this, I also enjoyed being involved in competitive sports. On the negative side, I was not content with the regimentation of school life and thus I suffered as a non conformist with much corporal punishment in both primary and senior schooling. This I accepted in time as a learning curve and soon figured that suffering in life was a necessary part of the getting of wisdom, growing up and living life to the full. My genetic influences had a lot to do with my writing poetry and stories. Grandfather George Cooper, my Mum's father, was a born poet who churned out lengthy stories in poetic form. Barney McPhillips, my childhood mentor grandfather was a grand storyteller who mesmerised the fertile mind of his grandkids with wild imaginative tales in his Irish way.

Uncle Jack, a younger brother of my father was an accomplished violinist and hands-on creator of useful things like fishing rods, which I got to test in the local river, when the fancy took him to take me fishing. My Dad was always so busy with his engineering works, public philanthropic gifting and new ideas, he hardly had time to be at home at all. When he was at home he seemed lost in the drink or playing the piano at which he was very accomplished or creating something with his hands. Like my Uncle Jack, he too was a dyed in the wool alcoholic. In fact as it turned out the McPhillips' brothers in time would prove to be mostly alcoholic and had a gambling streak too. There were exceptions to the rule that influenced me in a positive way in my family tree. Like that of great Uncle Reg who was an accomplished artist. He travelled the country doing commercial paintings for businesses, windows designs and cartoons for interested local characters. In time Caltex in USA offered him a position. I never did see great Uncle Reg take a drink in his life. His influence artistically fascinated me but I lost track of him when he moved permanently to the USA.

He had brother Bob, who ultimately headed up the art department at a Sydney TAFE college and had great skill teaching art. I tried my hand at it and did a couple of paintings which were quickly snapped up. It was one of those youthful impulses to do creative things. I ceased after I began to make films, but it was also a flash in the pan thing and like my piano lessons I lost interest in pursuing that line of work. It was inevitable that my poetic shadow self would ultimately over- rule the way of life I chose in the world at large. The world taught me to crush my creative self by following the way of the linear, rational, sequential, logical way of half brain living. Life thou has a way of pulling us up to the middle road, the way of the spirit and the imagination. It came to me late in life; It came in a song about my grandfather and me.

Every summer, up to 1935, the Baxters went to the mountains in their little Ford car for three weeks of holiday. They rented the Niger hut at the head of the Matukituki Valley, where the river divides to its east and west branches. It seemed they weren't enjoying themselves so they drove to Lake Wan-aka and camped by the shore. They trailed over the mountains where James later celebrated the memories of holidays their in his poem: "Poem in the Manuituki Valley." On many occasions the family camped as they liked by the lake or the river. James had fond memories of his father Archie doing everything whilst on holidays including the cooking and boiling the billy on two forked sticks hanging over a fire. Millicent's only chore was to keep the tent clean and tidy. They made the most of every holidays, visiting Mt.Cook, on the way to Lake Tekapo; tramping near the Tasman and the glaciers and enjoyed the many tramps through valleys in the constant changing weather. From those wonderful three weeks a year holidays, so many poems flowed for James from his boyhood family adventures.

My memory floats back from time to time over the past decade where I too camped where the Baxter's camped at Lake Tekapo. I've done many a tramp in New Zealand and walked to the snow line at Mt. Cook, climbed Mt. St John twice on two different occasions, camping at Lake Tekapo. The troubled mind of an alcoholic will try any method to beat the blues and the memories of the past. In all I traversed and tramped the North and South island of New Zealand in my coming to terms with the ego self and given time with nature to heal my body, mind and spirit.

Those tramping trails into the wilderness were indeed helpful, but as time goes by the quiet moments of just sitting with self is just as beneficial. It is a long journey from the head to the heart. Apart from New Zealand the thousands of kilometres I've walked over the past decade in Spain, Portugal and Ireland have been the most outward means of recovery for me. To this moment I've written many a book, poem and song as a result of those journeys.

John Macmillian Brown died at the age of eighty nine in Christchurch in1935. He left Millicent four hundred pound a year for the rest of her life with a clause that after her death the monies were to continue and revert to the maintenance and education of her children. At the time of his death, Terence was age thirteen and James just nine years old. The grandfather did not have any real emotional attachment to his daughter nor the grandchildren. He did spend some time with them all and grew to like Archie but apart from that he held little empathy with any of them. Millicent Brown was practical unemotional man who had more interested in academia than people. The annual income was very handy for Millicent and she saw a grand opportunity to travel to broaden her children's eduction of the world at large to increase their academic opportunities. For a while they moved to Wanganui for Archie health as it improved in the warmer climate. Millicent was pleased to get James away from Brighton Primary were James was thrashed for poor examination results by a cruel teacher. Unbeknown to Millicent, the teacher took out his frustration on James because of a relationship Terence had been having with a sixteen year old girl. They enjoyed their time in the North Island. Archie, perhaps as a result of his war experience, was often in a melancholic state of mind. When the next winter came around they decided to visit Europe.

CHAPTER 3.

FOND FAREWELLS AND NEW HORIZONS

They sailed for Australia and spent time in Sydney, Hobart, Adelaide and Perth, jumped ship at Norfolk Island for a time; sailed the Suez and were much fascinated in the area. Nearing Crete, the ship's captain sailed close to the mainland, explaining the history of the fabled island. He would have been surprised to know the impressions he left on the imagination of a budding poet.

Visits to Naples, Pompeii and the South of France added to the template for many future poems from the pen of James K Baxter. Then it was on to England and Plymouth arriving on a bitterly cold snowing day. They decided to settle in Salisbury Archie, still suffering from melancholic but over time his health began to improve. A visit to the old deserted Sling Camp where he had suffered so much during the war effected him deeply and he wrote of his war experience, in a book called 'We will not Cease.' It help him emotionally to journal his war time experiences in liberating him from the terror of it all. It first appeared in a 1939 addition of Gollancz's Left Book Club and was favoured in a review by the 'New Statesman and Nation.' James was particularly affected by his father's experiences, and this was later borne out in his writings. The effect of the wholesale slaughter of WW1 and his father's escape from death played heavily on his imagination. He seem to have a preoccupation with death in his poems and it all played out in his mind over time.

The boys were enrolled in the Quakers school at Sibford, chosen because of its avoidance of doctrinal teaching and its adherence to peace during the war. It was a co-education boarding school in a small Oxfordshire village on the edge of the Cotswolds. The dormitories were unheated and supper before bedtime consisted of dry bread and a cup of cocoa. One period a week was devoted to religious instruction which include the authorised version of the Bible. Each morning after breakfast, staff and pupils assembled for a hymn, a biblical reading and a short period of meditation. Worship on Sunday lasted for an hour and was held like a retreat into silence. James at the time was considered a shy boy of a likeable and sensitive nature. He was described by a classmate as slightly unkempt, idealistic, full of impish fun, but able to become serious very quickly. James enjoyed the school life there, liked the district but at times escaped to climb nearby high trees or steal farmers' eggs from the hen house for the fun of it. In July 1937, at the end of first term, the family headed for Denmark to attend the War Resisters' Conference in Copenhagen. The boys were the only children at the conference and kept their parents on their metal with their antics. At the Hotel King of Denmark, they ran pencils down the bannister groves and kept going up and down in the lift for fun. After the conference they travelled to Germany along the Rhine and through the Black Forest to Berlin. Then on to the Danube, beneath the steep cliffs with so many castles atop, and crossed the Black Forest.

Then it was on to Switzerland and France where they stayed for six weeks beside the still waters of the Rhone. James wrote many poems of his time there, of his puberty, of nature, of clouds and comets but this all came later from the mature poet. Early in 1938 they crossed the English channel and the boys returned to the Quakers school. James was encouraged at school to write verse and among his compositions at age twelve he received commendation for his poem : 'The Curse of War.' It was written against the historical background of the Spanish Civil War, fought between 1936 and 1939, and the growing rumours of a fast approaching Second World War. The children at the Quakers school at the time both boys and girls were encouraged to hold long discussions on pacifism, war and politics. James had written a good deal of juvenile verse by then and had acquired among the school students a reputation as a poet. A senior boy asked him to write a poem so that he could give it as his own to a girl he was courting. He obliged with some limitations as to the anatomy of the girls in question.

James later wrote of the Universal power of nature which reflected his emotions in many of his early poems. James school report in the summer term of 1938 records his english exam as 'exceptionally good.' The English teacher had added: 'He shows really promising work in poetry composition.' In his final term at Sibford, in summer of 1938, James overall work had really progressed and upon leaving school he marked the occasion with a poem 'farewell to Sidford.' It was a fitting farewell at the time, but from childhood to manhood it was a different story.

He remembered the barbarities of the dormitory in the beginning of adult life. The clear irrelevance of any external authority in the world of violence and self knowledge. The cruelty towards a German boy in which he shamefully took a part no doubt influenced by the approach of WW11 and the boys nationality. It was not uncommon to make a boy who was singled out for punishment to run the gauntlet. The peer group of boys would form two lines and make him dash between them. As he ran they would strike him with belts, shoes, or anything at hand. James because of his unusual approach to life got himself into some difficult situations, but he knew how to look after himself and was very courageous. If push came to shove and there was no other way out, he would resort to blows with his tormentors. He was really a true son of a pacifist and learnt from Archie Baxter's own war experiences to fight for ones' rights of independence despite what the masses of men or authorities dictated.

The family return to Brighton New Zealand with the approaching clouds of war in Europe on the horizon. As their Brighton home was still rented, they took a holiday home near the sea until the lease ended. Much of James's life was lived in reaction to the strict regime of his childhood and the strong personality of his mother who didn't know how to have emotional attachment to her children, I resonate with that, as like him I love my mother too, but like Baxter could never get any emotional mother son feelings of attachment with her. Without a doubt Millicent engendered James's rebellious nature that helped her son develop his linguistic gifts of expression He had the advantage also of a diversity of schooling in both Europe and England. Unlike him I got my worldly education and commercial know-how from my father. Mum was no academic, but was practical and hard working domestically. I gained a combination of these traits from my parents, of which I now have well earned poetic reasoning to pursue. This was more to do with Old Barney, my beloved grandfather who awakened the muses of creativity in me.

As for James Baxter, his literary talent came from his mother's side, and she was well educated and well spoken. James great creativity came from the Baxters. In his own words he believed his Brighton Primary education, rooted in English culture, created a barrier between him and New Zealand. The English boarding school increased that fact having been born in New Zealand. He had been out of touch with childhood companions during his English boarding days. I resonated with that having had the same difficulties of puberty, of cruelty of teachers and bullying imposed when sent off to a Sydney boarding school at the ripe old age of thirteen years. Baxter's childhood experiences were likewise expressed in his writings, in his urban connections with street people, in his close contact with nature, in expressing his powerful sensibility. He again like me found solace in nature. I found my greatest poetic influence in my grandparent Barney McPhillips and Baxter in is own father, Archie Baxter. He was a romantic poet of childhood memories of the Baxter clan, at a time when men worked with their hands and did not care for social acceptability, material possessions or worldly importance. He walked in the footsteps of the Baxter's world not the academic unemotional one of the Macmillian Browns from which his mother was cloned.

The brothers landed in the hustle and bustle of King's High School, Dunedin. Terence was the one who fitted the mold for the world. He was tall, good looking and popular with the girls. No one could be unfriendly to him. James was in a juxtaposition of image to his outgoing elder brother. He was bookish, had apparent schizophrenic behaviour pattens, felt he didn't belong to their world, and wasreduced to a nervous wreck like many of the authors he consumed in his tireless readings whilst still in his early teens. Like most private schools of the time, King's was entirely conventional, with a strict dress code and emphasis on military like discipline. Much like my GPS schooldays, competitive sport, particularly Rugby Union, was of major importance and a high level of achievement was maintained in fitness and training irrespective of weather conditions.

Baxter showed no display of good humour or conversation on the bus to and from school. He always seemed to have his nose stuck in a book or was creating crossword puzzles and word games. On occasions, he jotted down ideas on the ever present piece of paper he had the habit of carrying. Even the adult passengers considered him a little odd. Friends who knew him, would come to his aid by just remarking: " He is our poet."

James, would walk from bus to school with his class mates, but he was consistently late. He would just enter and say to the teacher: "No excuse for being late Sir." He was always given a mark of "Excellent" for any poems he wrote. When given a weekend assignment to complete, most boys managed four pages or so. Baxters assignments were never less than fourteen pages, for he went to great pains and depth of understanding in all his written words; it was in his nature to excel in these areas. Sometimes in the quadrangle, when other boys were talking sport, James would be seated alone reading or playing chess with a school club member. He was just not the usual kid who loved to play sport. Throughout his senior years he was mostly in the top 10 of students at exam time. Tops at English, fairly good at History, Latin and French. He was obviously a brain of a boy and advanced in algebraic, mathematic and chemical formula.

Of his subject matter, I too had high marks in history, top of the class in geography and proficient in algebraic formula. Unlike Baxter I was hopeless at languages except maybe Latin, and I would much prefer to talk and play sport then sit and play a game of chess. I did enjoy hiding my head in a book in the school library from time to time. My pet book escape was to catch up on biographies, mainly adventurers and explorer types. I managed to do this by pulling out of piano lessons all together, much to the disappointment of my parents. In Particular my father who was quite skilful as a piano player. Of course I carried on at the school as if I was on my way to music lessons but always headed straight for the library instead. I got away with that for a long time before I was caught out.

Baxter was in the main a well behaved timid boy and never made trouble. He escaped bullying by becoming the class clown when danger lurked. Caning for any minor infringement was always something that I copped though primary and senior school. I accepted this as I was viewed as having a rebellious nature by some teachers and fellow class mates. I took my punishment for various forms of disobedience as a means of toughening me up to the realities of the later world. I had experienced such cruelty from the day I first went to school in kindergarten. Such punishment in and after school activities were the norm as my understanding would have it. James Baxter's education was not like that, even though his schooling like mine had caning as an intricate part of the system. James rarely got caned and when he did it was applied lightly and any additional punishment for being in a teacher's bad books didn't last long. At school he was in the main a conformist and not considered in any way a rebel. It was when he entered the world at large that his views anticipated a late booming of non conformity, particularly when he discovered the benefits' of alcohol to sooth his nervousness and low self esteem. It had been noted by his teachers that he had enough trouble with his school companions to be singled out for further special punishment by the established methods. School boys are notoriously intolerant of eccentricity-and for a time Baxter was given a hard time. The bully boys began to accept his odd expressions and his class clown ways. Baxter had entered Kings at the start of the war and as the war escalated, younger masters enlisted and were fare-welled at assembly. The headmaster was often absent on military duties. Women teachers replaced men and old retired masters returned out of duty to the school to fill the gap.

The school was proud of its teaching community who were at war with the enemy once more. Archie saw to it that his son was exempt from the school cadet training as, like him he was a non conformist. He did not conform to normality in anything really. Neither in school sport nor community activity. In every way he was considered an oddity. He was generally considered a day dreamer. In every way Baxter was a loner.

I didn't buck cadet training at school, but I took a lot of physical punishment in cadets most Fridays for my stand against the futility of conditioning and training boys for some future possibility of war.

His peers did not understand Baxter, nor when Terence when he was called up, appealing against military service, especially when his case came up before the courts in Christmas 1941. The case was written up in the papers and Archie appeared as his witness. He was given a choice of non combatant service just like his father had been offered and he likewise refused it. He was sentenced to Defaulter's Detention and taken away as soon as he came of age. This was interpreted by the family as a still existing hostility towards Archie and his former objective stance in WW1. James, during this time retreated more and more into the world of books and wrote many a poem on faith and integrity, despite the fact that at heart he was then more of an atheist than a believer. He could not see the point of religion but he often retreated to the Bible for the lessons therein. It was at the time just another book to him. In the poems he wrote about war; they were all about its futility. James was entering more fully into the interests of his parents and their friends.

At the time of his detention, Terence was cast as the practical outdoor type, a non intellectual member of the family. He did however prove to be more reliable than his younger brother and was a greater help to Archie, giving him a hand around the house. By the time he was fifteen James was becoming more daring with risky activities. On a family holiday at Blackstone Hill, he rashly swam through a flooding culvert that ran under the roadway. He took ages to emerge from the other side and his terrified father, for the first time displayed his anger at his young son's foolishness. This didn't deter James in the slightest. He was often seen testing himself against adversity, swimming far out into Brighton Bay for the same reasons. Both parents were coming to realise that they could not trust his judgement on such occasions.

Climbing high into the canopy of a tree to rob a birds nest of a rare for my collection was not unusual for me as a boy. I didn't consider that I might fall as my focus was on the goal above me, for I was risk adverse back then Nor did I consider the risk of drowning when I went to the beach to catch waves. At that time I could not swim and would just wade out. I could dog paddle a little and let the pull of the tide carry me out to the point of the highest wave, then turn my body toward the shore, letting the exhilaration of riding the wave carry me to the beach. Climbing cliff faces and wading through snake infested swamps to examine whatever may be was another of doing what came naturally for a bush boy. I once, whilst away camping with school mates, took a dare with another boy and attempted to walk across the face of a fast flowing dam. Near the dam centre we were washed downstream and if it had not been for a broken branch of a tree protruding out a river level I might have drowned there and then.

My best mate, just before I was shuffled off to boarding school actually did drown whist we were both wading our way at high tide across a rising river. The fear of drowning for a time kept me out of the water. Once I learnt to swim enough to save myself I returned to the location where he drowned and made the effort to swim to the spot were he went down. I have always had a healthy respect for the dangers of swimming in the sea and river streams ever since. I am not a strong swimmer but still take a dip on hot summer days. When alcoholism took a hold of me I did even more risky activities, some of which just thinking about them now make my head spin. Playing chicken in cars with the risk of death ever present. Climbing the mast of a Russian ship blind drunk in a cyclone somewhere off the coast off Singapore. Entering the boxing ring to fight a professional boxer still suffering a hangover from the night before was another which resulted in two black eyes and a split lip. I could go on but suffice to say , I could only ever do these more dangerous activities when loaded up with dutch courage fuelled by alcohol.

At King's School his peers did not understand Baxter, nor realise his deep loyalty to his father and brother. Though he was considered unusual he was not ostracised. He proved to be respected for his intelligence and his ability as a speaker, because he seemed to be able to put great thought into his subject matter of oratory. In this he didn't take risks but made argument s that pointed out differences between facts as to the why's and wherefores. Despite some physical violence toward him for his objection to the war, by and large he experienced a degree of acceptance; especially as he advanced into higher classes. Baxters' earlier badgering and humiliations he later took to believe helped him as a writer. To his mind it taught him to distrust mass opinion and sort out his own ideas. Those school day experiences left a gap in him that was always filled by poetic expression. At graduation time he was not as yet decided on doing law, but was considering the role of a prophet, or a job as a literary critic.

Baxter was emotionally effected by the war. It was a topic discussed at home every day. The newspapers and radio broadcast on the progress of the conflicts were listened to and commented on by the family consistently. The mental anguish of relatives and friends, either in camp or in conflict with the community because of the Baxter's perceived unpatriotic views effected every aspect of James' life. As the war dragged on, Baxter retreated further into a private world, fighting his demons with a war of words. Some people turned to religion for politics, or pray for peace and to an end of senseless killing of humanity for the sake of so called liberty and freedom, but not James Baxter. With school now over he was looking forward to going to university. He realised the difficulty of writing and having the freedom to say what he wanted to say. The religious question is a case in point: "Religion to me is not an ardent need for belief in God, though in times of trouble I have been known to find one to murmur to. It is a brief in the sameness and continuity of life; thus, at any rate mentally, I would fear pain but not death, for I cannot believe in death."

The family took a holiday house at Naseby, a little gold mining settlement near Central Otago, for the Christmas New Year of 1944. Baxter, for the first time in ages became sociable. He joined the family and other holiday mates in tennis matches, swimming and rounders. However, he still enjoyed his own time away from it all in nature. He got away from his books and poetry for a time, but the notebook and pencil was ever present. Some new insights came to him though, as he took to reading Auden once more and remarked at the time: 'He is the best of the moderns..' It may well have been that Auden drew on mythology in his experiences and his writings which seemed to heighten the same inclination in Baxter which added to his later popularity as the poet of the 20th century, particularly for New Zealanders who were that way inclined. He read and amassed a lot of books which he added to his ever expanding library. The year 1944 in particular saw him reading the poetic works of Harold Munro, Siegfried Sassoon, and Gerard ManleyHopkins: "He is great, that is all one can say, except for reading him again and again, which helps him account for the tone of much of his early poetry. The long standing admiration and friendship with Ginn, one of Terence's friend during military internment, became another source of books he may not have otherwise read.

James read the lengths, breadth and depth of poems lent to him. Old King's School mates were surprised when Baxter did not try for a University scholarship. He had topped the class in English in matriculation and was top again in the lower years. He still didn't know what course to take, but expected at university he could talk to people about the ideas he was wrestling with, ideas such as the nature of good and evil. He was uneasy about the importance of academia and considered he could fire by himself with what mattered without joining the so called education system. It had a lot to do with the unease and admiration he held for his father, who to him showed utmost wisdom and courage; yet he was not academically educated - a simple ploughman, road contractor, and farmer who knew much more than most who had a degree from university. He believed that no one had more integrity or peace of mind than Archie Baxter.

It was James belief that the fact Archie's work with his hands kept him balanced and sane. He had literally made up his mind then to work with his hands, keep off the drink because of his alcoholism, of which he was then becoming aware, and he felt he needed time to find his own way of sexually explorating in the world outside of the classroom. Besides he had time to read up on the like of Wordsworth, Coleridge and had great admiration for Bronte's work especially "Wuthering Heights." as she had let the main character Heathcliff be his passionate self without clever intervention from her own self poetic ways. Although he couldn't take to Dylan Thomas initially, he found his poetic symbolism difficult but liked his prose, but felt his time would come to accept Thomas. I myself had great attachment to Dylan Thomas who seemed to endorse my own spiritual views of death in my youth. Perhaps Percy Shelley was more to my liking for he seemed to be reaching for answers that could not be had in my youth. These days I am more inclined to lean toward the Australian poets, like Henry Lawson and Adam Lindsay Gordon. This makes perfect sense really, as I am still a bush boy at heart.

Baxter enrolled at the University of Otago in English, Latin, French and Philosophy with the financial support of his parents. He was a seventeen year old youth full of energy and although not keen on the disclipine of fitness took to riding a push bike. The distance from the Otago university at Dunedin to Brighton was near twenty kilometres which he managed both ways on lecture days. The Macmillian Brown prize for poetry was up for grabs that year and the topic was 'Conveys.' Baxter had already written a poem on this subject before entering university and he just submitted it for the competition. He was awarded first prize and because he was the grandson of the founder of the prize the Otago Daily Times published it. It was his first brush with fame as a poet. Irrespective of faculty, students to varying degrees met at the local pub. The Bowling Green Hotel took pride of place and it was there Baxter met people and found an audience. In having had his fill of alcoholic beverage Baxter's usually made his way to the liver hash house where he enlarged his audience mixing with workers from the city. In his new found freedom from home, he began to drink heavily.

Undoubtedly it was in his DNA from his ancestral history, but the likes of Dylan Thomas pubs crawls and poetic influence at the bar over drinks may have had a little to do with it too. Thomas, incidentally died while drinking whisky at his local. He had consumed fifteen whiskies at the time whilst in his usual melancholic state had a sudden heart attack and died on the spot. Whilst Baxter was often seen in deep conversation with women he didn't have a girl friend nor had much luck in getting one. Women seemed to want to talk to him as he related well in friendship. Some of the senior women students lived in Huntly's St. Margaret's hostel and Baxter was a frequent visitor there. He enjoyed their company a lot, chatting and reading his poetry as though it was built into his Celtic character. Poetry readings were not common back then and Baxter, somewhat of a novelty, resonated with them it seemed. He was serious about his utterances but it was doubtful any women took him as seriously in his readings as he took himself. He was a fair scholar but not particularly gifted in languages.

Initially in that first year he was diligent in work and study, but as the year moved on his enthusiasm began to flag and he began to drop into lectures only when it suited him. The general logic of most subject matter was lost on him, preferring to delight more in the art of his own imagination. The lectures he enjoyed most were on Psychology, for it fascinated him. Unlike most students of Psychology, he didn't just read the potted versions of masters of intellectuals of this subject matter, he read the full versions. McDougall's experiences and that of Freud, Jung and Adler he read in depth. He knew his subject matter well enough to argue counter views with his lecturers over their interpretation. When the class was given an IQ test, Baxter scored as the most intelligent. He spent his spare time reading the works of Jesuit priest and poet Gerard Manley Hopkins from whom he learnt the trick of compressing his words into a strange method of letting go, which is the great trick of all poets. He was also influenced by the works of Wilfred Owen. By mid year 1944 he was feeling rather depressed and noted that his sense of writing had fallen off. He was enjoying university again but found that his expressions and readings only gave him some solace in the company of the bar crowds.

Baxter returned to reading during the winter months, turning to James Joyce's short stories and Tolstoy. From them he learnt the nature of death, the helplessness, the inevitability of the blindness of those living in the artificial light of the human experience ignoring the fact that death would ultimately claim them too. He realised that people might live without God, but they could not die without him. He was totally absorbed and obsessed by the idea of death. He was still too young to admire the style of 19th century novelists and the historic range of authors forecasting on matters of life and death. Baxter the pacifists and poetic genius of New Zealand produced a more sparingly colloquial style that suited local experience.

It may have come from delving into the world of consciousness of the authors he was attracted too, but religion kept coming to mind. He told his friends that he did not think he would ever become an atheist, but remain agnostic, although he often felt that vague foreknowledge of the something else. He reconciled that with the wholeness of the Universe, but never the presence or necessarily of a God. He was now doing the fairly hard hards at University and finish the year with a score of 85% with only two other students ahead of him in the finals. Baxter's excessive drinking and suicidal moments of behaviour reached his mate Ginn and brother Terence who were still in detention as conscious objectors. He replied to their letter of concern with the fact that he was 'feeling more solid than they might think and growing up. Not to regard that part of him showing erratic behaviour, drink and mood swings as the whole but just a partial not his entire being. He was more concerned for his brother's predicament than his own wellbeing. In August he travelled with his mother to Auckland and she took him to see Lawrence Baigent at Caxton Press. Millicent did the talking requesting the publishers to read his work. Baigent read the work overnight and was bowled over by his brilliance and agreed to publish JKBs work.

Baigent spent the next evening with Baxter and was surprised how well read he was for such a young man. They talked until two in the morning. Bailgent later said 'We went though virtually all English poetry from Shakespeare until the present day, backwards, forwards and sideways.' It seemed he had read everything and could recite them all verbatim. He had brought a little notebook with him and recited many a new poem just written in the previous few days. It appeared he was then writing at least six poems a day and at the time had amassed thousands of words. He was really on a roll. On the twenty first of November 1944, Baigent advised him that his *Beyond the Palisade* was printed but not bound yet, and the first one hundred copies would probably be ready by the end of the month. Baxter had planned to go fruit picking in Central Otago but the crop had been damaged by frost, So his parents arranged a job for him at Purakanui on a dairy farm on the coast, north of Dunedin. It was really a plan set by his parents because his heavy drinking was beginning to be out of control and they thought it would help him. Purakanui was an isolated location far away from liquor supplies. The routine of six in the morning start doing manual labour all day until early evening would help dry him out. Several times he had been found well in his cups and fast asleep at the back of the Brighton bus when it reached the terminus. Sometimes he spent the night there, though it was only a short walk home.

The fact that he had given up smoking and was in good health was a saving grace too. Like all true alcoholics, he didn't believe he had an issue but the grip of the grape hadn't as yet taken full control over his will power. The family he was living with belonged to the Salvation Army. He felt soothed in spirit by their humming of hymn and sacred rituals. He still carried his note book and pencil, and the old Salvationist farmer thought him vague and dreamy and warned his daughter to beware.

Baxter's one year full time at the University of Otago had modestly regraded him with passes in English and Philosophy, but he flunked Latin and French by failing to qualify for the terms of attending the required number of lecturers. He had been too preoccupied with sex and the fantasies that go hand in hand. Likewise lectures interfered with his drinking career. So in 1945 after only one year he dropped out of University to focus on his writings. He considered time at university a wilderness wasteland. Archie and particularly Millicent had road mapped his future in their eyes; to get a degree in English at Otago University then go on to Oxford or Cambridge to obtain a further English degree, become a scholar and teach English literature. He railed against this in argument with his parents with plausible arguments to be free to do as he pleased. In reality he was beginning to follow the destiny of becoming a hobo. He wept bitterly after a confrontation with his parents who were doing their best to encourage him to snap out of it and return to University.

James took a job in a foundry where he found work heavy, demanding and unhealthy. The inhaling of iron and enamel dust waa unpleasant. He took to visiting a ships quarters in his lunch break, climbing the mast and generally showing off. The ships crew remained aloof to him, so he changed his modus operandi and returned to visit the university and the pub were he once more discussed Hopkins and Chatterton. By drinking in the university pubs Baxter kept in touch with the social life of the university. Baigent the publisher had been concerned for James and his dropping out of University partly due to drinking sprees and he chastised him over his recent behaviour. Baxter as an intellectual always had an answer for others to justify his lifestyle, his drinking and his insights in poetic form. He wrote to Baigent parcelling those of varying intellect and classified most writers in the intelligent and unbalanced frame. He no doubt drew on his own psychological understand of human nature in doing so. Baxter indicated those he admired but could not be, but indeed wished to be. Again, drawing on his understanding of human psychology, he justified has own uniqueness and retorted that he knew what he was doing as if it was only a temporary thing. It was obvious that he had not yet recognised his own alcoholism. He still believed that despite his hobo mentality and erratic behaviours that he had acquired the insight necessary to change direction at will. A typical blind spot for one whose ego was running the show and not his higher self. *My own drinking was out of hand from the very first drink that touched my lips. Dad first introduced me to alcohol with Shandies, half beer half lemonade at the age of sixteen and by the time I had reached my seventeenth birthday I had graduated to full strength beer and spirits and had my driving licence. I was already in the grip of the grape and not my conscious reasoning self. The signs were there when I first raced the car playing chicken.*

Again when exceeding the speed limit through town, on the wrong side of the road and under the influence, being chased by the local motorbike cop. I had my licence just six months and I got out of that one because I was my father's son and the cop was sympathetic, but he did chastise me to wake up and lay off the booze. Back then I made promises but I didn't keep them. The drinking sprees kept coming all with memory loss as to what had happened during a black out. Later, at age twenty one, I hit the booze even harder due in no small part to a relationship breakdown. My then career in banking did't help as bankers had a daily drinking culture of boozing everyday after work. Drinking in my twenties got me into more fights than feeds in pubs and I wrote off a car or two under the influence too. Dutch courage always raised it head and it was common practice for me to do risky things whilst under the influence. More than once I ended up on the bar room floor in my attempts to pick up a pretty woman who was already in a relationship. I went were angels feared to tread and suffered the end of more than one man's fist back then.

Like Baxter I found myself waking in the backseat of a train carriage or sleeping blind drunk in a park for the night. Awakening in a not too balanced state of mind or physical shape. Once I remember waking up in my own vomit, being licked clean by a pack of dogs. I was a wild and woolly youth and it was not until many years later, in my getting of wisdom through the calamity of my life's trials and tribulations, that I began to wake up. I finally reached a point of no return, had my time in rehabilitation for depression and alcoholism. I eventually woke up to the fact that I was powerless over alcohol and I had issues of a spiritual nature that had to be faced.

James Baxter with regard to his dropping out of University was considered to be a dreamer, writer poet and was escaping reality by choice. He cleverly wrote about his demons without facing them. He understood through his university study of psychology, the personality types of those he admired the most; those intellectual and balanced few to whom he wished to be like. He however saw that he was not of that ranking at the time, but found justification in belonging to the lesser, the intellectual unbalanced. He was so well read and drew on the life of those poets and writers of the past that he admired and could justify as being like, in his own false self image. If one could draw on the true human balanced and real spirituality of a creative individual, then Baxter had it in his poetry, equivalence of speech as teacher and lecturer and his concern for the less fortunate. I struggle to simplify the meaning of the poet, the man, other than to say that Baxter in his understanding of his psychological explanations to those who were concerned for him was caught up in his eccentric explanation of himself, his creativity, lack of discipline in dropping out of university and his drinking to excess, he attempted to find psychological justification in his communication to speech to friends and family. Baxter used psychological expertise to explain away his then life and found in analytical self analysis just cause doing so. To be fair he was like most of us as flawed character living in the ego at the expense of really living our God given ultimate purpose.

He did find the way out by going inward as he matured and much of that came to him through the steps of Alcoholic Anonymous, but that was towards his end and will be discovered in a latter chapter. I hasten to add Baxter the poet was for the greater part of his life living entirely in his ego without the awareness of another self, although he found a mysterious essence in his poetry as all who read him do. Baxter was living in a kind of shadow self of his real persona, presenting an exaggerated version of self by wearing a mask in public, but when alone he was unable to face his own reality, except to escape in written word poetically expressed. On the surface it appeared to be that he really knew himself but could not face his own demons without a drink. He did not behave as one might expect. He showed surface signs of his better character but fell hopelessly into his defects of character. He wore the mask of the shadow self to convince himself and other, but could not go beyond the character of the darker side. He was in denial of everything one might call normal behaviour, casting it all into oblivion or anything and everything that the ego refuses to associate with. Baxter was unrealistic, unconscious of himself acting blindly on instinct, fooled by illusion of his conscious self coming to meet him in poetic form. JKBs some times assertive behaviour, convictions, strength and vitality could suddenly turn to aggressive and ruthless lack of care, impatience- the cunning and baffling disposition of a classic alcoholic. For better or for worse for the young man of poetic spirit, his collection of poems called *Beyond the Palisad* , equally worked on with his publisher Baigent himself and accomplished academic and poet, was to go on sale at the end of March 1945.

Whilst the book was being printed Baigent had fortuitously shown Baxters manuscript to Allen Curnow who was preparing an anthology of New Zealand poetry for the Caxton Press, entitled *A book of New Zealand verse 1923-45*. Curnow was impressed enough to include six of Baxter's poems in his book. He would have included more but considered he might steal the thunder of Baxter's book sales and being the charitable man that he was, wrote an additional couple of paragraphs to the already written introduction to James Baxter's poetic masterpiece. It worked miracles for the sale of his book for both Curnow and Baxter's books appeared in New Zealand book stores almost simultaneously. Curnow's anthology with its introduction, established him as the leading light and critic of New Zealand poetry, and put James Baxter's first book of poetry and prose on the the best selling list of all New Zealand poets. Lawrence Beigent printed five hundred copies of James Baxter's *Beyond the Palisade*. Baigent took great pains in the order and arrangement of the poems which pleased the poet. James Baxter wrote this book during WW11 and it was that period in time in which he was profoundly affected by it. The image of the book suggests the perils faced by the Baxter clan. Both victim and aggressor appears repeatedly throughout the book, The Baxter's common denominator.

CHAPTER 4.

THE POWER OF THE WRITTEN WORD

There are tragic symbolisms of his own short comings with violent regularity of his own preoccupation with death in his attitude to life and in his writings. He paradoxically likened poems in his *Beyond the Palisade* as a vocation as poet, as his life enhancing saviour. The book was considered by those of academic persuasion as lyrical and mournfully haunting.The book was a precursor to the direction he would take. He was on the road less travelled to some degree, in the company of Blake, Yeats and Auden, burning with imaginative creativity, guided by myth and symbolism. The book illustrated, according to the Who's Who, a masterpiece of technical skill and control of a variety of forms of verse. It was more than that, for it portrayed the open soul of a wounded animal who in his youthfulness went to great lengths explaining the mystery of his poetry. He was in his prime and he was now a celebrity. Whilst he claimed that he wanted oblivion it was nonsensical. At the height of Baxter's teenage book fame, Mother Millicent was totally preoccupied, collecting information on those sentenced to detention. She raised money, sent books and visitors to bolster the detainees spirits, no doubt mindful of her eldest son Terrence's plea, for he had been in detention for a some time. She was active in the Peace Council and the Howard reform league and worked hard to improve the living condition of prisoners. She help assemble material to send to the government, appealing on behalf of the detainees. Archie meanwhile spent much of his time counselling young men who had been called up for service, appeared as witness for them and when their appeals against military service were being heard. It took a great deal of preparation for each case. James, when on the home front become involved in the frequent discussion that went with his parents commitment. James isolated himself from the war which pained him and he sunk more deeply into his writings. James landed at Baigent's flat in Christchurch for Easter 1945 armed with a new collection of his poems entitled '*Cold Spring*' and considered them better than his *Beyond the Palisade*, but none of them were ever featured.

Baigent introduced him to his fellowship of personal artistic friends. It was to Allen Curnow to whom he was most grateful, for he was able to spend more time with him after the success of both their books. Baxter realised the status of this new found friend, for without his input and inclusion of the six poems he selected for his book of New Zealand verse 1923-1944, Baxter might not have had the fame that was imposed upon him. He also spent time over Easter with Basil Dowling, Rita Angus the painter and musician Douglas Lilburn, who agreed to set his 'University Song' to music. These artists all become personal friends, as did Baigent as the two got to know each other better. Both publisher and author were very talkative and they burnt the midnight oil as they talked over each other without drawing breath. They had the happy knack of hearing what the other was saying whilst at the same time talking, so it was a continual flow of conversation without a stop. They shared a room for the night and Baxter out lasted his new found friend in loquacity and either would not or could not shut up. Baigent fell asleep to the sound of Baxter still raving on.

After his return to Dunedin, Baxter told Baigent that he felt very happy with their friendship and that their Easter break together had done him the world of good. Some of his readers of his poetry in *Beyond the Palisade* considered his poetry too despairing and too full of death mood and self pity. I for one have a great collection of poetry books of poets works from medieval poetry to the moderns and hasten to say that death poems, those written of pending death and romanticism are the workings of the greatest of poets of all time.

James returned to his work at the Green Island Foundry, shifting from store work to the heavier work of range firing. His work mates were surprised at how well the young man was able to cope. The foundry workers, all older men, were hardened drinkers and he managed to keep up with them in their drinking sprees at the local pubs too. He was soon restless and planned to go up country to some fresh air and to work on a sheep run in the spring. He was keen to get back to writing poetry and develop a new style too.

Early Spring he sent Baigent another collection of poems and four sonnets, all of which were printed. At the time he had an affair with a young married women, and the husband luckily for James took a tolerable view but insisted the affair cease. JKB complied but insisted that the relationship had done him a lot of good, but could not explain how it did. He headed north to Wanaka Station in Central Otago in September 1945 working with the sheep, drafting and picking over crutching and dead wool in the paddocks. In addition, he took to the duties of top dressing, standing on the back of a lorry and feeding superphosphate into a hopper.

If he had a CV at the time, it would include his occupations as roustabout, gardener, lawn cutter, woodshed cleaner, ditch digger and swamp cleaner and sometimes poet. Whilst it proved to be a hard life he was fit and healthy and completely off the drink at that time. James loved the splendour of the country and its surrounds, the nearby lake, snow capped mountains, green willow trees under a huge blue sky. He was certainly not missing the iron dust of the foundry, nor the drink for that matter, but he was missing his family. He wrote home detailing the difficulties of working in the cold conditions, of his improved mood and the fact that his mind was clear and he had been doing a great deal of thinking. He loved to walk the mountain tracks, round up the sheep, absorb the smell of nature and noted that his life and love was far better than sex. He was not writing as he felt, for he had no need for self justification. A healthy simple life of good meals, plenty of fresh eggs, meat and vegetables sustained him as did the physical work on the Station. Millicent sent him some books he requested and he began to read again. He was also reading three books a week borrowed from the public library. Apart from the chores on the property he had to attend to all his own domestic duties including washing his own clothing by hand. A learning curve for one who had a domesticated mother to take care of these necessities of life in the past and the boarding school days of his teens.

He did a great deal of psychoanalyse to distract himself whilst plucking wool from stinking sheep. Like him, I clearly recalled events from birth until the age of five. A time of much personal hardship for me but a time of retreating into my own fantasyland too. Like Baxter, I would have been able to record some wonderful fantasy had I had the ability to write back then.

The way of life on Wanaka Station suited Baxter more than the world of academia at University. He had much more of his father Archie's character, emotions and common poetic feeling and in particular the Baxter clans attitude to physically hard work as an outdoor person in preference to four grey walls of discontent in study. Unlike the Macmillian Browns, who were all about controlled fixed goals, emotion had no place in their lives. James let his emotion flow on paper and he did that naturally. The outdoor work gave him plenty of time to reflect and he felt a new stability but missed the stimulus of intellectual company.

As far as I can recall I wrote verse from the moment I learnt to read and write. I use to write prose from an early age and had a habit of underlining text of interest in pencil from books borrowed from friends or libraries many of which I would forget to return. On the inside front cover I noted page numbers to turn to for future reference. it was the writers notations in symbolic references to suffering and death that helped my attention the most. I guess witnessing my Uncle John's death at age fourteen, when I was around four years of age had something to do with it. The drowning death of Kevin, my soul mate at the age of twelve when we were at the beach together filled me with further sorrow and pierced like a dagger into my heart, causing me even more to escape into the fantasy world of poets and adventurers.

No doubt the symbols and signs of the indoctrination of the Catholic faith and Christ hanging on the cross for the sins of mankind, as taught by the Sisters of no Mercy and regular attendance as an altar boy at funeral proceedings may well have set the template for my childlike understandings of life and death. I was soon enough shipped off to a private boarding school in Sydney, to be educated in character and soul into the vision of Marist education for leadership values, the common good, and to reaffirm the values and traditions of the Catholic faith. The aim was to prepare boys to manhood, to grow up with compassion, a good education and confident to face life on life terms in the wider world, once having graduated. To a great degree the methods adopted worked but some like me who bucked the system had to learn the hard ways of the big wide world in the university of hard knocks. Certainly I worked my way up the corporate ladder, but much to my parents disappointment continued to change career direction many time before I finally settled down and got married. The need to work hard for the man was over, so I resigned my corporate position, seeking a new vision to run my own business enterprises. This way of life continued for the latter half of my working life with an outward view to provide for my love ones. I did return to corporate life for a few years but could not settle back to that way of making a living and once more returned to the life of an entrepreneur.

It proved in time that working for myself was the right choice materially for my family and we become quite well off. My drinking career escalated during those years as I sold my soul to be a slave of working for work sake with ever increasing financial commitments. I sold my creative imagination to the linear side of my brain in business. I was on a treadmill of material success but personally I was not content with it at all. However, it seemed that I was locked in and so busy running two business ventures that I had no time to relax or consider any alternative to the outer world.

It all came to a head when, what seemed to be my lot in life was turned upside down by a series of tragedies that befell me. I was gutted by it all and was falling ever deeper into the pit of hell. The only residual parachute I had was alcohol. So like a bandaid on a cut I took to the bottle and the grip of the grape tightened.

James before his twentieth birthday had already concluded that he was not drawn to holy wedlock; perhaps due in part to his early sexual experiences with a young married women and female friends of university year influence. JBKs poetically philosophised as such in a letter to his mother in 1945, concluding that the normal social patterns were not at the heart of a poet, but to be found in the wind and the pollen fragrances, in the desolation of natures embrace. He understood the nature of the masses of men of quiet desperation in their slavery to be an upright citizen, to marry, procreate and educate offspring as an ever repeating process from generation to generation as if it were ordained by God. James could not see himself going down that married path, for it held little interest to him, but he had one proviso- until the capacity of loving another person became complete, then such a way of life may be called upon. In the letter to Millicent he added an adjunct: 'for even then if it happened to come to be, it mattered little for few loves are ever complete.' Being conscious of what his mother's down to earth reaction might be to his letter, he concluded that he was writing that which is usually left unspoken and summed it up with a reason of fact that he like all poets had a licence to be strange anyway. At such a young age that letter summed up what never really changed for him. The ever real tension between art and marriage, for poetry flourishes outside the normal patterns of social behaviour and most human love only results in disappointment. He confided in Baigent that he was growing up and loosing some of his adolescent attitude. He confided to his mother that whilst his poetry was somewhat gloomy, he was himself contented and it was the nature of a poetic soul to be melancholy, otherwise he wouldn't write poetry.

In the Summer of 1945- 46 life for the young Baxter men began to change. A young friend of Millicent, one Lenore Bond had met Terence and began to go out with him. The Baxters and James were keen to see the relationship flourish as Terry, although having many prior relationships, all had been short lived. By the time they were married in the following August, Lenore had felt she married the whole Baxter clan, for she had become the sister James had never had. For Archie and Millicent she was not just daughter in law, but for all intention purposes daughter.

James in March 1946 was working at the Burnside Freezing works and again drinking heavy. He ceased for a while on the advice of a medical student friend and was once more on the path of righteousness having read Jung's *Modern man in search of a Soul* and *Psychology of the Subconscious*. In a clearer head again, felt he had toughened up and at long last had separated from parental influence. However it was not too long before his heavy drinking broke out again and the habit of not coming home at night led to arguments with his mother. Archie seemed to be more understanding of his wayward son, perhaps because of his own father's alcoholism. Baxter was often seen drinking at the Captain Cook with his usual group and a female medical student to whom he held some attachment. She was more fascinated by the attention given her by the young poet than by any romance that might blossom.

During 1946 and 1947 Baxter's drinking problem reached a crescendo and he was sometimes drunk for days on end. He seemed to have completely lost direction and was showing signs of restlessness, irritability and discontent. On any typical day when he worked he would put in a solid six hours, collect his pay and go on a spree for a week or two. He drifted from job to job and was developing a history of being sacked time and time again. A student friend remarked that Baxter would spend the morning in the pub and meet him in the afternoon, embracing him with a suggestion to go on the booze for the afternoon. Baxter although so young was not a pretty sight on his benders, showing signs of the excess of the drink with deep purple features and white lines around the collar where the discolouration ceased. After he dried out he would start the day with a couple of raw eggs which he dropped into a bottle of milk taken from the front of a neighbour's door left by the milkman.

He drank this on the way to the bus whilst working at the iron works again. At the time he was freeloading on the floor of a flat where he often stayed the night. Baxter back then was in denial of his alcoholism but still held the floor at parties, paced the room with his head thrown back, sometimes supposedly nervously ruffling his hair until it stood almost upright and he would just talk and talk. In fact his active mind was still in full flight when his audience was passing out or leaving to go home. Terence had pulled him up more than once on his self obsessed conversations. . He seemed unaware that he was full of his own self importance which is the nature of an egocentric alcoholic. *I should know, I was no different to Baxter in that regard.*

Mostly his friends suffered indifferently from his fluency, but were impressed by his ability to reel off copious passages from Wordsworth, Coleridge and Percy B Shelley, then in the blink of an eye switch to the poems of Curnow, Glover and Thomas which he knew completely. Despite his alcoholism his reputation grew immensely at the time and people with similar literary aspirations would flock to hear him wherever he spoke. He drifted away from his relatives and close friends preferring to attend student parties and the annual Boat Club Ball. He was sometimes invaded by acute awareness of a problem with his sexuality. He mistakenly used as a template on the matter, his brother Terrence, whom he knew was better looking, had little problem in attracting female partners because of his sex appeal and had a much higher self esteem. In Terence's favour he appeared something of a romantic but elusive, which was like a magnetic attraction to some of the girls he dated. James had none of these attractions for women, and it was a quality in his brother which he greatly envied. It was even more painful to him because he was naturally demonstrative and affectionate. Terence was also an accomplished dancer and James did not have that ability. It seemed to him that dancers would sit around and talk with girls when not in the swing on the dance floor and of that Terrence was a natural.

James, from the female point of view was considered like an angel with beautiful blue eyes, golden fair skin, and a fascinating voice. The girls also seemed to be attracted by his poetic ability and his recall of so many writers works. In most instances he was not considered for his sex appeal .When he did see a girl who seemed to be attracted to him, it was as if she was just making an impression as much as a sympathetic ear. His self confidence was shaken and he often wondered about his sexuality.

JKB did have a brief homosexual affair with a university lecturer and whilst he did get involved briefly, it was to him more a psychological experiment. Baxter later admitted other homosexual episodes in his life, and although he could not be classed as homosexual in his larger life, he never the less took time to come to terms with his sexuality. It was not such an uncommon thing for a youth whose overcharged hormones found himself in close encounters of the same sex. Twice at boarding school other lads tried it on with me but I gracefully declined as such activities were contra to my desires and my moral code. Only once did I find myself in a difficult situation in that regard. It was a man of the cloth and family friend whom I had visited to seek advise about loneliness and the absence of a girlfriend at the time. I arrived at his office door in dire straights under the influence of drugs and alcohol. The close encounter on that occasion is buried in the dark recesses of my soul now. As I now recall, it was over five decades ago and It had left me morally shaken and near suicidal. I knew from that day that categorically I was not homosexual and not interested in the slightest in male to male bodily encounters.

Baxter at the time had a radical view on relationships with women and discussed openly his views on marriage and considered romantic love was mostly an illusion. The nearest he came to love was a romantic interest in one girl he met in a radical group of politically active students in 1947. The love God did ultimately show its favour in the person of Jane Aylward, a medical student at Otago University. Her appearance was strikingly beautiful and was undoubtedly very attractive to the poet. At the time Jane's father was one of the Labour Government's first special area doctors and was prominent in left wing politics. As an atheist he was particularly critical of religion. Like her father, Jane adopted atheism and her views on all morality were liberal. Knowing Archie Baxter's pacifist and social views, Jane's father Stanley wrote and asked him to refer a Latin tutor, as Latin was a part of the Medical Preliminary Examination. Archie recommended James, who despite the fact that he had not even passed first year Latin, relished the assignment. Upon meeting Jane for the first time, James fell passionately in love and so he began to haunt Jane's pad in Castle Street, and just could not stay away from her, counting the hours of her comings and goings. When Jane visited Millicent at Brighton, she found the girl good looking but not the right girl for James. Jane admired Baxter's genius but had the view that he was not right for her either. Later that year at a party in George Street, Jane fell in love with the man she would marry and James' most passionate and satisfactory relationship was over. The anguish of having loved and lost remained with him for a long time.

I knew that feeling having had my first real sexual experience with a nymphomaniac for the better part of a year. It ended abruptly when she married another within three weeks of the break up. She had obviously been two timing me all along. That girl surely had a huge appetite for constant orgasms.

It was not long before Baxter met the young woman who was to become his most significant female partner. Jacquie Sturm, a young Maori women had come to Dunedin from the North Island to study for a degree. Medical degrees were the preference of many a young serviceman returning from the war, and whilst Jacquie passed the entry exam her, the remaining places were prioritised to returned soldier male competitors. Her strength was not so much the scientific subjects but in the arts. She switched to a B.A. course and developed special interest in psychology. Baxter, in the mean time had a revelation with symbolic death poems and has fallen in love with the poetic works of Dylan Thomas. He carried his most recent published work *Deaths and Entrances* in his working coat and drunk or sober he would sprout Tomas verbatim. He had a collection of all Thomas's work in particular *Under Milk Wood*. He even went so far as to wear similar clothing as Dylan Thomas that he had seen in a photograph of him. Thomas's outlandish behaviour was matched only by James equally riotous ones. He once enlisted a young policeman to intercede for him at the bar when refused a drink because the barman had mistakenly thought he was under age. On another occasion he sat in the front row of a University lecture and challenged the Professor of English on Shakespeare. He was perhaps in his head challenging his dead grandfather who once stood on the same rostrum.

I recalled that Dylan Thomas had the same alcoholic gene as Baxter and me too. Thomas life experience saw him though depression in his teens and the Second World War too. His was an attraction to death and desolation not unlike Baxters nor mine. Whilst my poetic youthful expression was more centred on the Vietnam war and as a pacifist in the aftermath, I was not the creative poet that somewhat developed in my latter years for perhaps I had not suffered enough at the time. But I had a fascination with death and romance as did the man of my then admiration, Dylan Thomas. He was long dead and gone after his fifteen whisky drinking spree which killed him whilst in his cups at the bar, when I discovered his poetry. I think his *When all my five and country senses see: Especially when the October winds; After the funeral* and my favourite *Do not go gentle into that good night,* summed up how I resonated with Thomas in my youth.

Baxter to his contemporaries was a poetic genius in spite of his weird dress sense. Alcoholism had deeply affected his character in his twenties, and critics regarded him as self centred, self indulgent, pouting and posturing as a fake Dylan Thomas. Baxter's argument to the contrary was that everyone should live as they choose and not as others liked them to live. As early as 1947 Baxter had the happy knack of bringing home unusual people. Terrence in particular was resentful of James fostering strangers on his parents without warning. Baxter was in his own way, despite uncontrollable alcoholic behaviour, doing AA step work before he understand what AA was all about. As I recall I had a somewhat similar habit with friendships, bringing home a league of nationalities over time. I befriended Chinese, English, Polish, Serbian and some other dark characters to boot who ultimately ended up at my parent's home. Those were my male acquaintances but the female ones were of equal diversity.

James continued to write poetry which in his latter sobriety he rejected as bar room verses, a nonsensical and better forgotten. A wake up call came in a verse he wrote towards the end of 1947 when he likened his life experience to planting seeds. He reconciled that he had become a man of sorts in the process and in time the seeds would come to harvest. He made his way to Christchurch and started a new university career, with the hidden agenda to associate himself with a Jung psychologist. Baxter found it difficult to settle in, as he did not have the backing of his parents nor the security of home to turn too. He had made a clean break from his family influence and for once he was being adult. Unlike his former years this was new ground and he could not depend upon seasonal work for income, nor his parents. He had to rely on his own resources and he felt less sure of himself. Professor Sutherland had come to Dunedin from Canterbury University to deliver a series of lectures on psychology and Jacquie Sturm attended. She was suitably impressed enough to shift to Christchurch to study. At the time Baxter was an acquaintance who no doubt had designs on her. He begged her not to go but she went anyway. So it was much to Baxter's delight that he renewed his friendship with Jacquie. Whilst it was the first time she had lived outside a hostel they did not live together, but they saw a lot of each other.

Baxter fortunately had his base in Christchurch and had his Caxton Press acquaintances to turn too. He had a special relationship with his old friend and publisher Lawerence Baigent. The Caxton press had been a grand phenomenon for New Zealand. It had published many famous authors and Baxter's first book *Beyond the Palisade* as a forerunner to the *Landfall* was a windfall. Earlier in Dunedin the literary circle of many of the fraternity, especially those who believed in the poet's creativity were upset by one of Baxter's university lecturers. He had stated categorically that Dylan Thomas' genius stemmed from drunkenness. *I for one, who wrote a great deal of poetry and song in my early twenties, would only reach a heightened level of creativity after a bender.* So back then I would have, in all probability agreed with him. It was a different scene in Christchurch where Baxter the marvel was greeted warmly and made most welcome Those in the press, creative fields and university had high hopes and speculation about his promise in work output and fulfilment. There were some in the literary community who were aware of his habitual habit of getting drunk and they treated him with suspicion and some with jealously, but they could not fault his creativity as poet.

The shining light on the literary circuit at the time was a great personality, Rex Fairburn. Rex was not only a great poet but physically an athlete of commanding presence. He had been acclaimed as critic, humorist and raconteur. Rex was second to none in the literary circles of New Zealand, had a great voice as an orator and little effort making himself heard anywhere, even in pubs with bad acoustics. On a visit to Christchurch, when in full flight in a pub, everyone was attentive to his poems and any message that passed his lips. Whenever Fairburn visited Christchurch he was met by his creative friends and treated with great affection by those who worshiped him. Coupled with that there was a well established hierarchy which caused Baxter to have to make some adjustments to his top of the hoop former ways back in Dunedin.

Baxter soon renewed his friendship with former acquaintances in the Christchurch creative circle. He struck up a close friendship with artist Rita Cook and hung about the printer and calligrapher Leon Benseemann, who like Cook was an artist. These artistic and creative types were the people that Baxter loved to be with and converse. He also had a close friendship with Denis Glover, the printer and poet. Sometimes Glover would drift and drink the afternoon away with Baxter whose talk he thought brilliant. The young poet would talk over his poems with Glover who convinced him to be more sparing with words, not to work in the shadows of English poets of whom Baxter was influenced, including Dylan Thomas. It was not too many years later that Baxter had outgrown the Welsh poet anyway. Glover advise was as it should be, in not standing in the shadows of other poets and authors. An enlightenment dawned on Baxter that he was more intellectual than instinctive, but at the same time he was analytical. He expressed his anti-intellectualism by rejecting the tendency to be moderate by necessity, to be controlled and calculating which could be summed up in one word- academic. He had gathered this notion from identification of the Baxter freelance ancestors as opposed to that of his Mother's father, the academic John Macmillian Brown.

James was nourished by reading McDougall and Jungian psychology and in point of fact anti- intellectual, for he was in external rebellion of what was taking place within himself. Yet as early as 1948 he was still drawn to Canterbury University College. He attended regular lectures though he had not enrolled in any course. Sometimes he took a conspicuous part in the literal life on campus and despite his lack of academic qualification, he appeared as literary Editor in the first of the Canta that year. He had entered his editorial address as 'any pub.' In mid July 1948 Baxter spoke at the Literary Club on the poetry of Dylan Thomas and of his personal problems in self expressive poetry. He also pointed out that Thomas wrote not what he thought he should say but what he always wanted to say. He identified with the poet's explosive themes on sex, death and sin. James expressed the thought that Thomas's work was more a reaching out than a classification and he used symbolism as emotional content as a great poet only can do. It was clear at the time that he was identifying themes in Thomas 's poetry that he was attempting to incorporate into his own poetic style. That year he contributed three poems to the *Review*, the Canterbury College annual magazine.

The wounds from his infatuation with Jane Aylward had slowly faded by the end of 1948 but her ghost often appeared etched in his poetry still. James had grown fond of Jacquie Sturm and late in 1948 he asked her to marry him. Jackie's Maori parents had designs on her intellectual pursuits being fulfilled and were not impressed by a mixed blood marriage either. They even went to the Professor of the Psychology Department of Canterbury College where Jackie was a student to ask him to intervene. They had designs on a better match for their daughter within their own-race. The Professor suggested that Baxter might best apply for a post as writer on a pending Antarctica expedition, that might just be the catalyst to breaking the bond of wedding vows. Likewise the Baxters too held little enthusiasm for the marriage. Whilst Archie and Millicent had liberal views on marriage they could not envisage a marriage of their young son to a Maori.

Such opposition merely strengthened the resolve of the headstrong young couple. Jackie resented the interference of her family and Baxter just dug in harder and pursued the quest with added zeal. The courtship continued with Baxters intensity to pursue her ever increasing. Baxter's friends advised Jackie that Baxter would not be the ideal husband. He was too unstable in his ability to remain sober and it was a fact that he could not hold down steady employment. Love is blind and Jackie undeterred, through all the objections to the marriage took Baxter to meet her parents on a number of occasions. They initially were reserved in their meeting but grew to be more accepting overtime. Baxter, despite his alcoholism managed to hold down his job and his gloomy drunk behaviour and the holy bond of matrimony took place in St. John's Cathedral, Napier on 9th December 1948. Both families were in attendance and Jacquie's Maori father gave her away. She was twenty two at the time and James just twenty-one. Initially they lived with Jacquie's married sister in Wellington but tensions between between them all in a tiny living space made it impractical to remain there.

They soon found a quaint small cottage in the Western Hut Valley which was fully furnished. There was no heating except for an open fire, so Baxter collected and sawed up wood from the nearby river's edge. The facilities were primitive, with outside toilet and no light. For washing there was only a copper and tub. They had no refrigerator, but both were not troubled by this, having been used to a simple life in their upbringings and their living requirements were modest anyway. Baxter continued working at the Ngauranga abattoir on a regular wage. They were soon expecting a baby and Baxter had already an ancestor name for a boy, John McColl. It was a vastly different way of life that the drifter alcoholic poet now found himself in. He was working very hard at the abattoir, worried about paying the rent and the bills. Not having a car, he rode his bike to and from work. Whilst his general health was good, for some time now he had been suffering from irritable bowel syndrome. Neither Jacquie nor James had parents in the area to help them through difficult times. Baxter consoled himself that he was no longer alone and had a regular income. So with no worries over money, lodging and the concern of his relatives, they settled down to an initial married bliss. They were contented with their lot and enjoyed the friendship with their new neighbours too.

My romanticism in my early twenties afforded me much pleasure and equally burdened me with constant sorrows upon break ups. Mostly I had gaps of depression and anxiety in-between periods of sheer bliss and exhilaration. During the dark nights I wrote many mournful poems and in the spate of romance wrote love songs to my then intended. My drinking was mainly confined to weekends although I did drink after work with fellow employees out of sheer loneliness, when not in a full on sexual relations with the latest flame. The escape from family influence in work and play was a blessing on the one hand and a cure on the other. One year at home after leaving school was enough to turn me away from parental influence forever.

CHAPTER 5.

DAYS OF WINE AND ROSES

My mother continually nagged me about being of Catholic moral standings but weirdly encouraged me to become involved with any women of my choosing in the family home of which she approved, as long as they were not of native origin. Dad just wanted me to settle to a secure job, get married and have kids. It was the pattern of their life and they took it as read that it should be the same for me also. My father and mother were children of conservative large families, conditioned to the aftermath of economic depression, were exceedingly hard working and keen to have the best of the material world.

Like James and Jacquie Baxter, my parents married at twenty one and twenty two respectively and I was born a year later without a stamp on my bottom that should have read: "Other way up; warning- do not feed alcohol." It was their lot to believe the pattern of their upbringing should continue with the next generation. I was of a different age with a different mindset, in a time of free love, rock n' roll and a time of plenty including job choice. Needless to say, when I finally married the girl whom I then considered a prototype of my conception, they breathed a sigh of relief.

Jacqui gave birth to a healthy girl on 18th June 1949 and they christened her Hillary. Baxter eventually became a man about the house being more and more attached to his baby daughter every day. He was adjusting to his new family life and had stopped drinking all-together realising that he needed to stop playing the fool; that his illusion about marriage and frequent sex had been shattered. He found affection, marital harmony and domestic duties more important but continued to worry about money. He related to a new friend Charles Brasch that for the first time in his life verse was no longer the dominant force in his life but rather of limited necessity. Despite no time for fantasy he did keep on writing. Wellington was more a business city than that of the Christchurch of his university established friends and artist connections. He was however to meet people who would give him great encouragement in his future creative pursuits. Maria Dronke, a refugee from Hitler's Germany, together with her former German District Court Judge husband John had taken asylum in New Zealand after the war. She was known widely in the old German Weimar Republic for her expertise in exploring the best of people for theatre. Arriving in New Zealand in 1939 her reputation had preceded her as she was still at the height of her power and influence, and exhibited the manner of the grand dame who should not be crossed in any respect. Her public recitals of amazing projection and her work as teacher of speech and drama became the moving force in the culture of Wellington.

Maria was a vibrant presence and she trained some of New Zealand's best actresses. The gatherings in Hay street and New Lampton Quay of senior students, undergraduates, drama students, musicians and theatre people became a familiar sight; encouraged in no small way by Maria's influences. Her flare for language quickly introduced Maria to the poetry of New Zealanders. In public readings she included poems by Mason, Curnow and Baxter along side those of Keats, Shakespeare and T.S. Eliot. Many of the local Wellington artistic set of the period 1945-1948 owed their first introduction to poetry and plays to her. At the gatherings guests would read and Maria took part too. Baxter, in his usual bohemian style mess of dress and disarray would be introduced by Maria as a poet and the world seemed to generate a magic around Baxter particularly by the young in attendance.

Baxter was invited by Hella Hoffman to contribute to her collection of essays on the great short story writer, Frank Sargeson. James had more time to write and he finished his piece of the collection in three months. Sargeson was chuffed with Baxter's brilliance and that he agreed to contribute. In May 1949 Baxter addressed the Society of Victorian University College on the question as to why writers stop writing. He gave his answer as fatigue, lack of time but more to the point, writers are disgruntled by the inability to find meaning in the world. The solution he proposed was to embrace orthodox Christianity, though he knew that such a choice would be unpopular. Baxter paraphrased his answer with the fact that he was still writing all the time. He had embraced the Christian faith on creed, liturgy and the sacrament. Baxter was confirmed as Anglican in November 1949 by the ex-naval chaplain Bishop Owen. The Bishop took offence at Baxter's pacifist views and commented on them, comparing Baxter's anglican confirmation to the equivalent of entry into the navy. James was troubled that the metaphor of the Christian soldier made sense if properly understood. Pacifism he reasoned could find in Christianity the purest of motives without the risk of becoming sterile. He continued to occupy his mind with the problems of evil in human lives and in one letter on the subject speculated that a man's character drifted into defect mode, then the potentiality for good was then mis-educated into rottenness. He likened it to St.Paul's biblical quote : "for the good that I do, I do not, but the evil that I would not, I do" to prove his point.

Life's everyday problems loomed and the family had to leave their rented house at the end of the year. Baxter had the opportunity to enter Wellington Teachers College the following year. Archie and Millicent offered to pay rent for a house but he wouldn't hear of it. Instead he settled for a loan to pay a year's rent. Teacher's College he knew would break him into the academic world of which he formally despised, but now resigned himself to the fact that every job has with it a harshness of routine. He came to believe also that he never really belonged to the 'working class' even though he admired their virtues of patience, tolerance and charity. He much preferred the poetic devil of him who appreciates Shakespeare to the man of cool goodness whose mental facility was withered because of creative neglect. In 1950 the family moved to a farm house in Karori. They shared part of the property with an elderly widow whom they found most accomodating but who disapprove of some of their friends.

James collected wood from a nearby reserve for the fuel stove and heating in winter. He proved very skilful with an axe, a mallet and wedge. Baxter was also not too bad at gardening and growing vegetables. After Hillary's birth Jacquie had a miscarriage and did not keep good health, but she persevered with her degree. Baxter with low income and lack of financial resources felt that he was at the mercy of his landlords.

James Baxter did not go to Training College that year but continued at the abattoir, but soon enough threw that in to become a temporary postman. The new job allowed him more opportunity for poetry writing. He was still drinking heavily, frequenting bars and spilling beer all over the mail. Sometimes his friends would deliver the mail because he was too drunk to do so himself. He was usually too far gone to recall or thank them for their kindness in doing the deliveries. People would phone the Post Office to complain of his late deliveries. He lasted until 17th January 1951 when his boss found him asleep dead-drunk with his head on a full sack of mail in the Karori Post Office. Despite his dysfunctional behaviour Baxter had already resumed his studies at Victoria in Greek, History, Art and Literature, a course he had abandoned five years earlier at Dunedin. Baxter passed the term examinations which proved to him that his brain was not rusty. Professor H. A. Murray particularly praised Baxter for his answers on Homer which he considered exceptionally good. Jacquie had also returned to resume her studies of an M.A. in Philosophy. She passed with First Class Honours and was commended by the examiners as of exceptional merit. Baxter's own course did not interfere with his poetry writing as he studied only what suited him. He took the world of the desolate and uncreative moods which most writers cease to do and made it art.

Nineteen fifty one began with Baxter enrolling at the Wellington Teacher's College to train as a primary school teacher. The College was close to the University and down the road from the Arts and Craft and Science buildings and the student's accomodation building stood nearby. On entry to the first term Baxter struck up friendships with Louis Johnson whose first volume of verse *The Sun amongst the ruins* had appeared in *1951*. He had worked as a journalist for *The Southern Cross* and when it collapsed decided on a teaching profession; enrolling in the same crash course designed for senior students. Baxter and he as the oldest students on campus became friends. Both men were married and Johnson, with fertile ability in publishing, enlisted Baxter's help in literary establishment barriers.

In the battles ahead they were on the same side with Johnson blowing the trumpet and marching around the walls on subject matter, whilst Baxter mostly breached them. In 1952 Alistair Campbell who had made his reputations as a poet with his first collection returned to Training College and came to know Johnson and Baxter. Some of the emerging writers at the College felt overshadowed by the established writers but they soon felt they were left enough space to be included. The Library Club met every Thursday in an old prefabricated hut down in the Glen. It became the centre for what was known as 'The Glen Group.' Outside speakers like Denis Glover were on occasions invited to speak.

James already having literary contacts outside the college did not attend the Glen group very often. Sometimes though, he would address them on poetry and dissect it. They thought he knew more bout poetry than anyone they had ever met, and his range of reading astonished them. Club activities held little interest for experienced writers like Baxter and Johnson, who headed for the National Hotel in Lampton Quay. Alistair Campbell drank regularly with Baxter and thought he was more relaxed and amiable, especially when he had a few under his belt and there was no one to match him.

However, some of the younger students found his sexually explicit language quite shocking. As Baxter's drinking took flight Campbell found him less pleasant and inclined to be aggressive. Friday nights, the Grand Hotel in Willis Street was another favoured drinking hole for College students. Sometimes Baxter would drink the weekend away and turn up for lectures on Monday morning looking pale, red eyed and wearing the same clothing he had on Friday night. Friends encouraged him to shower and drink copious amounts of coffee before attending lecturers.

JKB managed to control his drinking during the week and was never seen under the influence during working hours. At times Baxter was exempted from some training courses. He spent that time writing poems, practicing "different poetic styles and usually what he wrote he sent off to the "Landfall" and more often than not they were published. College lecturers considered Baxter a deeply kind and gentle man. W.J.Scott, the Vice Chancellor of the Teachers College and lecturer in English considered Baxter's behaviour during his time in College impeccable, apart from drinking outside working hours. Baxter visited Scott on occasions at his home to discuss philosophical and moral questions that troubled him. Scott was astounded by his eloquence in these discussions. Baxter portrayed intense feelings for religious experience, and the contrast between good and evil in the world. Scott found he was more concerned with expressing his own ideas than listening, though he was capable of discussing a question and presenting a good case for what he believed in. He had taught more New Zealanders without a degree than any of the lecturers in the course he was doing for a teaching degree. Baxter was never at ease in Teachers College and considered himself a middle of the road manic depressive when under the influence of alcohol but he managed to retain his sanity when sober despite his addiction. On the 1st October 29th 1952 a second child , John McColl Baxter was born. James took his domestic responsibility seriously and felt shame when he let Jacquie down. Mostly, whenever she suffered from severe arthritis in her hands and had difficulty even lifting the baby, she left all the soiled linen piled up in the tub. James washed them all when he got home from work or College and did so without so much as a single complaint. He was living in two worlds; the domestic one with his wife and two children and the literary one where he received a great deal of praise for his poetry and admiration from far and wide. He graduated from Teachers College on 10th December 1952.

It was the same year he collaborated with friends to publish a joint selection of poems. The volume was widely praised by the Teachers College and his contribution to writers who passed through the College in the fifties was as a catalyst and animator. Baxter's stand in the literary world was the most brilliant. Baxter's lecture entitled *Recent Trends in New Zealand Poetry* galvanised the writer's Conference that year. Teachers and writer attendees were were impressed with his youthful idealism and grasp of the problems confronting New Zealand writers.

The lecture was confined to the years since Curnow's 1945 Caxton anthology, and concentrated on five events that marked a significant evolution in New Zealand poetry. First he established *landfall* as the most significant vehicle to promote poetry in New Zealand. He followed with Alistair Campbell's first book of poetry, *Mine eyes dazzle*, Basil Dowling's third book, *Canterbury and other poems*, Ursula Bethell's *Collected Poems* and Allen Curnow's verse play *The Axe*. He related all five to the history of New Zealand poetry and argued that the nineteenth and some twentieth century poets were unable to meet the country on its own terms in their verse. He indicated that the poets of the thirties and paid tribute to Fairburn, Curnow, Brasch and especially Glover. He argued for the new and valuable stereotype that was being formed: the view of national history held by the poet who has grown up in entire acceptance of his environment, truest of humans inhabiting the country. After evoking the images of the city and the wilderness, he made the famous statement that the modern poet: 'should remain a cell of good living in a corrupt society, and in this situation by writing and example attempt to change it.' The Conference's was the first large gathering of writers since the war and the sense for a new start was widely felt. Baxter, with his youthful appearance was considered the one to show the world the new form which New Zealand writing might become.

Teacher's College allowed Baxter in 1953 to go on full salary to further his education at Victoria University College. He passed Latin 1 and Philosophy 11 but failed English 111 because he simply had not done any study of Old English, which was a must for a pass. The same year Caxton Press published his third major collection '*The fallen House*' which was his most accomplished book to date. He showed the capacity to adopt a variety of roles and carry them all out with an assured proficiency. The dominant theme of the book is loss and the feeling that holds it together is grieving. This evolves largely from an acute awareness of the loss of innocence and vision possessed in his poetry. Themes of the memory of a magic world of childhood; those of childhood instinct with perceptions over those of adults, poems of innocents that succumbed to grief of experience and sharpened by the poets yearning for a lost paradise.

Baxter completed his year at Victoria University College and was appointed Assistant Master (Scale1) at Epuni School in Lower Hut. He was on a salary of forty five pounds a month which was a far cry from his days at the abattoir on thirty two pounds of back breaking physical work. JKB consider himself blessed with his new role; he was one of four new teachers who taught children from primary to Standard Four. Headmaster John Clifton Ward knew Baxter, who had already been at the school as a trainee teacher. Ward was aware of Baxter's reputation as a hard drinker, but admired his powers of application and the way he related to the children. He was happy to have him back on a permanent basis and James had a class of thirty two young school children between age seven and eight years, and was conscious of the fact that they were still like young babies and had to be nurtured. It was his job to make them less so and teach the basic skills of reading and writing. Much of his time was taken up with keeping up a routine though he preferred their outdoor periods to the class room activities. He was conscious of the fact that the best students were the ones who got the strap, which was applied by the headmaster and not him. The difficult child, the outsider, was always a priority in Baxter's attitude to teaching. He did not have a good record of discipline in his classes but the children loved him. He could always spark their enthusiasm, especially teaching English. In particular with poems some of which he wrote especially for them. He showed them the fun they could have by building up verses together. The verses that he had written for his own students were collected and used in other Hut Valley schools. The poems he wrote for children appeared after his death in "The Tree House," published in 1974. In the playground he was oblivious of the children fritting about. He always seemed to have his head in a book as he walked slowly around the playground. He was like the Pied Pipe of Hamelin with a trail of children following him about.

The Department of Education found Baxter's style of teaching a concern as it was unconventional and he did not appear to follow the rule of discipline to their liking. It was more the problem of class control than his ability's as a teacher, for he gave more of himself and his energy to his students than his system could sustain. In addition to his role as a primary school teacher, he was invited to give a series of lectures at the invitation of the University of New Zealand. These lectures were endowed by Baxter's grandfather and were known as the Macmillan Brown lectures. He granted the endowment with the proviso that lectures were to be on his book subject matter gathered from the reading from them. Baxter gave these lectures in June 1954 and were published the following year under the title *The Fire and the Anvil*. with a dedication to the works of story writer Sargeson of which Macmillan Brown was well read.

The three lectures, in all, comprised the formal aspects of poetry, figures of speech and personal criteria for judging a poem; the nature of poetic inspiration and significance, and Baxter's personal philosophy which dealt with symbolism in New Zealand verse, drawing on a wide range of New Zealand poets works. He did not so much sustain an argument for analytical criticism but took a more impressionist approach allowing him to follow his own interest in literacy, social and psychological opinion. He did not come over well in an academic sense, but it was his personal response, rhetoric and more persuasively unobtrusive manner on the stage and the earnest way in which he spoke that his published lectures were well received. Baxter's lectures were shrewd observances with genuine concerns for the future of poetic expression in an educated spiritual sense for the community of New Zealand. Interestingly, Baxter's own critique of his *The Fire and the Anvil* was confused but sincere in expression of what he felt and to his own admission written between or during wild bouts of drinking.

Not long after his address at the Writer's Conference and just weeks after the three lectures he by invitation gave at the University New Zealand, he stated that they were all just ' charts of progressive knowledge of aesthetics rather than statements of dogma. He had a remarkable insight into his own personal development, family life and potential as a writer. He was conscious of the danger of being too egotistical, driven by materialism, preoccupation with religious views and lack of control in all things when under the influence of alcohol.

I was not born for academia, though some of my career did channel that way. My first job, while awaiting my school L.C. (leaving certificate) results, was holding up truck gear boxes while my engineer father bolted them into place. Various duties around the motor works included handing the right tool to mechanics working on engines, cleaning cars, serving petrol and working the motor parts counter away from the grease monkeys. I was so glad to get my L.C. results as it qualified me for the second intake for Teacher's College in September, but what to do in the meantime There was no way I could continue working in the motor vehicle business. Dad had kicked me out of the workshop for an error in judgement when I forgot to engage the hand break on a customer's car. It became a run-a-way, travelling driverless and backwards on the highway crashing into another parked vehicle that had just been panel beaten back to perfect condition for a customer. Both vehicles were extensively damaged and I was banned from the workshop forthwith.

Dad was jubilant with my L.C. results and took me out on the grog with him and some of his mates to celebrate. The only job I really wanted to do was to become a dental mechanic but the entry to university was restricted to higher marks than mine, so teachers college seem edto be my only option.   I begged to repeat the L.C. year to improve my pass and qualify for my career choice, but Dad would have nothing of it. A letter of congratulations from the Commonwealth Bank offering me a start at eleven pounds a week was an immediate way out. The basic wage then was nine pounds and the extra two pounds I was paid was due to the fact that I had my leaving certificate. Those of banking rank and file didn't like it, that a young upstart was entering their holy grail-I sold my soul to the banking career with a push and shove from my father. Mum didn't seem to care much what I did for a living as long as I stayed off the grog and away from wicked women! The teachers College idea went out the window too. In fact it was a second option for dentistry had been my real goal. A year in the local CTB branch of my home town and various country moves saw me rise in the banking ranks to savings bank examiner.

I finally moved to Sydney, with a shattering of relationships and increasing my daily quota of alcohol which escalated to a crescendo over the three and half years in banking. I was suffering from melancholy, irritability, discontent and the extremes of loneliness. My father was on the next plane south to chastise me. I explained that I never really wanted to be a banker and only joined the bank because he wanted me too.

Dad wasted no time in seeking another career for me and I found myself, once more with his push and shove, in line for a flight steward job in Qantas. I had in the meantime found myself a job in R.K. radio working as a technicians assistant exempt (meaning unqualified) doing area strength measurements for Television, climbing towers, measuring signal distances from studio to towers and travelling far and wide, always with a drink not too far from my hand either. This came to a head for me with a week of drinking on an assignment which included upside down aerial antics with a wild man in a Piper Comanche aircraft. The aftermath of my last episode in that role was a stay in hospital with alcoholic poisoning. It took less than a week of recovery to be back at the bar again as I had not twigged to the fact that I was alcoholic. Job Security loomed and the old LC results carried some weight back then, as most non university types only qualified at intermediate standard. I joined the third division of the public service remaining with the PMG, as I liked the people and the life-style too. Besides I was having a raging relationship with a young woman. It too ended in disaster but it was not long before another girl came a trotting into my life b ring more pain and sorrow.

Half way through my PMG career the Public Service Board approved my entry into the Prime Ministers Department as a Clerk Class five, but I ultimately declined as I was having too much fun partying, being involved with a young lady and the job had some great job lurks and perks too. Besides, I concluded that I didn't want to live in Canberra, it was far too stuffy for the likes of me. I was working in primary works and the job involved my being the second in charge for signing off on engineering jobs including the coaxial cable which ran under the harbour to join up telephone networks on the north side of the bridge. The other major works at the time was laying cable up George street. Both jobs were signed off over beers at the NSW leagues club with attention given to the amount of overtime that could be had for all participants from engineers to the cable layers. There never was an official plan applied to any public service job back then, just a sign off for work completion stretching out over as long as possible to gain extract overtime. Like all chickens that come home to roost, the two major jobs caused nightmares when the city underwater tunnel was built as the tunnel engineers discovered a spaghetti like entwining of coaxial cable under the harbour. When telephone failures occurred with exisiting cable, it was far to difficult to find the faults. so we simply fed another lot of cable from a barge across the harbour and joined it up on the North side with existing works.

Likewise there was no official plan for the George street cable either. This applied to gas lines, as well so when the current tram way was being built they struck more than one cable or gas main that they had no notion of it being there. All these plans are no-doubt buried somewhere in the bowels of the GPO. Earlier, I built an engine's library for the chief engineer who took me under his wing. He gave me a new role after completing the engineering references books to his satisfaction. I became his driver when he inspected TV equipment locations for the broadcasting Commission. As a dogs body I was then looking after the telephone exchanges for administrative requirements and occasionally riding shotgun on the pay car.

After three and a half years, like my banking career, I left the job for what I perceived greener pastures. An AMP representative sold me an Insurance policy and suggested I would be suitable for the role and that I would be my own boss. The company was very generous with their commissions, extraneous fringe benefits which included low interest housing loan and interest free car finance too. It was not long before I had accumulated income and a client base that afforded me timeout for a three months holiday in Europe. In some way it was an escape from a likely 'shot gun wedding.' The likely 'bride to be' family were against the relationship from the word go, as I was considered too much like a close relative, particularly in the mother's mind.

II was seen as apparently irresponsible, a gambler, a dreamer and an alcoholic. I protested, but eventually took umbrage at her assessment of me. In point of fact it all proved to be true over time. I was doing my utmost to live up to the standards of my Catholic upbringing, I.O.G.D.(In Omnibus Glorificetur Deus) - 'In all things may God be glorified', which the Sisters of No Mercy from my earliest primary school days insisted be written at the top of every page of schoolwork. It proved for me to be I.O.G. D.- I often get drunk. Not long after my return from overseas where I figured I had sown the last of my wild oats, I was on a different career course again. This time I had a clear cut goal and after reaching the dizzy heights of sales and service to clients I applied to become an AMP Manager. I was the youngest manager ever to be appointed to management at the time with a stigma of being Catholic to overcome in an indoctrinated work ethic of a company that bordered on freemasonry. The company was attempting to change its former policy of only recruiting managers from within the organisation and taking a new ecumenical stance of inter-denominational employees. It proved to be in their best interest and mine , as I took to the tasks of managing a region that was at the bottom of the pile. As Time proved it became profitable and I turned it all around to being the top region for the company.

Reward for effort was the catch cry and the organisations motto of "amicus cereus in re incerta'- a friend in uncertain events proved real to me, as it did to many a client of those times. I had married Penelope, the girl of my dreams, manifested as the prototype of my conception and our first child, a son Scott was born in the first year of my appointment. The delight of a father to have a son was quickly followed by another son Peter and the world for a time seemed to be my oyster.

However, my drinking got out of hand and I made a fool of myself on more than one occasion. The Company who were happy with my work ethic and results in recruiting, training and motivating new representatives, and managing the old and bolds, overlooked my drunken behaviour and my apparent occasions of sinfulness.   During this time I attended a course that AMP insisted I complete in my new found ability to manager people and ultimately I completed a Harvard Business management course that was well above the standards required by the industry as a whole. My office wall was plastered with ego driven qualifications that meant a lot in the industry but were of little worth in the world beyond. After a time I got itchy feet again and returned to the road as an AMP representative. I wanted to see if I still had it in me to write new business. This I did for a year, setting a weekly target of new client business which I did without a blank week in sales. However, I was spending far too much time away from home in other country towns seeking out business. In point of fact I was back in the same pattern as when I was recruiting agents and decided to turn the tide back to management again.

It meant leaving the region I had built up and moving to another that was at the bottom end of the pile again. I gracefully accepted the challenge, lifted its performance over a three year period but again began looking for greener pastures. All the while I continued my alcoholic drinking habits and smoking upwards of forty cigarettes a day. I had not at this time recognised that I was alcoholic, but my overall behaviour proved otherwise.

I was a loner at heart, preferred writing poetry to working at academia, not unlike the masterful James Baxter at a similar age. Sometimes I got into fights, ended up accepting a challenge to step in the ring after a night on the booze, thought I had the horse racing betting in my control, as I seemed to be able to pick winners when I attended the track. All this proved fruitless in the long run and as I began to see the writing on the wall and needed more income, I began to manage a news agency at weekends for extra money. Ultimately I resigned from my AMP career and begged, borrowed and cashed in my insurance policies to purchase a News-agency in a small country town The sad loss of Sarah Catherine , a daughter still-born, caused my then wife and I much sadness.; so with mixed emotion we buried our feelings and looked for another way on freedom road. It was another good reason for leaving the job and doing a geographical in taking up the new life in a new environment. Soon enough a third son Samuel was born with much joy and ceremony. He seemed to us a gift from God at the time after our former sadness. After the loss of Sarah Catherine, my then wife and I still hoped for a daughter and God in his wisdom granted the gift of a gorgeous little girl, Emma Mary, some decade later.

The experience of being in a retail business was a new lease of life for me. Back then the business was very forgiving, as the profit margins were good and with a sale and return policy for non sales of newspapers, magazines and books, one could afford to make mistakes and still make a reasonable profit. As time moved on I expanded the business, took on a Dick Smith electronics agency, sold computers, two-way radios sets, jewellery, guns, ammunition, and reloading gear. I also employed my mother in-law who was an ardent reader and we began to build up quite a profitable book business with her skill in doing an on the spot synopsis for customers of any book she had read, and book sales, like the rest of the business multiplied.

I had always intended to get three years good profit then sell out and move on to an even bigger business. News-agencies like pubs and chemists were worth gold back then and with Goodwill plus stock, one could name one's own poison with buyers lined up to get into the business. It wasn't so easy in my case as the oldest of employees who had seen the back of seven former newsagents who sold out and moved on, was milking the life out of the profits. I dug my heels in and had a cockatoo on the look out and I uncovered a chain of activity that would have sent me broke if I had let it continue.

Upon investigation of the theft, I uncovered another staff member in on the racket who was supplying under cover of darkness another retail outlet that was dwindling my inventory. So, not wanting to draw too much gossip or attention to my customers, I paid out and sacked the two offending employees. It was during the worst drought on record, and the business soon increased by $200,000 o per annum for the next three years. despite no increase in sales income. It took a year of due diligence on the business by the next purchaser before I got out of it all. No sooner had we exchanged contracts and the sale gone through, the drought broke and he sold the business at double the profit in just one year. In hindsight, I understood why the seven previous owners sold out. I stayed, fought the good fight and won the day, but my drinking got worse and for a good while I suffered the effects of a bleeding stomach ulcer as a consequence. The running of that small business set me up for a future career as owner manager of small business enterprises, but not before I had another crack at the Insurance industry again. To be fair, the small town experience honed my skills in a number of areas, as for a time I was town delegate for the National party and later first secretary of a new branch of the Liberals. To keep the balance though, I was, like in my youth, a member of state labour, as I found the local member always seemed to get more done in the community than state representatives of the right, liberals or nationals when in power.

As an added extra and further interest I joined a committee to help boost business interest locally. So before leaving town I brokered a deal for a community fair event which I learnt from my fathers involvement in community activity in my youth. The annual event expanded from a one day carnival when I was still in town to later becoming a three day event with people more skilled than I growing it. Despite all this I was restless, irritable and discontent.

The remainder of my time I focused on seeking a position back in the Insurance Industry and as luck had it I found what on the surface appeared to be the ideal job. Not being able to keep away from the Insurance industry I returned to manage MLC for the Lend lease group on the coast from Taree to the Queensland border. It seemed to me that the Dusseldorf, the little dutchman with the entrepreneur business acumen had introduced his Lend Lease style of management of people and was, to my mind, buggering up a great industry of past era. I had a cruise of a job, got paid a grand salary, had all the lurks and perks of a dream role and to boot was paid an additional monthly bonus for non tied agents to encourage their general insurance clientele to the MLC fold. All I had to do for this was call at their offices along the coast and smile, checkout if they had any issues that needed to be solved on behalf of clients and pass the information on to head office. Yet I was not happy, as it all seemed too easy and living back in Coffs Harbour were I had been stationed for a time in my Commonwealth Bank days did not appeal, nor did it for my family. I resigned after one year, moved the family to Sydney and started back as a sales representative with AMP all over again.

I soon found that the Lend lease style of management was not the issue, it was the whole dam industry that was going through major unstable financial management changes. I rented a house for a time and from the sale of our country property and the business sale profits we purchased a house and a mortgage in Sydney.

It was not long before I took on a financial planning role with the ANZ Bank looking after customers investment interest. I was still unsettled ,and although the salary package was fair, I could not recapture the former glory of my earlier AMP career. I was then on a treadmill for a period of three more years of job changes, looking for the golden rainbow. The next eighteen months I worked as State Sales Manager for Legal and General, but could not recapture the motivation to achieve at my former level of work load. My drinking was in the way of any chance of glory and was on the increase for I was a very unhappy man. Next, I found the dream of a job as the National Training Manager for Friends Provident. The role involved rebuilding their sales and marketing material from scratch, training sales managers to compliance company standards and working with actuaries and lawyers with new contracts; writing sales scripts, converting mathematical and technical material to sales speak. It was a job I enjoyed doing, but the worst part was travelling around Australia to check out how State and Sales managers were doing in their job, then writing a report on their performance to determine who should stay and who should be sacked. One of the board members of the company approached me after eighteen months in the role to enquire what role I would like to do next in the company. It was apparent that there was to be a reshuffle of State Managers in the new year ahead. He asked me if I would be interested in that role and which State would I select if I was to take on the job. I nominated western Australia as it appealed to me as a place like my former A.M.P. regional roles, i would enjoy. He stated . "Mum's the word , but you've got it!"

For a loner, far from the eyes of head office in such a far away location, I would have the freedom of being as near as was possible in the corporate world to be ' my own boss' again and looked forward with renewed enthusiasm for the coming year ahead. I figured with the culture of the company some internal spy was critiquing my performance on a similar basis as I had been charged to do interstate with fellow managers. I surmised that despite my excessive drinking I had impressed the powers that be with my work ethic and performance to date and was on my way up the ladder of success even further in the future. The crunch came with the take over of the company by a European consortium before the year was out and like all other employees I was out of a job. I transferred my financial licence to a stockbroking firm and began to sell share float deals for a time,. It helped a little with some cash flow whilst I searched for the next career move.

I had attempted to build an accomodation centre and resort in the country were I had some land.The idea was to encourage Japanese tourists to stay and play golf on an adjoining eighteen hole golf course. It proved disastrous as it was the beginning of the 1990 recession; the Japanese went home and I was left with debt and acres of empty land. I was granted approval by the local council to sell it all as housing blocks, However, the recession had hit hard and people in the bush were just not buying, so I had to sell the land at a loss. Another golden dream turned to ashes and once more I was back at square one.

Psychologically I was not sure if I should pack up the family and go bush again or stay put in the city until something broke in my favour. We decided to stay put, as we had a home we could call our own. It was not ideal but it was ours. I had kept some powder dry for any business opportunity that may come our way, but as cash flow was running out fast and with three boys at private schools and Emma still a baby I had to find work soon. So with a reference from family connections in the pub game, I completed my publican's licence and considered this career move. I tried to broker a deal to buy a pub but this came to nothing. Besides, I soon found working behind the bar was not for me. I much preferred the customer side were I could sit and drink with friends.

As luck would have it, I had some excess stationery stock left over from my days in the news-agency which had followed me around and was in storage in our garage. The need for cashflow was getting desperate and I wanted to delay dipping into the dry powder (cash reserve) that I had stored for a rainy day. I could now see storms clouds on the horizon. and knew I had to move fast to find a job or buy myself one. My answer to my work dilemma had come along just at the right time so it seemed. Trevor Morgan who purchased my excess stock had brokered a deal with the receivers of Link Line, the parent company of Ancol, the newsagents association, to sell off the stationery stock for brokerage on a commission basis, as it had gone bankrupt. Trevor accepted his fee in stationery stock had initially opened a 'pop up' store selling a lot of stock in Parramatta then Northbridge and finally he opened up in Lindfield to sell off the remaining inventory. With nothing better to do, I worked the store front and after a few weeks Trevor offered to sell me the remaining stock at less than wholesale price. It made sense as I knew stationery from my previous business days in fact was enjoying being back dealing in tangibles again.

Soon enough I had handed over my dry powder to Trevor, purchasing his stock and granted free the market tables he had made to display stock. Now totally dependent upon walk in trade I marketed by letter box drop and the business began to grow. The then State Bank was the only one interested in giving a start up business an overdraft to ensure survival, and as they did I was once more on my way to business success. Luckily I had no major competitors to cut into pricing so with my family help, and an ever flowing customer base we built a very successful enterprise. It lasted for fourteen years of progressive upward profits and I found myself able to purchase a second business, as a Paper Merchant. The business had a customer base Australia wide. We broke even in nine months and I sold it after eighteen months for a tidy profit. It appeared we were now on the gravy train. So at least for the next fourteen years we raked in the money. Our profitability afforded us a large home on the harbour, two motor vehicles and boat, good regular resort holidays and private education start for our children. All seemed rosy in the garden but in time it proved to be the opposite.

On latter analysis, It was ultimately my drinking to excess, working long hours to gain even more material wealth and possessions and hardly ever being at home for family time that became my undoing. The catalyst to all my itchy feet and drinking habits was glaringly obvious when I came to face it all years later in a state of long term sobriety. Whilst I had always the appearance of one who was supremely confident in all I achieved; deep down I was fearful and had low self esteem. God had his own way of working on a lost soul and he came my way by the route of calamity, psychological collapse into depression and ultimately a cry for help by me, which was answered in my letting go the control of my life and handing over to the God of my own understanding. It took a lot of doing over a decade or so but I ultimately found the way that had eluded me for the major part of my life. It came via tragedy, rehabilitation, shock treatment, AA and walking the Camino de Santiago. Like James Baxter my shadow self, the real me was hidden until I found my true calling, set my ladder of life on the right wall for once and began to climb a new way up and forward. Like Baxter, I needed to remain sober a day at a time to open up to spirituality and follow my dreams.

It was the way of AA that led me to sobriety, to learn to hand over to a God of my own understanding, to find some semblance of what life is really all about. It came more from what I learnt in the twelve steps of the programme and more recently in the twelfth step. For like the founder Bill Wilson, I realised no greater joy nor satisfaction than doing the job of the twelfth step, once one has the power of all the steps under ones belt. To watch and see the eyes of men and women come out of darkness into light, to see their lives unravel with a new purpose and meaning, to watch them awaken to the presence of a loving God in their lives; these things are the substance of what we receive as we carry the AA message. Its is by seeing the program at work in my friends of the fellowship and to in some small way practice what

I preach that I remain sober a day at a time. As Bill Wilson himself once said: "Gratitude should go forward, rather than backward. In other words, if you carry the message to others, you will be making possible repayment for the help given to you."

James and Jacquie in the late summer of 1954 moved house in Wellington to a rambling old school house away from the difficulties and influences of sharing facilities with other families as they had done for the previous four and a half years. The empty old house echoed the voices of the children as they ran about freely. The place had the effect of freeing up the whole family. Both parents shared the responsibility of the children and they were happy about their lot most of the time. Jacquie was almost through her degree courses and had time to return to her writing. James was doing his best to remain faithful to her after some indiscreet sexual encounters under the influence. He hardly had time to feel much guilt as he had been busy with Charlie Doyle and Louis Johnson in developing a new periodical called *Numbers* as a competitor to the *Landfall*. Their mission was to feature a great number of New Zealand writers in print and promote to an international audience the strength of local poets and writers works. Between 1954 and 1959 they managed ten issues of the paper and to some degree achieve the mission, but it never had the triumph of the *landfall* quarterly. In James's contributions, the poetry reflected his alcoholism, his growing commitment to Christianity and the issues he faced with life, his art and a discontent with the need for solicitude in writing his verse. He had lots of distractions in his domestic life responsibilities and remaining faithful in that regard.

At year's end James was exhausted due in part to the extraordinary lengths he went to in his teaching duties and at the time had taken on part time university courses. He had passes in Latin 11 but failed English 111 for the second time as he had not studied the subject matter to the level required to scrape a pass. The in-depth nature of the man and his poetic expression also had a great deal to do with his tiredness. More than anything else though, was his alcoholism which was bringing him undone. The excessive bouts of drinking increased and his sexual irresponsible exploits increased too, particularly on his visits to Auckland. By 1955, his most frequent drinking buddy on those visit was the printer and editor Bob Lowly. They would virtually live at the bar and on one occasion drank on for two weeks without so much as a break.

I recall My 'best effort' in a a drinking spree lasted for eight days and resulted with a stay in hospital with alcoholic poisoning. I was still young enough to put those experiences behind me, straighten myself out for a time, but I continued to return to the drink once recovered enough to do so. I had no idea back then that I was an alcoholic. If I had been introduced to AA at the time, I would not have darkened the door. I had the believe that I could stop drinking whenever I wanted to and didn't want to then. However, over time the grip of the grape got the upper hand and ultimately I cried out for help and God answered through the help of AA.

Bob Lowly frequently held bohemian like parties for the social set of artists and writers at his home on the slopes of One Tree Hill in the mid fifties. It was a time of excessive drinking bouts and sexual exploits for JKB. It was open house for the Auckland intelligentsia with the flow of copious quantities of red wine flowing and conversation, with fellow well known writers and with Baxter the great raconteur in the thick of things. JKB was considered the wild Dylan Thomas type bad lad with red wine stains on his clothing, up to his usual drinking and verbose poetic utterances, he was often out of control and had no problem getting sexual partners, be they female and sometimes male.

On other occasions outside of Auckland, Baxter was observed as quite well behaved, particularly when in heavy sessions of drinking gin. He often frequented the Britannia Hotel in Wellington getting roaring drunk but did not so much command to be the centre of attention any more. James did sometimes boast of his sexual conquests but it was more in his imagination than in reality. He was often a little child-like, acting the part, watching others to see if they were watching him. Baxter was care-free and careless with money often taking home naught of his pay, having spent it all on alcohol. JKBs out of home activities put a big strain on the marital relationship. The main burden of care for his two children was left to wife Jacquie to be the responsible one. It is a small wonder the marriage lasted as long a it did.

JKB was living a life of illusion but longed for reality and responsibility to take hold. He made many a resolution to stop drinking and eliminate his extra marital affairs but fell short repeatedly. Self analysis of his lifestyle sent him in a morbid set of self criticism. When sober he was appalled at his behaviour whilst under the influence and even admitted his use of violent language, rape of women with whom he had relationships and disgust of his homosexual exploits. Baxter's better nature when sober had more of a Christian soul appeal with much concern for his fellow man. However, the darker side of his nature took hold from the moment he returned to drink. He was certain that there was two personalities within him. The one that turned schizophrenic under the influence and did any amount of despicable things and the other James, when sober being of functional disposition and sound mind taking on an all-together different life-form being creatively effective, responsible and self giving. Unfortunately, he turned more and more to the dark side as booze began to effect even his sober moments more often than not. Baxter was going down the slippery slope of alcoholism ever more deeply in the 1950s. He was more troubled by his lack of control in sexual conquests outside of marriage. He thought at the time his issue with alcohol was secondary to his other 'isms,' and was troubled by use of vile and violent language that seemed to be more free flowing under the influence and contrary to his genuine controlled and gentle nature when sober. He was back then even more troubled by his tendency to entice hostesses at parties to sexual activity and on more than one occasion reverted to rape to get his way. Contrary to his better nature too, he was encountering a recurrence of homosexual activity which seemed to go against all he considered pure within him. These repeated encounters he finally gained control over when he stopped drinking. The relationship with Jackie was strained as he had a false picture of what love and marriage was all about. Sexual encounters with Jackie developed into forcing his will on her which often resulted in a pitiful and sorrowful situation that ultimately resulted in an end to their marriage.

CHAPTER 6.

FROM APATHY TO EMPATHY

Henry James Senior, was an American theologian and adherent of Swedenborgianism, a new church of several christian denominations influenced by the writings of scientist and Swedish Lutheran Emanuel Swedenborg. According to Swedenborg, he received visions from Christ of new revelations over a period of twenty five years. Henry James Senior, apart from his brilliance as mathematician, and mining engineer is best known as the father of philosopher William James, novelist Henry James, and diarist Alice James. In midlife he had a crisis of conscious and went on to travel far and wide researching the religions of the world. He wrote five books in all over the next thirty years of a religious, theological and philosophic nature, the most in-depth and complicated being '*The Varieties of Religious Experiences*' written between 1902-1910. It contained the elixir for a religious conversion for him.

In the 1930s, Bill Wilson, the co-founder of Alcoholics Anonymous, read James's book on his own search for spirituality and cleverly summed up James work in three critical insight into the awakening of man to the spiritual. Wilson's natural ability to decipher share values, having investigated the assets and liabilities of a company, its management, its product and services future potential proved him to be the best catalyst to examine and explain James's work and to break it all down into the understanding of the journey to sobriety and living a worthwhile life of spirituality. Henry James, long in his grave, without every knowing it became a cornerstone of AA for Bill Wilson and his founding principles. James' work is seceded and written into the AA programme as equally as Dr. Silkworth, and the Oxford Group principles. Whilst James's book consisted of very large numbers of religious conversion experiences and was underpinned by the professors studious analysis, Wilson cleverly used certain common denominators that seem to cover all the bases of spirituality that worked, irrespective of which ever way James's had presented them. In Wilson's analysis it seems that there are three critical common denominators on the journey to spirituality.

The first common denominator is calamity. Nearly every recipient in Wilson's study described how they had met utter defeat in some controlling area of their life. Every resource of courage, understanding and will had failed them. Each had been beaten into despair upon a wall and had seen no way over, under or around. This was an essential condition of the experience to follow. The next common denominator was collapse; bearing that an admission that from the depths of defeat was utter and absolute. Each individual had admitted that he simply could not go on under his own steam. The third common denominator was the cry; an appeal to a higher power for help. Bill Wilson had concluded that the appeal could take innumerable forms. It might be accompanied by a faith in God or it might not, but an appeal it had to be.

The cry for help could course through religious channels, or a despairing agnostic could look at a growing and reflecting tree and respond to the laws of nature and he, in his humanity, might then raise his voice to the God of nature. Then the transformational experience could set in, something like a thunderbolt, as with St. Paul on the road to Damascus, followed by repeated appeals, or the individual would slowly grow in a new state of consciousness and release in utter defeat, the complete admission of helplessness and appeal. This is but the beginning of a new way of life. To quote Henry James: "Every man who reached even his intellectual teens begins to suspect that life is no farce; that it is not genteel comedy even; that it flowers and fructifies on the country out of propounded tragic depths the essential dearth in which the subject's roots are plunged. The alcoholic who has reached the bottom in his cry for help knows this all too well. This sense of powerlessness and awakening to the spiritual new inner journey is herein quoted by Wilson: "We perceive that only after utter defeat are we able to take our first steps towards liberation and strength. Our admission of powerlessness finally turns out to be firm bedrock upon which happy and purposeful lives may be built."

James Baxter at his most critical alcoholic state had turned, like ever so many alcoholics into a schizophrenic egoistical madman, a genius who had lost his way completely and in his defeat it appears divine sources led to the steps of Alcoholics Anonymous. It was a late December night in the summer of 1954 that Baxter found himself seated on the front steps of a stranger's home in Wellington where his AA journey was to begin. In a state of despair he rang the door bell and the owner opened the door. The stranger he sought direction from was a leading light in the AA movement and shall not be named here to protect his anonymity. JKB had masked his cry of help on entry to the man's home by bursting forth with Francis Thompson's poem 'The Hound of the Heaven,' which the dramatically illustrated ex-drug addict's evasion son guilt and final conversion to Christianity. Baxter ultimately would follow a similar path, but from the moment he had not fooled the AA man, for he was altogether used to ego behaviour but perceived that he had a real live one of literary genius to now contend with.

Baxter was soon seen around the meetings of AA, reading with great concentration the Big Book of the programme, as it is commonly known, during meetings of the fellowship. To put the AA programme into perspective, the movement assumptions are that alcoholism is a disease over which the alcoholic has no control, which matched Baxter own experience. He was, through his reading and the guidance his new found friend in the fellowship, attracted by the assurance that anyone who really desired to attain sobriety could o so through AA steps.

Bill Wilson wrote innumerable insights into his own alcoholism and set down a set of suggestions in the steps of AA and its associated traditions to live by for the benefit of fellow alcoholics. The first six of the steps are from the Oxford group and the remaining six may well have been God inspired for Bill to include the spiritual consciousness enlightenments found in the works of Carl Jung.

Whilst Bill's wrote much of the enlightening guidelines for fellow alcoholics, it was the simple approach of AA co-founder Dr Bob Smith to the programme in its infancy that I, as a an alcoholic, tended to draw more upon. Dr Bob Smith encouraged over five thousands alcoholics to sobriety by his simple approach of three key principles: 1. Trust God, 2. Clean house and 3. Help someone. Maybe James Baxter got this simplicity in his latter days at the Jerusalem commune he established. However, in my opinion, one has to put the twelves steps of AA into practice before such a simple approach to helping the still suffering alcoholic maintain sobriety is entirely possible. JKB like most of us driven by ego and puffed up with self importance, particularly of an alcoholic persuasion, take time to reach a spiritual level in our lives that we can really let go to a point of sacrifice for others. This in turn benefits the giver of such fair tidings of great joy even more so on his or her journey to recovery. letting go alcoholic behaviour is more than stopping the drink.

Baxter quickly got it; that one alcoholic can help another in harmonious support, because any alcoholic having been to hell and back in the depth of their alcoholism understands the disease. The biggest challenge for James the alcoholic was the claim by AA of the need for total abstinence in leading by example. AA quite rightly points out that it matters little be you sober, one year, ten years or more, you are only ever sober a day at a time. In that sense you can logically conclude that you are but one drink away from being drunk. As is commonly quoted in the programme: 'its the first drink that does all the damage.' Another of the sayings in the programme to bring home the message of total abstinence is "One drink is too many and a thousand not enough." JKB had unrealistically promoted the concept prior to entry into joining the rooms of AA, the romantic notion that artists of genius conceive the best ideas when in their cups. The new as well as the old hands of AA are confronted by the necessity to have a head free of substance in order to live the twelve step programme. Whilst, to the newcomer, it may appear to be a little like the ten commandments of Christianity, it is more of a methodology of suggested steps to sincerity and spiritual wellbeing and not a black and white method of teaching. It's a hand over job to surrender to God that is the crux of the matter. From the very first step of acceptance that we are powerless over alcohol or any other 'ism' and could not manage life on life terms any more. Until that realisation and acceptance happens spiritual progressing serenity in an alcohol free state cannot be maintained.

James had great reluctance to accept that he was alcoholic and could not manage life with the kind of attitude he had previously based his life upon. When he, with the help of his fellow alcoholics and the steps of the programme, came to realise that he was powerless over alcohol and when in such a state often abused his friends, became violent and could forced sex on those who appealed to his desires. Its was the realisation of his defects of character and of coming to terms with the first step of powerlessness and the second, of coming to understand that a power greater than himself could restore him to sanity that he began to hand over his will to the unknown God, forgo his atheism and trust in the process that now befell him. He was not fully fledged in the programme but for the first time in his life felt free of all depression, anxieties, and fearful dreams of being judged for his past life and actions. Things started to fall into place. He was thankful to AA that he was not in gaol, in a nut house or worse still, dead. For a time life seems to take on a black and white appearance but as the clouds lifted the world seemed to be fairly good mostly but James had no ambition to preach the AA doctrine to others.

He was not finding the twelve steps an easy road though and it took another seven years of haphazard sobriety, reluctance to master the steps and he wasted time in delusions of grandeur and personal deception before the penny dropped and the compulsion for alcohol was removed for good. Thus he then found a workable alcohol free pattern for daily living and a need to be of service to others unconditionally.

James Baxter left a lasting impression on his fellow alcoholics when called to speak at the regular Thursday night AA meetings in Wellington. He spoke with sincerity, originality and often very quietly. It is a common pattern when asked to share at AA that one tells their story of what life was like prior to going AA, what changed and what it is like now. He made his story even more colourful by blending into his testimony his personal philosophy and added a great deal of humour and self irony into the process. He never really became a group representative, preferring to blend into the back ground to listen and observe. However, he was to become a respected presence in the whole AA movement. He came to realise that he, by sitting back and listening was becoming less egotistical. It was noted at meetings when he was called to share, he was fond of pointing out that there was no 'I' but 'We' in the programme and stressed that alcoholics can not recover without help. By then with a family inheritance and a home of his own, he had adequate monies to live on. He was known to be a soft touch for the fringe elements of AA who were there more for the free food and cup of tea or coffee. Those were the ones who hung about more for a monetary handout more than wanting to gain sobriety. James seemed to get the one promise of AA that : "We will loose the fear of financial insecurity, " and took it upon himself to hand out his money freely. Baxter seem to do a Christ like move in the acceptance of being influenced by a power greater than self, to help those who were powerless in their alcoholism and were suffering the consequences of their addiction. The deep belief in people made him vulnerable but had him living the twelfth step: "having had a spiritual awakening as a result of these steps, we tried to carry this message to alcoholics, and to practice these principles in all our affairs."

James was a born counsellor and in that regard he fitted well within the framework of the AA movement. He spent many hours with problem drinkers over coffee and a chat. He showed great compassion to those who seemed to be living a life of complete desperation and far outweighed even the most seasoned members of the fellowship of AA in his living the steps for the benefit of others. He had already conceived of the idea of a shelter for those living on the street so that they had a place they could call their own. He had no difficulty with the men who came to him for sponsorship and a listening ear and was discerning in evaluating individual's problems. However, he had great difficulty in counselling women as his natural inclination was to become emotionally involved. Early in 1957 in a letter to his mother indicated that he was learning to manage, to cope with the reflexes of the nervous system and his imagination, uncharacteristically indicating his intent on prayer for pure intent and his acceptance to ignore his reactive actions without thought, and not to take himself too seriously, that he was learning to laugh at himself more than ever.

On frequent visit to the local prisons with fellow AA members, JKB observed that most inmates crimes related to excessive drinking. Whilst some prisoners would not attend the AA meetings as they seemed to think they were being pestered by prison officials to do so, they always accepted Baxter. He seem to have a knack to get them on side; spoke their language and they liked the fact that he was sincere and frank in his efforts to help them in their sobriety and rehabilitation back from the brink. From the first visit until the time of his death Baxter made prisoner visitations a regular part of his life. Baxter tried to help the underdogs of the prison system, especially the Maori. He invented many a ballad based loosely on fact to empathise his plea for those lest fortunate and the movement of AA helped him on his evangelistic course. Baxter struggled with his ideal of total abstinence and displayed all the irrational fears and mental disturbances of the alcoholic drying out. He noted that some of his fellow alcoholics obtain freedom from the obsession within months whilst others like him with their own mental process of the difficulties of letting go seem to take years. He eventually achieved sobriety and it came with a sigh of great relief for at the time he had also found God, a power greater than himself to guide him. Whilst loosing the desire for alcohol brought freedom from the bondage of the drug, it did not solve his personal problems. AA was foremost in his life, but his marriage in particular was under great strain. Jacquie found the process of James's focus on his sobriety very difficult. She did her best to keep her feelings of expectation to herself. For all too often in the past he had let her down and let himself down. She no longer wanted to go through the disappointment which sometimes resulted in a rage within her. It made it difficult for James also, for he suffered with the guilt and did not want to let her down again. In addition, she had to live with his AA commitments which to all intention purposes took precedent over everything else in his life, for he had overcome his drinking problem and solved it, but this meant an even deeper commitment to AA and to others.

When one lives life as a blind man, he cannot see nor experience the light. My journey to AA and overcoming the grip of the grape in my alcoholism came with the three ' C's.' First there was the calamity- I was riding high on material success, hard work and basking in the sunlight of my own self importance, doing all the right things as it might appear to the world at large, but then came the crunch. The mother of my children left me for another after near three decades of marital bliss. Well, to my mind at the time it seemed so, but in reality it wasn't. There were faults on both side, there always are, but mine had one major glaring impediment which outshone all the good of my true nature and that was my alcoholism. My real self was kind and considerate of others but this was overruled by my irritability and discontent and tendency to turn to anger with my then wife and my four children when I drank. It made for an unhappy life for the household. I was too busy for apologies and regrets as I was the master of the house and home so it seemed to me

My justification was that I had business responsibilities, and provided the best for my loved ones with all the trimmings of a modern home, private school education for the brood and the best of material possessions money could buy. In God's eyes, I must have been a hard nut to crack, for when she left she took with it my heart and home, but it was not the end of the calamity.

The lawyers came on hard as I attempted to fight the divorce settlement. Within the year a good friend committed suicide, another died of a heart attack on his way to stay with me, then my mother fell ill which ultimately led to me having to confine her to age care. It was not all over, the worst of calamity happened when my second eldest son committed suicide. I was at complete loss and devastated, suffering health issues and sort refuge in the arms of lovers, I had three short relationships apart from those, the only real crutch I had to keep me from going crazy was alcohol. It was my lifeline, my band aid and it seemed to me, my only friend. In time it proved to be my worst enemy. I battled on to beat the onslaught of the divorce but it was hopeless. The home went with the settlement, the business I had no choice but to close down and pay out my creditors for I was a lost and bewildered soul and was incapable of going on. I fought hard to start again in another business venture but it was no use. The second 'C' had come to be, the collapse. I had awakened in a drunken state of terror and had an uncontrollable screaming fit. Days passed nursed by my friend Christine, and I ultimately saw daylight, ceased my drinking out of fear and now in a depressed state of mind, headed North to find a place to hide away and lick my wounds. I cared not if it be a tent or a cave, I just needed to find a way forward and recover. I dared not drink for fear that I would kill myself and was mindful of others close to me who had done just that under the influence. Living near the beach on the mid North Coast had some healing aspect to it and in hindsight I am grateful for being led there. I had enough income to see me though the next six months without work, had time to take in nature and do my best to rest and recuperate without drugs or alcohol and I wrote a lot of dark poetry for therapy.

In a way I was living the life of an anchorite but without the spirituality. For I was in great mental anguish without the fix of my drug of choice and the embrace of a woman. I did have a drug of sorts as a medico had prescribed a sleeping pill and it knocked me cold every night for about seven hours. My typical day comprised upon arising, before the depression sucked me in again, toilet duties, putting on shorts, T shirt and joggers and heading for the beach to walk a few kilometres before returning to meditate for a half hour, eat a light breakfast and head out again for the day. I simply tossed can a baked beans a spoon, an apple and bottle of water into a knapsack and began my tramp into the bushland. After eating my rations wherever I may be I reversed my direction, returning to my 'home near the sea' to do household duties, prepare some dinner and write poetry until bedtime. My contact with humanity was once a week on a Tuesday helping out at the aged care centre were my Mum now resided. The connection with nursing staff helped to a degree but I was really too unwell to be doing the chore, which was mainly serving cups of tea for the old people in their final days on earth. It was not exactly a joyful place but it was an experience that I was drawn too, particularly as it got me closer to my mother than I had ever formerly been before. There were three other activities I eventually became accustomed to. Friday mornings I joined a pottery class and learnt a little of the art for it allowed for creative expression which was soulful healing. The other in the same vein was to join in a men's group discussion once every week with other wounded hearts like mine.

By sheer chance I also met a group of walkers and joined them on their weekly excursions too. All his helped to a degree, but I was so severely depressed and contemplated suicide on two occasions despite my improved human contacts. I got close to the edge but somehow, something inside me drew me back to the necessity of working my way through the pain and suffering in my attempt to live a sane life again.

The lease was running out on the property I was renting and I was desperately lonely. By now I was seriously into depression medications prescribed by my mother's GP and all I wanted to do was escape. I tried a number of alternative remedies, like barefoot meditation practice, guru therapies, seeking alternate Gods, campouts in the bush with other wounded souls and even driving up and down the highway at night talking to strangers camped along the way in my lonely desperation. I drove to Queensland on one occasion for crystal healing. The guru told me she had shifted a lot of negative energy from my body, but I felt nothing except the eighty dollars she extracted from my wallet for the experience. I returned to Sydney for a week doing a live-in mediation seminar and felt better on my return to the coast for a few day, but the depression returned. Then came the third 'C', the cry. The hours and days drifted slowly along and my depression seemed to deepen even more. Another geographic loomed on the horizon as a way forward for me. I packed a bag, headed for the airport and flew to New Zealand in a desperate effort to find another focus. The cry was not far off, for I had yet to learn that praying was one thing, meditation another, but letting go was the key.

I landed in Auckland, hired a car and drove the length and breadth of the North Island over the next week. The journey finished in Wellington where I climbed aboard the morning ferry to the South Island, hired another car and repeated the process of journeying all over the South Island before returning to Queenstown for the flight home. It proved nothing but I was fully occupied having adapted a routine of driving from daylight to dark for the two weeks I escaped. The journey over, I returned to my beach retreat and the madness started all over again.

To distract myself from my dilemma, I began to develop a habit of collecting smooth stones on my morning beach walk. It gave me something to focus on outside my head. It was a simple action of one stone a day collected , then returning 'home,' to place it in a dish. When the dish was full, I began to take one stone at time out and return it to the beach again. It was just another thing that kept me on the planet, apart from writing my poetry. When the poetry pages of the book were full too and I had enough of the stone routine, I simply closed the poetry off, took the remaining half dish of stones out the front door of my place and tossed the lot into the garden. Soon I packed my belongings and headed south again. Six months had passed, money was running short and I was desperate to find some work. I had no idea what I would do nor where I would live, but I bit the bullet and headed back to Sydney. The cry for help and the answer to follow was not far off. I found a place to live, sharing the digs with another alcoholic to help pay the rent. It worked for a time when I was not drinking but once I began to feel better, I went on a bender and I was back down the depression hole again. Somehow I managed to work short term work in a call centre. I resigned after two weeks as I was just too ill to continue. Then things started to change for the better and I found contract work as Business Development Manager in my old field and once more I was gainfully employed. However, my state of mind was not at peace and I went down the hole again. This time I landed in rehabilitation and it was from there I found my sanity, a guiding light to a new way. The cry for help led me to AA and a God of my own understanding.

It also led me to walk the Camino de Santiago for the first time. Therein I discovered a rebirth of my creativity and a new way of life emerged. God had heard my cry and led me to a of a life of sobriety, clarity of mind, freedom from medication dependence and the gift of service to others.

Baxter's empathy with the fellowship of Alcoholics Anonymous had him writing numerous poems and idealistic invention ideas. Sobriety did not come easy but he persevered and eventually succeeded, remaining sober for the rest of his life, despite the effects of his earlier excessive drinking remaining with him. He returned to study and eventually passed English 111 with the help of a tutor. He graduated with a BA, conferred in May 1956. JKB had no real affinity with higher education and regarded it as a requirement only of making a living and nothing more. He had it with teaching at the Epuni Primary school. James loved the children and caring for them but disliked the regiment feel of the education system. He resigned his position at the end of the first term after his BA graduation and become a sub editor for the Department of Education. He received a glowing reference by Principal Ward for his honesty, integrity, and his natural ability to get along with all his colleagues. Ward also stated that the children taught by Baxter had a privilege that was second to none. James was not of the disciplined type that the system demanded. He did not like to reprimand the children and the regimented routine of school life did not suit him. The temperament of an alcoholic is one of individualism, restlessness and discontent. A long term career was not on my agenda as it was not on Baxter's either. Looking back on my own career over a lifetime, I changed occupations mostly around the 5th to 7 year mark. Baxter it seems had the seven year itch too.

A career in School Publications was a new beginning for JKB. The idea was a new development during the depression, to provide locally written material for schools in New Zealand in preference to European. It was considered more beneficial for future generations of Kiwis and better than anything else available at the time. James began his appointment in May 1956, publishing bulletins and journals for post primate school children. It had from its inception recognised the importance of native authors of a particular genius to be successful and Baxter certainly fitted that to a tee. Whilst numerous journals were produced for children between the age of seven and that thirteen, only six bulletins per year on average were produced during Baxter' seven years at the branch. He wrote a series of bulletins between 1957 and 1960 and compiled a glossary of Maori words, as he had a soft spot in his heart for Maori children and encouraged the publication of Maori children stories too. Baxter's main role for the Department was as editor of the junior section of the School journal. As a writer he considered Maori myth as important as ancient European myth and more important to local audience. He had spoken with a great deal of feeling for the Maori at the time of his appointment.

Baxter's admiration for the Maori people increased as he travelled around New Zealand in his role to initiate new projects into the curriculum. The influence of Jackie, his Maori wife and own children with the native blood in their veins may had an influence too, but it was the visits to Maori villages to see first hand the plight of native, nature and the environment that had the greatest effect on him.

CHAPTER 7.

THE WAY TO ORTHODOXY

Baxter spoke at a teachers' conference in 1957 of the 'Motukiore in the Hokianga Harbour surrounds of the river in the far North of New Zealand; of the mangroves and the sea impact on disappearance of the lands.' From the trip North he wrote the poem 'At Hokianga' and 'At Atiko' and was influenced by Ruth Ross's pioneering bulletin, Tinti O Waitangi which challenged the European version of Treaty with the Maori people. He had stayed with the Ross family up North, enjoyed the company of the parents and two ten year old boys at the time. Much hugging and tears follows when he left there. It was the seed that blossomed in his heart for the Maori that later led him to establish the commune at Jerusalem in 1968. James encouraged contributions from many an author to the school bulletins. He was keen in his instructions to them to aim their composition to the level of a five year old child. He wanted the balance between information and interest to be maintained and expected accuracy in all bulletin information. James Baxter had proved to be a very responsible editor. Of the articles he contributed himself, he displayed independence of mind, remarkable technical expertise and an imagination of mind for the benefit of the children, even in the necessity to imitate what was dictated by the Department of Education in periodicals he wrote. The role necessitated the need for a child like modelling of moral vales. It was by 1957 that he was preoccupied with original sin, death, sex, grief and humanities need for love. This was also a time of him being a good family man and he spent a great deal of time with his children reading them children's books which resulted in family plays in which the whole family took a part. Apart from the works of the likes of Dr. Dolittle and Rudyard Kipling's "Jungle Book" the parents invited children's authors, like Barry Crump and Jean Watson home to feel their stories. Both Archie and Millicent Baxter had encourage James and Terrence as boys to read a lot as they also did,James proved to be a creative hands-on-parent who produce many a homemade toy from odds and ends around the home, to the delight of the children.

Baxters general knowledge was quite exceptional and he passed this on to his own offspring. He typed away almost every night at home and he often walked through the house quoting lines from the latest poem he was working on. During 1957 he completed his poetry collection 'Songs of the Desert' which was first published in the *Nightshift* with works of some of his author friends. He was writing with varying degrees of success and whilst he had remained sober, but was not content with his work, his life nor his religious belief. He had a number of years up in sobriety and his attention to the Anglican religion, but it was not fulfilling his needs. In late 1957 he decided to become a Catholic, but had varying degrees of difficulties in doing so. Private feelings, including the breaking down of his marriage and his intellectual pursuits, pulled against his conversion. A fear to the acceptance of Orthodoxy was modern intellectual arrogance. He asked friends to pray for him and figured divine intervention was the only way he might make it into the new found spiritual desire to become Catholic. For some time now he had been attending regular visits to St.Mary of the Angels Church in Wellington. A priesthood congregation founded in France in the early 19th century. . All the early missionaries in New Zealand were French and drew on their distinct version of spirituality from their founders.

On 17th September 1957 Baxter knelt in the Church before a statue of the Virgin Mary and lit a votive candle and then made his way to the presbytery to keep his appointment with Fr. George McHardy SM, a curate of the parish. The priest was neither intellectual nor literary and had not read even one of Baxter's poems. The priest recognised him as a young man whom he had seen often at Mass and praying before the altar of Mary.

The goodly Father, in his simple way, after listening to James for sometime remarked that he needed to follow the thermal method of conversion through the creed, the commandments and the theology of the sacraments. He used the basic text of the the latest revision of "Catechism Simply Explained," first published in 1897. It was pre Vatican text, which was still widely used for adult instruction. It was characterised by shades of black and white expressions of article of faith and morals, as is the way of catechisms. It certainly let the hopeful catechists know where they stood in taking a step into the way of the Catholic Church. James attended the weekly instructions for September 1957 to January 1958. Father McHardy recognised that James had read widely on Catholicism and had gained more insight with the help of Pat Lawlor, a Catholic with deep convictions of piety of the traditional way. He wisely decided to let Baxter sprout what he knew and only commented when it became necessary to do so to keep him on track. Whilst JKB had no difficulty of a doctrinal nature he asked many a question on Catholic belief on the Eucharist and the forgiveness of sin and the place of the Mother of God in the plan of salvation.

Baxter had no trouble in recognising the misconception that Anglicanism had on the nature of Mary in the Catholic Church with regard to having equal place with Jesus on the divine plain. I had often been drawn to explain to Protestants that Mary as the Mother of Jesus was jut a catalyst to prayer for Catholics. We were even taught as children that we could pray through Mary to ask her to intercede on ones behalf for a special intention that needed an answer, or to ask her for help with some personal perplexed sexual difficulty in our teens. By way of example, like any mother might do, Mary had interceded in asking her son to perform the miracle of turning water into wine at the marriage feast of Canna. It had been a simple request to her son of 'they have run out of wine' and as a dutiful son he did something about it.

It had been the simple humility and compassion of Mary and her bond with her fellow man that had drawn Baxter to her. He had read deeply of Thomas Aquinas the Italian Dominican, Catholic priest and Doctor of the Church and an eminent influential philosopher of the 13th century. Also, the works of Jacques Maritain, French Catholic philosopher who was raised a Protestant like Baxter, was an agnostic before converting to Catholicism in 1908 and wrote more than 80 books, reviving the works of Thomas Aquinas in modern times. In his conversion he was drawn to discussion on Jung's fatalities of human psyche in intellect, feeling, sensation and intention to produce his poems and therein he linked Mary with the intuition and sensation that lead to writing poetry. Baxter had felt like me that Mary was the ideal mother he had never had in his youthful abandonment and a female spirit to whom he could relate. I too took that on board in early youth and like JKB felt that virginal motherly love without complications.

It was the physical relationships with women that James was bedevilled by and it made life complicated for him. The Mother of Jesus spiritual contact was his road to a kind of freedom from bondage to some degree. Back home the marriage was on its last legs so to speak. Both James and Jacquie had worked as a team when times were tough and they struggled financially. However, more prosperous times had arrived and they did not need to lean on each other for survival and tended to go their own way more often that not. Jacquie had somewhat come to terms with Baxter's turn around as a non drinker and full time member of A.A. He was more than preoccupied with recruiting members to AA and his new devotion to become a Catholic which seemed to leave the burden of child raising more to her than him. She was shocked to find his new bent to the Catholic faith as she was a devoted Anglican and daughter Hillary had been going to regular Anglican Sunday school. Son John had also been indoctrinated and baptised into the Anglican community. It was the last straw in what had been a marriage of 'injury and injustice' by Baxter and more often than not a clash of temperament between them. He wrote it all in his poetry; the death of the marriage in his fiction and it all rang true. The marriage ended in October 1957.

My own life flashed before me like a kaleidoscope of colourless sequences. being by my fourteen year old Uncle John's bed just before he took his last breath; learning the latin as a five year old on a stool with fellow kindergarten kids, a one eyed fiery irish priest cracking a stock whip over our heads whenever we got a sacred word wrong. I was never good at languages but I could spit out latin in fear like it was natural to me. My childhood flashed before me, running freely through the bush bare footed in search of hidden treasures like frogs, lizards and snakes and surviving to tell the tail. Crossing a river when I could barely swim and being there when my best friend drowned as a boy just beyond the age of reason. Crazy games of chicken imitating James Dean in the film ' rebel without a Cause,' initially on my pushbike. Playing kissing games with young teenage girls and doing my best for one in the bush which eluded me until my late teens.

My youth was not unlike James Baxter to a great degree, but I was not as well read as he was. An average student who wrote poetry as child, had my head into Shakespeare but more so into comic books. Rugby league football in the winter was the norm and the beach and tennis the pastimes of summer days, birds nesting for my hobby and cutting corkwood for pocket money up to age twelve. That was before being shipped off to boarding school were Rugby Union, Rowing and regimented school cadets were considered the essentials outside of schooling. The Marist brothers were no different to the Sisters of no mercy; they thrashed the hell out of us boys. Whilst I did not much like academia, I graduated with enough education to choose my own pathway. I found the pleasures of the flesh more suited to my taste as women, gambling and alcohol become more a part of my being in overcoming loneliness. I was always striving to better myself but more often than not was held back by my attraction to the shadow self and not the light.

Ultimately I found sales and marketing to my liking as career choice for a time. Once having the freedom to be my own boss I made enough money to set up my own business ventures and travelled overseas for a time. Then having sowed my wild oats returned in my late twenties, got married and so for the next three decades did all the usual things that a so called responsible father of a family of four kids does. I grew an even bigger business, got a bigger house, flash cars and a boat. Nothing pleases a wife and mother more than to see her husband overburdened by a huge mortgage. It kept me working day and sometimes night, away from the temptations of the flesh so to speak, to provide for the family, educate the kids and build a retirement package for a hopefully blissful retirement one day. Of course, this was not to be, as my 'isms' became even more suppressing. Workaholism, extreme commitment to my customers at all hours in preference to time with the family and drinking became my prime pastimes and I was still taking a risk or two dabbling on the Stockmarket.

At the hight of business success and material reward I found myself on an ever increasing treadmill of what seemed important at the time. It all ended when the so called prototype of my conception of marital bliss left me for another, then a good friend suicided closely followed by my son Peter doing likewise. The three 'Cs' of calamity, collapse and the cry to God for help ultimately followed. I tried to find the answer to my dilemma by running to the arms of lovers instead of God and my communion of choice to soothe the savage beast that lay within was alcohol. It could only end one way, utter defeat and even after my retreat to the bush and the beach for a time, finding work, and being dry drunk, I ended up in rehabilitation as a mental and physically exhausted wreck.

The breakup of the Baxter marriage caused much heartache for James and Jacquie as a whole. The children were distressed and missed their father terribly. Whilst Jacquie had the better of it with the family home and children under the same roof, the mortgage still had to be paid. Jackie took a second job and James did his best to help support them too. James' place of abode was not the best but it secured him some freedom that Jacquie did not have the luxury due to family commitment. JKB's new found Catholic belief was a catalyst to him remaining sober despite the marriage break up and his entrenchment into helping other alcoholics. James felt the need to quieten his mind and find some way through his dire situation. of guilt and remorse. Approaching Christmas 1957, he stayed for a week at the Catholic Monastery of Our Lady of the Southern Star at Kopua, Hawke's Bay. He was very much taken in by the communal life of constant devotion to God in prayer, silence and the simple pleasure of physical work again to maintain food and shelter for the religious worshipers.

Whilst Baxter had been baptised into the Anglican faith, he was baptised again into the Catholic faith in January 1958. He did not wish to have the in-depth remission of sins that may well have been inflicted on him by the sacrificial act of a Cardinal or Bishop of Christ of the Redeemer, but rather settled for a rather gentle old Marist priest of a local parish in Wellington for his initial Catholic confession and Communion. After the wise old man had James examine his consciousness and confess, he administered communion.

JKB for an elating moment felt the great freedom of letting go to the hands of God, much like Bill Wilson, the founder of AA had experienced in his own vision of enlightening insightful freedom from the bondage of alcohol decades before. The ideal of forgiveness of sin, regular confession with absolution of his sins became a feature of Baxter's belief from then on. The Mass which reenacts the sacrificial death of Christ for the redemption of mankind also became an integrated part of his life also. He became a daily communicant in the order of the 'saints' of old who had chosen the Lord over their lives and had great appeal to him.

Unlike Baxter, I was not moving further spiritually towards my childhood indoctrinated Catholicism, but to the contrary I was in search of a new way of life after so much of my mind was destroyed in painful life experiences. For a while I did try to find an answer within the faith but it proved to be of no avail. I attended Sunday Mass on a regular basis, confessed my defects of character. 'Sin' in the vernacular of the faith of our fathers holy faith and sometimes received the Holy Communion. However, it did little to lift my mood, left me feeling even more guilty for my continuance of drinking and craving the need of extraneous sex. On a visit to The Jesuit priest who presided over the Mass and burial of my son, I asked for his wisdom in the matter of adulterous sexual activity. At that point in time I was still not divorced but needed the touch of a warm body next to me so desperately. Father Peter's advise was "it is o.k. to have another relationship Doug, but that doesn't give you permission to bonk ever bird you meet. It will profit you naught and may well cause you more sorrow and shame." Time proved it to be so. Still not satisfied with my state of being, I visited a regular parish priest, after attending an unsatisfactory Indian meditation event. my visit to the so called Christian religious seeking further advise on God's word in the matter proved worthless too. He was more interested in drinking his whisky and watching his favourite TV show than listening to a dry drunk in so much mental pain and physical exhausting tell his story in a search for a way out. The way did come eventually, but not through the order of Malchizedek in that way of the cross, but more like Job of the old testament. my spiritual awakening ultimately came via my second rehabilitation, resulting in my regular AA attendance and my first tramp on the Camino de Santiago.

In time I drifted away from the Church altogether except for an occasion attendance at a group meditation instead of Mass attendance. The theme being a mindfulness, mantra, a key to spirituality it seemed to be in a word. It was inspired by its founding Father John Main, based on a fifteenth century Indian method and converted by the goodly father to a Christian methodology. It helped me for a time and set in motion a state of stillness, chanting" Maranatha." The technique was to breath in and out with the word in equal syllables of 'Mar...rar....nar...tha.' The meaning being in the old Arabic language " Come Lord Jesus Come." In time, as I recovered I gave up the practice, but in a way I have never really let go of the scaffolding of Catholicism in the home of my soul. The signs and symbols of the faith are still there, particularly in the Mass, as James Baxter , in his spiritual practice took on board. Maybe one day I will return to the faith but for now it is it not so, for I find my new way of life in creativity and regular AA meetings in the fellowship of alcoholics being spiritually satisfying for the present.

James Baxter, through his dark night of the soul, his spiritual enlightenment and new found Catholic faith had become more humble. He regularly prayed the Rosary as devotion to the Mother of Jesus asking her to intercede in times of trouble in his life and often entered the church to walk the Stations of the Cross that adorns the walls of all Catholic Churches. It afforded him the opportunity to relive Christs way to Calvary. As Baxter meditated on each station of the way, he like other devotees could be heard praying: " We adore thee O Christ and we praise thee, for by thy holy cross thou has redeemed the world."

The initial religious euphoria left Baxter and he struggled in his sadness, expressing his absence of religious emotion and had a belief that he was being slowly but strongly influenced by God to take a more balanced view of himself and his Creator. It did not worry him so much, for he had come to the conclusion that God had him or life now disputed his own sinfulness. He often meditated on the Resurrection of the Body. He found it impossible to be happy without God in his life now and likened his way to that of St. Paul, who often spoke of his sinful nature. " What a wretched man I am! Who will rescue me from this body of death. Thanks be to God, through the Lord Jesus Christ! So then, with my mind I serve God, but with the flesh I serve the law of sin." (Romans 7:24).

James Baxter felt domination because of his pride and his need to express himself wilfully. Thus he often expressed his Catholicism doctrine of faith with flamboyance. He was once sighted at Seresin's coffee bar in Lampton Quay overlooking the street making a huge sign of the cross and whispering the grace before meals before eating. It seemed this expression of a new dimension had overtaken the character of his poetic utterances of the pubs in his drunkard haphazard past. He once appeared at a society wedding and performed the Stations of the Cross whilst the wedding ceremony was taking place. He was both self absorbed and Christ like in his outward spiritual expression of his faith. To any observer he would appear to be an actor in a play and a spiritual Catholic overburdened by his womanising and at the same time doing his best to help those less fortunate of the street, particular souls of Maori persuasion. The Catholic Church of Wellington, and indeed New Zealand at large didn't know what hit them when they had to confront the character that he was as a result of his conversion. He was sometime like St. Francis of Assisi in the streets of Wellington counselling street alcoholics and doing his bit to relieve the burdens of the drug addicts. He was his own man in the persona of a Matthew Talbot, the Irish Catholic of the Dublin of the latter part of the 19th century who was somewhat revered for his poetry, charity and mortification of the flesh. Like Talbot, in New Zealand at least, he became like the patron saint of the alcoholic. As well as the Catholic rituals JKB lived and breathed the suggested steps of the AA programme.

As true as his Catholic doctrine of faith and morals, and his twelve step work in AA was his poetry. He revised the first of three sections of former work into a new book. Then his comprised earlier work and his uncollected works, no doubt kept on pieces of paper he had somehow kept for future reference. The third part of this book was confined to the religious side of his nature. Somehow he had not yet mastered the ability to write religious poems. In that regard his poetic brilliance was left wanting.

Baxter's brilliance was in his ability to piece together poems that were flashes from the past or experiences of the street, not unlike Bob Dylan's way of creating a song from disjointed rhyme roughly assembled on scraps of paper or Dylan Thomas's mournful cries on parchment after far to many whisky at the bar. JKB had attempted in the third section his ' *To God the Son* ' *(1955)* revival but it still proved his lack of a religious connection there. In any event the book In '*Fires of No Return*' was not well received by the critics. He did not have the illustration of his latter work ';*Auckland,* ' which happen to be his last. James had lost the glittering perceptions of his assembly of words, the colour of prospective and the controlling ideas which he formally had in his more youthful poetic expression seem to have vanished. It did come back eventually but in the meantime he sometimes wondered if he return to the drink he may well open up the well of his poetic soul that for the present was denied him. Typical alcoholic thinking in early recovery.

    Baxter had formally a lyrical sequence in his dramatic gift of seeing and feeling in his expressive poetry. He produced a play in September 1958 for the New Zealand Broadcasting Service called *Jack Winter's Dream* which was written for the speaking and singing voice of radio, as it was the days pre T.V. It was a masterpiece of an unusual kind and contained songs in different voices, accent and pitch. The voice parts of narration by Bernard Kearns, the gravel voice of Ballarat Jakem and the soft Cornish accent of Will Trevelyan, the Scottish accent of Lowy made it a resounding success. The play was a conversion of a dream into a nightmare and it made an ideal story for radio which Baxter had tried to write it for. He was much influenced by Dylan Thomas '*Under Milk Wood*' from which the idea may well have come from in the first place. Before broadcasted the *N. Z. Listener* gave it as a main feature article and the production itself was enthusiastically received by critics and audience alike. The response more than made up for the lack-lustre response of JKBs *In Fires of No Return.*

    The story of *Jack Winter's Dream* much paralleled   Baxter's former life of a drunkard, rabbiter, swagman, station roustabout and that of his Grandfather John Baxter, who like Winter found gold "in them there hills." The play mutates from dream to nightmare much like the poets own life and that of his alcoholic but loveable old grandad. JKB, also infused some delightful characters who resonated with the Baxter clan of old; those life hardened interesting rough and tumble types and the down and outs of society, that James had grown to embrace in his own lifetime. The play embraced themes of age, death, murder and love held together by the threat of a something of a spiritual nature hidden in the plot. The introduction of the spiritual was no doubt an influence of James new found love of God, the need for penance and sacrifice and the idea of giving of oneself for the benefit of others. It was a theme he carried into his late communal life.

 Baxter for a great deal of time after his separation from Jacquie went through lots of grieving. He was always hopeful of a reconciliation with his former wife, but knew he had to wait for a time for his past failure as a husband, drunkard and womaniser would take time for her to gain some degree of acceptance and forgiveness.

His moment of some reconciliation came when he was granted leave to take part in a conference in Tokyo to discuss school textbooks and to include Indian equivalent in NZ school publications. It was his hope to infuse Asian material into the school bulletins to give children a broader view of the world beyond the education system of New Zealand's then limited scope. JKB was granted leave on full pay and he asked Jacquie to go with him and put the past behind them. She willing accepted his invitation.

Jacquie was brave to accept his invitation considering his former life and known sexual encounters which she now had full knowledge of. The fellowship to attend the conference provided expenses for Baxter alone, so to ensure his family could attend at least part of the conference, he arranged for Jacquie and the children to meet for the second half of the conference relating to India at a later date. He seemed to himself to be more humble and at ease since giving up the booze, embracing Catholic belief, and being involved in helping other still suffering alcoholics to maintain sobriety. Up to the time of his departure for Japan, James keeps up his daily Mass practice, prayer and meditation and delighted in frequent confessions, feeling the relief from his perceived sinfulness. As the priest provided him with absolving him of his sin in the name of the Father, Son and Holy Spirit, James always felt renewed to start again on his spiritual journey. Time would prove this a blessing and a person curse, but as the record would prove to show, he never did return to alcohol as a crutch to his ongoing mental and physical torments.

CHAPTER 8.

THE GEOGRAPHICAL TO JAPAN

The flight to Japan on 16th September 1958 was to be an eye open for James and help lay the seeds of his future communal living and guidance in the future at Jerusalem. JKB arrived in Tokyo as typhoon Ida hit the coast flooding streets and houses and blowing roof tops sky high. Whilst Baxter himself was not in any danger, as he was staying far from the centre of the trouble, he took to heart the courage and determination of those that were effected. He noted how resourceful they were in quickly going about the task of rebuilding their lives from this misfortune. James took on extra tasks at the conference, writing a paper for the UNESCO delegate from Paris on visual aids, keeping notes for the French delegate when he was absent from meetings. He also took on the task for a Japanese professor who asked him to proof read and edit his paper and improve it in English whilst drafting conclusions also. Baxter had written a poem on the typhoon which was translated into Japanese and it was widely circulated among the attending delegates with great acclaim. He won the friendship of the anti colonial delegate from Iran inviting him to enjoy a non alcoholic drink with him. Baxter had Japanese professor Karasawa held in frequent discussion on Buddhism which initiated many a lengthy conversation. He managed time also to send a quantity of notes on the conference to his NZ office.

Baxter's capacity to work was always at the extreme and he paid a price of physical exhaustion as a consequence in his efforts at the conference. He did a final report to the Director of Education in New Zealand who was instrumental in his gaining the opportunity to travel to the conference in the first place. Included in his report was a lengthy letter of his impression of Japan, noting the technological advancement of the Japanese tertiary systems and their completed democratic methods of education. These were advancing despite the background of widespread suffering of the people caused by economic difficulties and the dislocation of traditional patterns of living after the war. It bewildered him and other delegates how Japan was moving so fast materially and education wise, especially among the young. A group visit to a training college of students endorsed this observation even more so. He was taken by the fact that they had ultra left wing views politically and socially without this being of a Marxist nature. It had not the stable middle of the road leftist views of his home country. JKB found Japan with a vibrancy that was static at the time in down under New Zealand.

Whilst the peoples of Japan portrayed a militant appearance on the surface, behind this shell there was a manner that was simply beautiful and very much alive. He was very much moved by the vitality and warmth of the country people. On visits to local villages there was cleanliness and tidiness even amongst the poor. He had taken it upon himself to learn their ways, taking them into his confidence without seeking to exploit them. A meeting of minds so to speak in half way exchange of ideas for the future. JKB had pointed out in his letter to Director Beeby, who was in the midst of planning the next UNESCO conference, that the Pacific countries who would attend should be on an equal footing as their New Zealand host country. Baxter advocated that the mission should be one of inclusion not as teacher over pupil so to speak.

He suggested that a lesson might be learnt in that regard by the local white population of New Zealand and its outlook on the Maori people. Baxter considered their point of view had not been considered sufficiently enough nor understood in all matters and in particular education. He concluded that some Maori should be included in the next conference workshops.   During the Japan Conference Baxter was invited to the United States to work for summer months on a children's encyclopaedia for Asian countries. Whilst the funds to do so were available he was not one for personal achievement and declined the offer, for he felt he should be getting on with the job in Wellington on his return. The offer to attend USA as an educator confirmed how highly regarded James Baxter was at the Japan conference and back home in New Zealand.

By the time the conference ended Baxter was once more exhausted from his extraneous duties and extreme input to the conference. He made his way to a distant fishing port at Chois City and was accommodated by a Columbian priest who met the exhausted and disorientated Baxter at the train station. James related his spiritual journey and discussed with the priest how God was working on him as a channel of peace. Baxter seemed to have a view like that of St. Francis in his prayer; " Lord , make me a channel of thy peace...." Baxter also discussed his marriage difficulties and spoke with much love and affection for Jacquie and his two children who were suffering too as a result of the breakdown of the parent's relationship. Baxter pointed out to the priest that the next faze of his conference journey was to India and the outcome of this visit with Jacquie and the children was crucial to their marriage surviving. The priest was deeply concerned and soulfully effected by Baxter's vast knowledge and believed it was because of him that he was to become a better person. Baxter left Japan after the three weeks and spent sometime in the Thai capital of Bangkok. He loved the green land of canals and friendly dark people. Whilst there he found he could not sleep much at night due to the stifling humidity and high temperatures. One evening he met a young girl who approached him for a sexual encounter. He explained to her that it would only make him sad and reminded himself of his past way of life of sexual encounters that had been instrumental in his marriage breakdown, apart from his alcoholic self indulgences. The poor girl poured out her troubles including that she had been jilted by her lover and had no money. Baxter, with a sympathetic ear, gathered his remaining monies and gave her half of what he had left. He had honourable intent as he walked with her in the cool of the evening. However, when they reached her shack with but a mattress on the floor they fell into each others arms and made passionate love. He had contented himself sexually, but later admitted the experience had left him sad.

It was five years after I had given up the booze as a result my mental condition at the time and in acceptance of the steps of recovery in my daily life of the AA programme, handing over to the Master of my destiny, a God of my own understanding. Whilst I was still suffering bouts of depression they were less frequent and my first rehab some four years before had helped to a degree in settling me down emotionally. The contract work had been going well and I had enough repeat business from my employer to take time out and still receive my agreed contractual income.

So in mid May 2013, I headed for Paris and winged my way to walk the Camino de Santiago. An escape to Spain to sort out my head and let go the tragic events of marriage break down and my son's suicide that still plagued me. The rehab and AA had helped but not solved the pain and torment I was still feeling. The thought of walking The Way of St. James seemed like a good idea at the time.

My Camino started out with a further burden than the overweighted pack that I carried. I had stayed on one previous occasion at the 'Welcome' hotel on the Rue de Siene in Paris, but my entry through the main door on this occasion was both fortuitous and memorable. I had only had one previous stay in Paris for a wedding but remembered how to find my way to the hotel using the Metro system from the airport. Full of pride I step into that foyer with my sun glasses still on to shade my eyes from the sun. In the dark entry I had forgotten about the small step just inside the door to the foyer and tripped head first with my heavy back pack projecting me forward like a rocket. I hit the deck of tiled floor, cut my nose on the glasses as they broke on impact. I had landed face first without time to reach out with my hands to soften the impact. Half stunned I raised my head and was assisted by the Concierge, who quickly went about his business to clean up my blood off the tiled entry. I sat on the step waiting for his attention to detail and then he focused on my wounds, tracing my cut nose with Ia cotton bud dipped in iodine. A rather large band aid was applied and I thanked him and headed for the lift to my assigned room for the evening. Examining the damage done, in the bathroom mirror, I looked like I had just finished ten rounds with Mohammad Ali. Both eyes were already swollen and around the bottom eye lids to the base of the damaged nose, it was all turning a brighter shade of purple.

After a fitful nights sleep, I did my best to patch up and lick my wounds before heading for a light breakfast of coffee and croissant at a nearby patisserie. I was in no mood for sight seeing and headed for the nearest main rail station , Gare de Montpamasse, to board a train for St. Jean de Port on the french side of the Pyrenees mountains where I planned to commence my walk of The Way the next day. It was to be a slow train journey through the north of France and would take until late afternoon to reach St.Jean for my overnight stay before heading out across the border to Spain the next morning to climb the Pyrenees. As my head was throbbing with a splitting headache, I decided to distract my attention away from the head pain by writing a poem about my grandfather. Listening to the rhythm of the train on the rails in tune with my verse, the poem came easily. Once finished, I filed it away in my knapsack and thought no more about it until two weeks later.

The old fellow alcoholic patient in the next bed to me in rehab had given me sound advise. To put my boat of personality upon the waters of life, trim the sail and go with the flow, accepting what ever happened as meant to be. My journey so far had proved that by letting go I was freeing myself from worry and my headache had somewhat eased As I climbed the stairs to the attic and my bed chamber for the night, I looked up at the foothills of the Pyrenees mountains and wondered what was in store for me when the sun rose the next day.

I awoke early to a summers morn of 38 degree centigrade celsius. After replacing my pack and eating some breakfast, I headed up the mountain to commence my Camino. The degree of heat at 9 a.m. that morning was 42 celsius and for the next month on my Camino journey it never dropped below 40 degrees. It never rained once in the whole month of 'The Way.' It was an arduous task to walk that first Camino in my 68th year. I learnt a lot about the necessity of being reasonably fit for such an ordeal and what to pack for further reference and the necessity to have adequate medical supplies and drink plenty of water too. Along the way I shed 5 kilo from my back pack and lost 10 kilo of body weight by the time I reached Santiago. This I documented in a new website www.-caminoway.com.au for future reference for fellow pilgrims of the way and of course as a timely reminder for myself for future ventures.

At cafe, bar Abergues -pilgrim hostels where I stopped, I wrote down all my experiences and documented the locations of each stop and end destination of the day, taking from each a snippet of life on the road, on my up hill and down dale along the Santiago way. My daily diary and poetic jottings proved to be a great help as a template to work from when I later documented my book of poems and wrote my first novel on my experience of that first of my Camino. At the time of this my first real inward pilgrimage were I learnt love from others on their personal journey; the art of giving freely of myself in a more charitable way, of humility and the pain of letting go, the gift of unconditionally unburdening my soul to perfect strangers from every corner of the globe. More than anything else, I began to learn acceptance for whatever transpired in my life on that journey.

There is something about one's Camino that is miraculous in its rewards for daily living. My most cathartic experience came one night high up on mountain top singing songs with a couple of young people I had journeyed with over the previous week. On this particular evening I had been listening to a young German rock musician who became like a younger brother me in my then search for meaning. Robin Marion was the lead singer and guitarist for a well known German heavy rock band. He was at the time contemplating a change in direction to folk music as it was becoming all the rage again in Europe. An old guitar he borrowed from the owner of the Albergue where we were staying and began singing rock n roll songs to his captured audience. We all sang along with him with much fun and gusto of the memory of youthful days of the past and sad songs of tomorrow land and past loves. Just before the nights activities reached a crescendo, Robin sang a most beautiful ballad he had written about a lost refugee who had come to Germany to start a new life. I commended him for his ballad and suggested he should write more. It was then I remembered the poem I had written on the slip of paper I had in my nap-sack and he asked me to read it to him. I read it to the sing a long audience but nothing more was said about it, so I just filed it away in my pack and forgot about it.

Then about one month after my return from the Camino Robin emailed me asking for the lyrics of my 'Boundary Rider' poem, as he thought it would make a grand ballad. The intention was for Robin to add music and record it on his group's next album. I wrote a reply advising that as I did not have a chorus for it and would put some time into writing one before I sent it to him. I accompanied that reply with two other poems I had written that I thought he may have an interest in. Sure enough, one of those poems was centred around my drinking days with my Father and his fall from grace as a result of his alcoholism. Robin liked the lyrics and recorded it as a song on his newly formed band "Master Mint.' Meanwhile I had written a chorus for the 'Boundary Rider.' It was then I realised that I had an ability to write songs. So I set to work and wrote sixty all together. It was like a lotus flower of creative ideas flowed from the depth of my being. Meanwhile Robin had recorded my " Dad and days gone" that I had sent him, altering it with an entirely different music theme than I had in mind. So it was that my new life began to unfold. I set to work and recorded my first album of songs 'Country Camino' with the help of a group of professional musicians. This was followed by a book of prose and poems called ' From darkness to light.' I then got to work immediately on another project of a novel centred around my first camino entitled "the Sword of Discernment." It was my actual physical journey overlaid by a goal of a man seeking an outward sign of his inner discernment. It took a lot out of me as it was another form of letting go my inner feelings of loss as well and it was rewritten four times before I felt it a satisfactory manuscript to self publish.

   If that was all I had to focus on it would have proved a grand obsession that could have just as quickly faded and I could have just as easily drifted back to my three AA meetings a week, healing mediation and yoga sessions. I could have then contented myself with the contract work I was doing quite successfully without causing me any depression nor unnecessary anxiety as a consequence. I would have learnt to just take things as they come and over time live a life of acceptance. and maybe serenity of being-ness, whilst assessing others on their spiritual journey too. But that is not the nature of this alcoholic and so I returned to the frantic pace that drove me in my drinking days. Whilst I was making the album and writing the first novel, I completed the sale of one renovated property and took on a second property renovation, whilst riding the stock market's cut and thrust of the derivatives trading of "puts' and 'calls.' I was living on three hours sleep a night and still holding down my full time contract work as a Business Development Manager as well. The writing was on the walls and I once again fell in a heap and ended up in rehab. This time I was only coming back to some kind of normality through a series of sessions of shock treatment and mind bending anti-depressant drugs. I needed to change and that could only mean for me anther return to the Camino. Despite the lessons of driving myself too hard with creative activities and the hard soulful lessons of past relationships, I felt it may be different this time around.

Whilst my first Camino was to let go and let God to speak, I reckoned on the fact that another Camino, this time on the Portuguese route, might do the trick. When I faced the facts of that journey in retrospect, in truth I just wanted to find another woman and get laid.

As time proved I did find some peace of mind and a romance that in the long run proved another heartache. However, I was soon to fall victim to a serious viral illness as a result of my arduous physical endeavours in going beyond the boundaries of endurance and to make matters worse, before I fully recovered, a further deep depressive episode landed me once more in rehab. I arose to some peace of mind and vision to climb another mountain. So after my Camino of letting go the first time and the second of seeking answers through romantic attachment, at long last I woke up to the fact that it was time to do the Camino for myself without any agenda and decided then and there to go cold turkey of the heavy depression medications I had been prescribed. So, at the ripe old age of 73, I returned to the French route to do another Camino. It took a week of walking to rid myself of the withdrawal symptoms of heavy medications. This time I walked the way in the cooler months of April- May and it never stopped raining. So having contracted a flu virus again and after beating the addictive habit of heavy medications and having no alcohol to lean on, I steeled myself to nature and slogged on through the cold winter days living in wet clothing and ever wet boots for weeks on end.

At the end of my French Camino, I had a couple of days rest in Finisterre to reduce my flu and fever and to gather some strength to then return to Santiago where I caught a flight to Ireland. There I commenced another mountainous hike. A week walking the Wicklow mountains, another few days walking up the coast of the Aran Islands and riding a push bike down the west coast, I returned to the mainland to commence walking the Burrow Way. An exhausted old Australian returned home to Australia having walked near 1200 kilometres over the previous six weeks. I returned to my Business Development work for a few months and stayed to the end of the contractual term that year before retiring to write more books. This current book is my seventh and I have since completed another album of songs with the help of my professional contacts. None of this would have been possible without giving up alcohol, returning regularly to AA and having a belief in a power greater than self.

Jacquie and the children arrived in Bombay India on board the *S.S. Stathmore* three weeks after the conference in Singapore. Baxter joined them on board ship and they discussed their many differences in an attempt to a possible reconciliation of marriage. Their religious differences were not reconcilable, so they figured it would be best to build a new relationship in a new country in preference to returning to New Zealand, away from the prying eyes and advice of parents and friends alike. They took up residence in a small house in New Delhi in the Muslim Quarter and employed a servant to cook for them. They travelled widely during their time there and were mostly troubled by the poverty, particularly in Calcutta and they also found the heat, the smells and the dust almost unbearable.

James began to assimilate himself into the village environment of the people and familiarise his consciousness with the ethnic minority. He was fascinated by the joy and bright eyes of the lowest classes in Indian society. Despite their suffering and primitive conditions they absorbed their suffering with dignity as if it was ordained by God himself or herself, depending on ethnic belief. James learnt so much and begged to love as they did in showering it upon one another. The poor and starving were constantly in his mind in both India and Japan. He later recalled a lot of this experience in his Jerusalem books. Baxter ventured to Bombay, Madras and Calcutta in his work for the New Zealand education system. He was entitled to travel first class in an air conditioned carriage but chose to travel second class and even third class so he could mingle more with the poor and outcast of the land. Along with the people he slept on the floor of the train, he shared the money he saved on the first class ticket with those in dire straights. Baxter would often go hungry to feed another, giving all his savings away, he lived on dates he scrounged at railway stations en route to his next destination. He was never satisfied, believing all he gave was but a drop in the ocean and he was often in despair over beggar's suffering, never once seeing that at the time he was in the same boat. The exposure he had to bad hygiene and poor diet damaged his health considerably. He had constant bowel issues since his time in Thailand and his condition grew worse.

He had suffered much in giving up the booze but health was a big issue now. He knew he had to focus on his soul more than body and this was a grave mistake for the constant bowel problems plagued him. Despite his physical discomfort and mental torments, JKB displayed an intellectual toughness and shared his knowledge and educational experience with the ordinary folk of India. He was no doubt gearing himself for a future life of service to others which he learnt through his AA counselling of the still suffering alcoholic. The seeds of a commune back in his home country was in its embronic stage in his subconscious soulfulness. He was shocked by the flagrant unnatural reality of misery which struck deep with intensity within him. India suffered the indignant arrogance of a British landlord for decades in both political and industrial rule only to be then overshadowed during Baxter's time by industrial unrest due to the threats of China looming over them. Street gangs were fighting in the cities. The Indian communists were gearing up for a revolution and if they where to win the next general election then China would be invited to take over were Britain had left off.

Baxter was caught up in the turmoil of it all. Conversations by Communist writers and artists he communicated with deeply challenged his resolve. His mode of dress had him sometimes mistaken for being American but more often than not his cultured voice had him mistaken as being English.Neither helped his cause when advocating for the people. The wounds of the past British rule which had ended just a decade before Baxter's travels in India still caused a raft of reactions to the British Raj and made his purpose in helping even more difficult.He was passionately desirous to belong to the Indian peoples. Baxter was keen to know more of the nature of India and its people. He ventured forth on a thirty hour train journey from Calcutta to New Delhi with a determination to live outside the bounds of his official connections.

James travelled second class, conversing with passengers and stopping over in the villages along the way where he found the people warm and friendly with a spiritual wholesomeness and in their hospitality he was able to glean their political leanings. He was surprised to find they seemed politically well informed and up to date with the current industrial unrest in areas of the cities. The villagers were poor and were deeply committed to family life, the community and unlike in the cities, conscious of their local environment, living in harmony with nature's law. JKB was partially taken by the Holy man of each village revered by the people. The men of heavenly realm he found to be intelligent, broad minded and practical men who had all trained for a least twenty years in their yoga and meditative practices. The Guru status of the holy man was demonstrated in their attitude to animals in the same light as humans. Such similarities Baxter later introduced in his Jerusalem commune as he did with the modern Ashram he attended. He was particularly fascinated by the study of religious devotion performed and the venerability of the Guru who resided there. It was the Guru's instructive talent as both teacher and poet, political leader with unusual talent and integrity that attracted him.

Baxter saw himself as having much in common with the Gurus he met. On a practical level the Holy man was a playwright and poet with similar romantic notations as his own. The idea of psychological freedom of expression and the loathing of anything reeking of academic education he admired in their attempts to revive the first schools of old India over the British style of education. The harmony of concern for the individual mirrors Baxter's own concerns too. Its was the Ashram of Rabindranath Tagore that fascinated Baxter the most. He portrayed the values of study, education, religion, nature, decision making and understanding of universal law that Baxter learnt so much from in his time there. Whilst much discord flared up in the post partition riots of 1947, when Muslims killed Hindus and vica versa, idealist like Baxter and his new found friendship with Guru Tagore overlooked such complexities of a country diverse in relationships, with so many different views and closed of by certain boundaries of creed and culture. What was significant to Baxter was his personal perception of India that was to shape his ideals which he would try to replicate back in New Zealand. The lesson of horrible living conditions of places like the city of Calcutta focused his attention more on the benefits of living outside a city where the reality of New Zealand's city life had a general worthlessness in his eyes, in particular to that of the Maori peoples.

Possibly the greatest benefit the Baxter family gained from their Indian exposure was that it drew the family closer together as a consequence of living there. By the New Year of 1959 there was a great deal of happiness and joy in the home. James realised his past love for Jacquie had not fully filtered to his heart. During their time together in India he saw her kindness to the sick, the care she took of the children overlooking her own needs in the process. He soon came to acknowledge that her relationship with others was much better than the one they had together. He was learning from her, as the marital vows and the Christian faith dictated, as 'two in one flesh' and he looked forward to more time with her in a happy life to come.

What he recognised more than anything else was that what he felt for her was not passion and it may not have even been love, but a more mature coming together in harmony, overlooking the small irritations and the crisis of life that inevitably could come their way. Yet, later that year, back in New Zealand he had expressed to a friend it was the first time in a decade he realised that human affection was temporary and that solitude was the real seed of freedom for him. It was a weening of the need for another that he was expressing and felt that it was a growing up experience that he was now learning for the future. The overseas experience had broadened his outlook and in his discovery he believed he had changed. Like most delusions of us of poetic expression, we often live in a Disneyland of mythical belief that the road ahead may yet be smooth; our vision for the future will remain happy.

Jackie was of the belief on their return that they would never split up again and that the whole family had learnt much from their Indian experiences. The Baxters missed Adam their cook in India and despite their own financial hardships sent him money regularly to help support his family. The Indian experience had taken a lot out of Baxter and he was now in poor health as a consequence. The illness he contracted in Asia may well have been the beginning of deterioration in his health that shorted his life, for formerly he had a strong constitution. The experience of Asia had given him a new social conscious. Writing was no longer the main thing in his life. His chief focus from then on was his family and people in need. Of course he had this to a great degree for others the moment he accepted the AA steps and in particular step 12: " ...having had a spiritual experience as result of these steps, we proclaim this message to other Alcoholics..."

JKB felt a new affinity with his homeland. The air seemed clearer and cleaner and he felt he had fallen in love with New Zealand more than ever before. The reality of looking through rose coloured glasses soon dawned on him. A letter to N.Z. Listener had asked a pointed question. As a writer, was it necessary to narrow ones vision of life to the point where 'no published works could risk offending an unstable thirteen year old or an unlettered journalist?,,,,,, The shadow of Calvin rests still upon the heartland minds of our countryman, dividing grace from nature, and refusing our artists their legitimate entry to the garden of a mature vision of life.'* Baxter continually fought against literary censorship which was transmitted in his poetry as far back as 1952.

Baxter's Asian experiences were recored in his poetic collection of *Howard's Bridge (1961)*. He had written on the dust jacket: "The first part was written some time ago by a man who thought he was a New Zealander and the second part lately, in the past two or three years, by a man who become almost unawares, a member of a bigger, rougher family. The poems in India mark this change."* The book presents a man of disorientation in need of finding his bearings.The former poems acknowledge his origins in trying to come to terms with what he inherited from his Scottish had for bears, the high points in his life and the low ones, in a state of consciousness, childhood memory poems leading to the latter poems reflecting in his choice of humanity over the natural decisions because of his life in Asia having confirmed those choices.

Like me, Baxter had a devotion to 'Our Lady of Perpetual Help' which seemed to be my guiding light as a young man before I too fell from Grace and gave up that devotion. Baxter on the other hand continued his devotion, even finishing his "Howards' Bridge" book with a poem to his vision of Our Lady of Perpetual Help, giving it special emphasis. Baxter saw his Christianity not as an abstract, but a matter of great personal relationship. I never did quite get there. Baxter often prayed to Mary of his spiritual weakness for she had the power to help him heal and in his vision a beauty beyond measure.

* Extracts: Life of James K Baxter, Frank McKay text 1990.

CHAPTER 9.

A MAN OF LETTERS.

Baxter's poetry had not moved far afield from that of Dylan Thomas even though he had matured to a great degree in his writing. Whilst he had that Dylan like poetry of images, related and unrelated, engraved in his every line, for they emerged as they occurred to him, without thought of structure as to the ending, he was somewhat different in that his definition to clarity of intent was more pronounced than the doomsday approach of Thomas. Whilst Thomas was more focused on death in his works than Baxter, their poetry had that mournful appeal to those who thought deeply about the end being near or the spiritual rub of it all coming to nothing. Thomas ended his life with the drink, Baxter continued with his with suffering and clarity of thought without a drop of alcohol on his breath from the date he joined AA until the day of this death. Whilst he lived as a teller of tales romantically, he did have that mouthful carriage like one who had the weight of Christ's cross on his shoulder and the stone on the Master's grave removed so that he could express his intention poetically to replace him there at any moment.

There is always a contrast in comparison of writers of poetic verse. Perhaps the best of contrasts is in comparing two of New Zealand's internationally best know writers to get a more in-depth picture of the one to whom I am devoting this book. Baxter certainly was New Zealand's great romantic poet whilst Curnow in contrast was the most distinguished modernist. Baxter's pitch was for the broad church audience whilst Curnow was of a limited view; Baxter wrote untimely, Curnow obsessively controlled. Curnow's verse was groomed and perfected whilst Baxter, on the other hand undisciplined, scattered his verse across the page. One wrote with perfection, the other didn't really give a rats' arse so long as he got his message out there.

In my own early poetry writings, I give no apology for writing the feeling, the rhyme or reason that took hold of me. It always assembled to be a grand release to write a verse or two of what inspired me at a moments' notice when the verse arrived out of thin air.. Never did I give much thought to grammatical error, like 'where' when it should have been a 'were' or in my haste to get a line out of my head I overlooked the last 't' in thought. In my first book of poetry, I was conscious of this but never bothered for a proof read other than alter what I saw on first reflection. I just printed the thing. After all to me it was just poetic expression and my life did not depend upon it, I had, and still have, greater fish to fry. I feel sure that Baxter, to a great degree in his poetry, in his manuscripts and in his lectures is offered the same fate and would agree with me. I feel safe in the assurance that there has never been a monument built to a critic but many a statue, book or work of art that stands as a tribute to the greatest of creative genius. I like the words of Charles Bandlaine, long since dead french poet, who defined the work of genius as 'childhood captured at will.' I believe Baxter had that child like genius that matured to expand to honest creative criticisms in his latter poetry, play and lectures.

Baxter's works were often deep rooted thought expression against the establishment and soullessness of those of the status quo. Works that are still object lessons for justice and freedom of expression, of spiritual understanding and betterment for suffering souls.

Throughout his lifetime, Baxter's achilles heel was his relationship with women. This is even more poignant in his relations with Millicent his mother for in his letter to her he more than once expresses his feelings of disconnection with her and his infatuation with other women. His honest assessment of his sexual perversions and the intolerable humiliating want of physical relationships with women he didn't even like. JKB struggled with this throughout his life and suffer much for his indiscretions. He more than adequately denotes displeasure in his short term marital 'bliss' with Jacquie, his Maori wife. He wanted so much to make the dysfunctional marriage work and did his best to make amends but the relationship was an inevitable failure in the end. James sometimes violent imagery he jotted down in note books as he dictated in the turbulence of his " Mr Baxter' Evening Liturgy,' and the ' Spring Song of a Civil servant.' The time and years of these note book jottings is unclear as he did not date them , but it more than indicates his difficulty in unworthy sexual bondings. It is even more understanding then that a poet of his worthiness would lean on the vision and prayers to a perfect Mother of Jesus Christ as he drew deeply into his soul to overcome his suffering and attempt to lead a more chaste life.

One Christmas, Baxter drove his family up to Rotorua with Jacquie's mother on board to stay in a rented house there. He had only secured his licence in August 1959 and was most anxious about the safety of his driving with his precious cargo on board,. He endured this time out and many others as he continued to jot down notes of his living hell. In his ' *Numbers* ' of 1957 he had fortuitously written; ' one who will never be content this side of the grave, for the spirit of turbulence, asking from man and nature an impossible harmony. Yet his songs are the fruit of that harmony, which he knows best in the pain of absence. He will always jerk against the yoke; and will always find him hard to bear.' * Oh! how I can relate to those words expressed here. It is as I have written in a poem of my aboriginal brother within my soul that relates so much like some itching underneath the skin. Baxter's insatiable restlessness I also carry deep within my nature which has continued to disturb my life for as far back as I can remember. It has not been made easier by my giving up the drink.

Baxter's next play was '*The Wide Open Cage*' which he and Richard Campion review, for Campion had reviewed and produced "Jack Winsten's Dream'"with some success as audiences found the story appealing. It was a grand attempt by Baxter, for in the play he had told his own former life story. Thus reviewed by Campion the '*Wide Open Cage*' was once more returned to. Baxter with notations for correction. Baxter came back with his own invention on Campion's work. He had allowed his warmly love of people, for life and sex, to flow in the play. When the play finally opened to a full house in Wellington, Baxter had introduced in the cover sheet of the programme: 'The play has no message. It simply holds a mirror to certain relationships among people. *The Wide Open Cage* is life itself, or, if you like, the inordinate love of creatures. The people in the play are each in their different ways trying to find happiness in other people, except for the priest, who is out of the running, and Hogan, who loves nobody. The fact that three of the people are Catholics is really incidental. Catholicism brings to head certain problems of freedom and involvement which are latent in all human relationships. To those inside the cage release seems to be the death of love. *

The characters in the play live in sordid surroundings and are rather seedy, but their vitality is left never in doubt. Nor is there any doubt about the presence of important elements of Baxter's own character and his difficulty in relation to women being worked out. He was attracted by them, they liked him, yet he was unable to establish an easy relationship at a deep level. This tension added greatly to the force of the play.* In a discussion after the first performance of the play, Baxter said he had deliberately rejected a neat plot in favour of a poetically satisfying scheme of 'the eclipse of the forces of light by the forces of darkness.' and that his approach was psychological rather than sociological. Like his *Jack Winter's Dream*, the play had a strong element of melodrama, something Baxter found attractive. Campion mounted the play in a small studio in Drummond Street, Wellington on 7th November 1959. ' This funny old converted house' seemed to Campion ideal 'because it was at the heart of Jim's country- odd, derelict, cops, priests, things happening; booze-ups , and violence round every corner; his kind of country. ' Staging the play in a tiny theatre, where the audience was close to the action, was an advantage for a play with such intimate material. And of course it was as much to do with things of the spirit as with murder, sex, and the rest of it. To add to the realism, Don Ramage, the art master at Wellington Boys High school built an open sided cottage on stage of rusty corrugated iron. This gave the audience the feel that they were watching the actions as if being in the street where it was taking place.* Those of us who have felt the pain of abandonment running through our veins from our first breath tend to suffer a crying need to the depth of our being. Baxter, Bill Wilson the founder of AA and myself, all had this feeling and constant yearning for the love that was denied us as our birthright. From my childhood a silent cry from deep within my being emerged in three distinct waves of expression. First was sexually expressed in the accumulation of many female encounters, each with a varying degree of temporarily satisfying the need for affection and love. The second was the pleasure of alcohol, as it falsely fulfilled a settling of body, mind and spirit but the feeling and the craving followed and rewarded me with an addictive habit even greater than that of a sexual nature. The third was the satisfying release of being able to express on paper in poetry and song all that ailed me in my former life of abandonment, loss of love and direction in life. This, as previously expressed , all came first as a calamity , a collapse and ultimately a cry for help. That is when a God of my own understanding changed it all for me. It is uncanny that James Baxter and Bill Wilson had a similar life path in this regard as I did. I may hasten to add as a final point that my Mother , in her own way like Millicent Baxter, did love her offspring but did not have the capacity in her makeup to know now how to nurture nor teach the art of love. Bill Wilson likewise expressed this in his writing as did Baxter in his.
In the Drummond street theatre the play continued to a packed house night after night.The season could have easily been extended. Campion was intent on it being a film as John O' Shea of Pacific Film was enthusiastic to do it; but the plan was ultimately abandoned more for lack of funds than the brilliance of it all as project. There was a fanfare of publicity in major media about the play. It was reviewed and talked about as the most explosive and valuable insight into exposing areas which New Zealander's preferred to conceal if they could not evade.

* Extract from The Life of James K Baxter- Frank McKay 1990.

The play was later performed by a small company of a Washington Square, New York theatre 1st December 1962. Baxter had visions of thousands of dollars pouring in from TV or movie rights, but did not believe it would happen in reality. In point of fact he received nothing but applause for his creation. Campion revived a manuscript for Baxter of a new work *Three Women and the Sea* in 1961. It was a play that disturbed the waters of the mind and feelings. JKB wanted to communicate once every now and then a special someone who comes into one's life. The person who reshapes people's lives and then vanishes. Finally a last play Baxter collaborated with Campion on was entitled *The Spots of the Leopard* written in 1962 but it was not produced until 1967. It depicted characters drawn from the Wellington streets and didn't amount too much but for its impressionist approach. At any rate Baxter had come into his own as a Playwright which in literary circles was considered by some as of greater public appeal than his poetry.

JBK genuinely liked to please his audience and considered his plays more appealing in that regard than his poetry. He appreciated the fact that the audience could hear the voice of plot as opposed to only reading it in poetic form. Like his life he felt that in a play there was no going back over the words and amending that which had been proof reading what was said. He appreciated his collaboration with Campion and took great delight in working together. Campion as the director in turn liked the way Baxter believed in the Shakespearean tradition of sacred text and respected him for sticking to the knitting in that regard.

When things were getting altogether too heavy in a plot, Campion liked the way Baxter could throw in a joke or something very human to break it down a tone. Baxter had learnt from the master himself for Shakespeare knew how to introduce not comic relief but only humorous intensity. Baxter was often seen at the back of the theatre with is hands thrust deep into the pockets of his old gabardine raincoat which he wore with regularity. He seemed always to have a cigarette hanging like Humphrey Bogart from his lips. James would just listen to the dialogue of his play with eyes half closed from the action wearing a bemused expression on his face. Campion considered him some kind of a magician. A poem by John Weir, a Marist priest, published a poem in the *N. Z. Listener* entitled *'letter from Waimarama'* which he addressed to Baxter. This was the beginning of a life long friendship between the two men. Baxter from then on wrote to Weir every week and the priest likewise responded. Weir later wrote a thesis on JKB's poetry based on their extensive discussions and correspondence and ultimately he was the editor of Baxter's Collected Poems. Then Allen Curnow's *The Penguin book of NewZealand Verse.* In 1960 Curnow's book caused much controversy as it involved readers comparisons with Bennett's anthology of New Zealand verse, published by Universal Press just two years prior. Curnow had originally allowed but three of Baxter's poems in his 1945 anthology. Baxter himself thought that a reasonable representation of all he deserved at the time. However, Baxter's poetry had since been published in no less than eight of various poet's works between 1952 and 1958.

95.

By December 1960, back on the home front, Baxter was still having trouble in his own written expression and he was struggling to make his marriage work too. He considered he and Jacquie stood equal in their offering to each others commitment in marriage and in their suffering. In their own way they loved each other dearly and the bond was gathered by their devotion to their children. It was the glue that bound the marriage together. Jim wondered what Brasch would make of the recent poems he sent him to review and added that his domestic situation was making it difficult to write. September 1961 saw Baxter busy with the progression of six bulletins he was working on for the NZ Primary schools. He was editing and rewriting as a most conscientious exemplary editor. For writers of bulletins he would go through the manuscript page by page, prune and reshape where needed to help the author with a masterful end product. Baxter's relaxed manner with contributors to the bulletins encouraged personal response from contributors. He found editing hard work and he described it as having 'three brains and six hands to keep all the bulletins moving forward smoothly at the same time.' *

Some people thought the job required little or no work and it was a Government benevolence to keep JKB writing. He was looked down on by the Director of Education as 'somewhat of an amiable donkey who occasionally excreted lumps of gold.'* To escape from the gruelling job of editing he would occasionally venture forth with a poem or two to discuss over tea break with colleagues. There was also the AA types who would appear on the scene for personal counselling. James as an AA sponsor would have these men appear for help without prior appointment. James always gave preference to them at the expense of his official work.

The poetic types in the Department were considered a bunch of wandering minstrels and Baxter and another man were once reprimanded by the Chief Editor for being derelict of their duty in being absent from office. The other man stood sheepishly taking on what he was being advise but raged internally. Baxter, on the other hand accepted the reprimand and quietly slipped out to the pub for a non alcoholic drink in the company of other renowned wayward poets. Official reports on Jim Baxter were always favourable. He was considered by his boss as strongly qualified for the position he held and did an excellent job. He was very reliable and an extraordinary facilitator who could do the job with ease. Baxter could do in a day what would take another person a full week to complete. He worked quickly and could type rapidly. Once he commenced his work nothing would distract him until the job was finished, unless it was a fellow AA who was in difficulty or a street kid who needed his help. Baxter's relaxed attitude made him an easy person to work with. He did not attend staff parties nor become enveloped in small talk around the office. Colleagues found him rather abstract but pleasant to be around. It was noted by a fellow lecturer that Baxter was kind of remote from ordinary life. He seemed to prefer to be wrapped up in his own thought processes.

Baxter continued to write to his mother and on 7th November 1962 advise that he had completed another novel called *Horse*. He described it as a tragic-comic novel with a certain element of self portrait. There is more of a conscious fallen Adam in the book's story than of Adam in the Garden of Eden. It had clearly a Dylan Thomas like influence with language and outrageous situations. The title may well have been after a suggestion by Carl Jung who spoke of the unconscious side of the human psyche, the lower part of the body. James had read deeply because of the Swiss psychiatrist analytic psychology theories. Also Baxter ultimate influence by his belief in the steps of the fellowship of AA to overcome all with a trust in a higher power greater than self being a key to the theme of the novel. It might be noted that it was not Jung that advocated this belief in a higher power but Bill Wilson, the co founder of AA who had an enlightening experience as a result of following the six steps of the Oxford groups and the conscious beliefs advocated by Jung. Bill's conversion from atheist to a believer leaves no doubt in my mind that James Baxter felt the same as I do; that Wilson's enlightenment and conversion and the adoption of the six steps of the Oxford group to which he expanded to twelve suggestions for sober living were God inspired. But I digress.

James K Baxter resigned his position from the school publications on the 27th March 1963 after much consideration as to the consequences of his action. He had told his priestly friend John Weir of his intentions as as the preceding February 1962. 'I am tired of lending my brain to Caesar and having to return it to fagged and filthy ..... now it seems that he (God) requires a better thing - that I should sell only my labour, not my brain, in the urban brothel, and be free to look on the face of other men and praise him when I so desire.'(* Extract from Pig Island letters.)

This enlightening of will to serve others in preference to one self has overtaken me too, as the moments move into days and days into months and now years. I am still working on what that direction will be. For whilst I wait it is not a clear vision but to see through this glass darkly. I see the door open ahead, but still wait for the opportunity to afford me as God dictated purpose. Meanwhile, I serve as opportunity evolves towards my direction home. As much as I once would have thought it be my will to determine my goals and the benefits I expected as a result, it is now in God's hands to determine, for all of me and what talents remain are for his doing not mine.

James joined the permanent staff of the New Zealand Post office on the 11th March 1963. The duties were simple and clearly defined, and were to be fulfilled without any personal concessions. Baxter liked the duties as a postman as it gave him time to think, to compose and write poetry and to continually pray. It was outdoor work and he enjoyed walking and keeping fit.

My previous decade of ever day walking and meeting people in the course of my duties, as well as regular bush walks inspired me to write many poems and books. In this regard it was not the product of my inspirations but in common with Baxter; the unresolved occupational duty of being an ordinary man.

Baxter reported to the old Post Office in Featherston Street at seven o' clock each morning, sorted the mail into streets and conversed lively with the other fifty or so sorters in so doing, He was notable for his resonate voice talking in the dialect of the locals and was good fun to be with as fellow workmates warmed to him. He was laughingly known as the most brilliant of obscene people in the place. It was interesting to note that his work associates in the sorting room at the time of Baxter being there were young university graduates of similar stages of personal development as him. One became an accomplished musician, another a film maker and censor, another a Mozart fellow in music and one bright fellow a poet and publisher. They were all destined for a place of importance to the world at large, but not Baxter. He for one had a deep seated notion of not falling for the trap of the masses of men and had designs on doing something or other of greater importance, but at that time, if questioned, he did not know what.

At the time of their employment with the Post Office they were all seeking a new direction. To be fair, so was Baxter, but his was of a spiritual basis, being in this world but not of it. In Baxter they found an inspiring mentor. It was possible to discuss any topic with him without the slightest hint of embarrassment. He could articulate their problems and aspirations and knew Jung well. The fact that his answers were not preconceived and he was devoted to them with an insight that did not necessitate any commitment by the hearer was a further attraction to him. One person had remarked that Baxter was a good confessor who understood himself well, even his own fears and lack of courage.

Baxter shared himself as an example by leading for his audience. The Post Office staff liked him a lot and were proud to have him as a fellow worker who was a well-known writer and a university graduate. Despite this he displayed no strains of intellectual snobbery and was open to talking to anyone. James had a habit of stopping strangers in the street and inviting them to join him at any nearby cafe for a coffee and a chat. He often plunged into lengthly monologues and then suddenly take flight and walk away. He was more in need of an audience than needing friends. It was once stated by a poet friend that Baxter's monologues were a sense of his own isolation and it was this that he needed to communicate to a sympathetic listener.

All posties had a different walk area to deliver in the Wellington city and surrounds. Over a period of time Baxter managed to walk and deliver in all of the seven hilly walks of Wellington. The hills, the valleys, the occasional glimpses of the harbour and the walks were attractive to him inspired many poem en route. He made friends with dogs and masters alike, fed the dogs that gave him trouble and in idle time had lengthy chats to people as they collected their mail. But it was obvious to all that he was living in a world of his own making. He often didn't start the delivery until late and was once chastised for a late delivery; he simply remarked that he had started the mail delivery from the end to the beginning that day instead of his usual way. He was once observed doubling back to deliver a letter he had overlooked. He could have delivered it the next day but that was not Baxter, he was too conscientious for that to happen.

Contrary to this however, circulars were often heavy and if he found then too burdensome he simply didn't deliver them. Baxter had a secret desire to understand militant unionism, which was possibly the most powerful force in New Zealand at the time. The Post Office Union had a rather passive laid back approach to the needs of the worker.

Baxter for a time considered he had no gripe to serve up to them for the benefit of employees. He did get his chance to understand unionism during the '*Soap Powder Lock-Out*' of July 1963. It all, came about when Lever Brothers the soap manufacturers arranged to send free samples of Surf soap powder by mail. The samples were a quarter of a kilogram each and Posties were expected to deliver fifty samples to households on their appointed rounds. This extra weight in the mail bag on top of the mass of letter to be delivered meant the posties had to do more than one trip per round and thus extra hours of work without extra pay. Most of the posties refused to deliver the samples. It was argued by the Chief Postmaster that the samples fell within the limits of regulations covering mail and must be delivered. The Union Post of Administration said no progress could be made until the posties resumed delivery. Volunteers were called in the meantime to do the deliveries.

The week old dispute ended in a compromise; vans would take the soap powder samples to walk sights and posties would then deliver from there after their normal delivery. The authorities then assured that the delivery regulations would be re- examined. This 'strike' happened only four months after Baxter had joined the Post Office, so although he had no worker union authority nor experience in such matters to make a stand, he did write a short poem on the matter which received great acclaim. He also did his bit to support his fellow workers during the lock out by writing letters and spoke of great excitement in fighting for the cause. The support from the general public also encouraged James and he felt a personal link to them as their mail man. He also felt their anger when he sometimes delivering the mail late causing them anxiety when it was a bill that arrived late leaving little time to pay as consequence of his actions.

Baxter thought like a unionist from a political standpoint and wanted to see every factory in the country run by a syndicate of workers. He was always concerned with ideals, not with the strategies for action. It was typical of Baxter, much like his poetic expression; it was his notion of love, of dispossession, of the concept of the belief in something other than the status quo. James thought his letter on the lock-out sounded more communistic but he clarified his belief that he could never embrace that belief. He was really stating his doctrine of faith and morals. He had a grand vision of love as the supreme basis of solidarity. He continued to write a great body of poems and letters expressing his feelings. The three years as a postie had been good for his soul, for the depth of expression in his poems, but the yearning for God and his future work was not far from becoming a reality.

By the beginning of 1966 Baxter was weary of his work as a Postman. He successfully applied for that year's Robert Burns Fellowship at Otago University and was successful. The Post Office gave him year of absence. From its establishment in 1958 to commemorate Burn's Bicentenary, the scholarship had been founded to encourage and promote imaginative New Zealand writers at the University. A Fellows obligations were linked to the Department of English and were not demanding. The study provide a full years salary like that of full time university lecturer.

It was not the first time Baxter had returned to Dunedin since moving to Wellington in 1948. He was now to take up residency there after a lapse of some twenty years. Life circumstances were now completely different than from the time of his youthful self and the last time he walked the halls of the University. He was now married with two children, had mortgage commitments, was a recovering alcoholic and had moved from an agnostic belief to that of a Catholic and to boot, he was now a most famous writer in the public eye. Baxter was a different man than that of his youthful self, he was more centred than ego centrical, and was not that loud, out of control, sex hungry drunkard poet that he once was. Whilst he still struggled to keep his fly done up, he was more mindful of his intent and actions than his old ways. Jim was a changed man indeed and could be seen around Dunedin, more likely at a coffee lounge than a a pub; a quiet brooding man now in his fortieth year, highly conscious and obliged to the fact that he was now facing the second faze of his life as a non drinker who was more intent on his personal contact with God than impressing his fellow humans with his own brilliant light. The image of an alternate life of service like a New Testament Paul of Tarsus was a constant in his life these days. Doing sponsorship work in the fellowship of AA and his recent Asian experience had embedded in this new man the view that his previous life, his poetry and his past glory counted for naught in the scheme of things. Of course, deep down he had a different view of his writing ability but for the greater part of his remaining years it was no self seeking that was important to him but sacrificial service, devotion to God through a prayerful guidance of the perfect woman, Mary the Mother of perpetual guidance.

James did enjoy his relationship with fellow members of the English Department at the University during his one year course. Students loved Baxter's lecturers and his ability to put his own slant on some other Master's genius. Fellows at the University, because of their many duties were not as available to help students as was Baxter. They brought him poems for comment, but he never showed any sign that they were using up his valuable time. He loved the work and applied for a second Fellowship grant extension and got it. James was a born leader and teacher of students but his calling was to be in another direction in the long run. Meanwhile he was well supported by the English Department and the representatives of the selection committee. Somehow he managed to write ninety new poems, in a semester which would normally take twice that time. He also joined in discussion groups as well as competing his assigned studies with distinction. In *Landfall* and in the University of Otago he published a book of talks that appeared in *Man on the Horse* published in 1967.

In term three of 1966 Baxter proposed an editing of his grandfather John Macmillan Brown's memoirs which were still only in manuscript. The extraneous duties he took on meant that his proposed editing of the Macmillan Brown project was too much and it was left to another come it. In truth, the subject matter of his Grandad's memoirs was probably of little interest to James and perhaps that is why he abandoned the task. Much of his time now was taken up with travelling, giving lectures at Invercargill and Alexandra, addressing the Arts Festival at Massey University which he entitled ' *Shots around the Target.* ' Though he felt great affinity with staff and communicated exceptionally well with students, he sometimes said outrageous things that sounded more from the head of James Baxter and not from sound research.

CHAPTER 10.

THE CALLING OF THE PACIFIST

   The Vietnam War broke out in February 1961 and the town of Dunedin, being alive with students ripe for protest, became very active. Baxter was in the thick of it. Like his father Archie and brother Terence who both spent time in war zones as prisoners because of their anti-war stance, he was a pacifist.Those of professional, religious and political persuasion as well as militant activists were present in the Otago Museum auditorium on 1st May 1961 to discuss the ethics of the Vietnam War. James was introduced to the packed hall as a guest speaker and "Burns Fellow of University of Otago, well known New Zealand poet and a member of the Catholic Church." He presented his case for having a purely pacifist viewpoint on the war, which involved in his own personal history a great deal of difficulty. He related the point made by a Maori Chief who once related that he was Christian and as such the shedding of blood was a sacred thing; as in Christ shedding his blood on the Cross. He knew that such a viewpoint may not be convincing enough to those who felt threatened by the far of loss of life themselves, he then went on to examine the justification for war and as to fact or theory of just cause on both sides for such an action. He put forward the proposition of negotiation in preference to out and out warfare using the consequences of both actions historically.

   Baxter used the biblical notion of war being unnecessary in any circumstance, being the annihilation of human life as non permissible, relating it all to the then Vietnam war. He implied that the stance to be considered on the grounds of this war as to who is the aggressor and who the defender. He raised the examples of the bombing of Hiroshima and Nagasaki, the bombing of Dresden and equally some of the bombing by the Germans of England. The bombing in Vietnam in Baxter's view was no different to these WW11 bombings. He pointed out that obedience to the State was no defensive as was proved in the Nuremberg trials. He concluded by quoting Pope John XXIII, who had done more for peace between communist and the so called free world than any western man had done in the past fifty years. On 20th October public demonstrations followed with the first being a march to the Museum Reserve along George Street with three guests speakers in an open air forum. The first speech was from Eric Herd, Professor of German at the University, the second was Archdeacon Miller, the Anglican Vicar General of Dunedin and then there was Baxter.

   The speeches were held below the statue of Robert Burns which presided over the Octagon, where a crowd of four hundred had gathered to listen. Baxter assured the crowd that had Burns ben present he would have surely been on their side. He associated the Vietnam War as being much like his own wayward character. He did not speak with passion but quietly enough for the organises to insist he use a microphone. He did not refer to notes but seem to speak from the heart a testimony of a man who pondered what he says with true commitment. He related the pacifist history of his family, but the real reason that encouraged the crowd was his appeal as humanitarian.

To this very day James K Baxter is not just remembered for his ability as an orator, but more so for the awe of his standing as a humanist and writer. The need for medical aid to Vietnam was a call to assist by those of the poetry group of the University. On 1st August 1967, Baxter took part in poetry readings in the University Common Room to raise funds and two days later he was a speaker at a symposium on *"The Church and Human Needs in Vietnam"* Those that took part included medical staff, Buddhist and Christian speakers. In March 68 Baxter published an article in *Vietnam Quote & Comment:* The poems , *'to speak truely,' ' The grand Tour',* and *'a death song for mr. mouldybroke'* was publish there too. Baxter continued to lecture and speak to students on the War. As a man of the people, a powerful speaker against the Vietnam war, a champion of student rights, as a man who was always capable at an instance to come up with a yarn or a poem to endorse his belief. As always Baxter was greatly appreciated. As a leader he was colourful and charismatic with an aura of great achievement about him. In that tranquil sheltered environment of the English department of the University he always stood out. He would have done so in any capacity of any other Department of academia in New Zealand at the time. All good things however come to and end, so by the end of the second year of his fellowship Baxter was once more out of a job. Far be it from me to make any grand reasoning of my abilities of being likened to Baxter and his unique abilities as writer, lecturer, student adviser, poet, humanist and pacifist, but can see some parallels in my life and writing as one in the shadows of Baxter. My brush with the duties of fame and experience was from fortitudinous circumstance that imposed upon me some justification as to my cause of what I was about and what I have become. I could reason there was a parallel in my dubious abilities.

At the ripe old age of sixteen I was 'encouraged' to tag along to labor meetings with a dogmatic believer of left wing causes, my father. There I sat listening to communist utterances as the youngest member of the local labor Party. Dad had never shown signs of left wing leanings to my knowledge but was a staunch supporter of workers rights and in that regard he put his money where his mouth was and supported the left much more than the the right in matters of workers rights and political decision making. Dad was a generous supporter of the cause of then Union leader Bob Hawke, who was to become our Prime minister. Needless to say that Hawke would never have made it to the top job if it had not been for the financial support and direct influence of Sir Peter Ables of transport fame. Ables then with his political acclaim and connections, ultimately took a post on the committee of decision making within the Reserve Bank. Hawke won out in every way with Sir Peter as his mentor. Bob was a loveable larrikin who influenced the votes of union rank and file in the transport industry which was un knowingly the cause of Sir Peter. In hindsight it proved to be a great combination for Government and private enterprise that served the best needs of the generation of the working class. Student assistance and countless hand-outs came at a time when the country would have been in dire straits had we had a tight fisted conservative government in power.

Here I am again of course, as it was about my called ability and predisposition that I was hitherto writing. The influence of the political left I soon learnt was more about the doing of the local political working class and having a local member who was more of the vein of a St. James philosophy of life; "That actions speak louder than words." This came to pass for me too as not too many decades later, I found myself as the local town-delegate for the National party in my capacity as a businessmen. My old man possibly would have turned over in his grave at the very thought. It was but a few years later that I was succoured into becoming the first secretary of a new State Branch of the Liberal party. So those of political persuasion who somehow thought me the right man for the job encouraged me to be federally more right wing. It proved to be true that my interest were of selfish motive as it helped me in my business to associate with that so called elite class of people.

I still had many common man causes in my veins though and attended the regular meetings of the labor party voting that way politically in the State elections. Later I took up a post in another township on the New England and was asked to become a member of a Church committee as decision to build a new Church in town was under consideration. I was the only one who voted against the project, as I thought that the existing church was adequate and the funds could be best used more effectively elsewhere for the benefit of the schoolchildren. The church was ultimately built and has become a central part of the local community in that town. The town has grown to a point that the need for the Church proved paramount to the faith an d faithful.

Not to be outdone, I was later asked to join a committee for refugees fleeing from Vietnam by boat at the end of the war. We arranged for a house to be purchased , funded with community and government help , the vision was thus well in play when the first load of boat people arrived in the township. The locals were not impressed and on many occasions I had to defend our position and intent of assimilating a war torn people into our community. Ian Sinclair, the then local member for New England, attended our meeting and offered to help with blankets and clothing of which there was a shortage. He was a grand help and did a lot behind the scenes which speaks of his own human kindness in organising this.

Ultimately the whole thing failed. The Vietnamese people found it difficult to assimilate and most of them had lost parents and loved ones. All had never known anything else of their lives but the rule of the gun. They were lost and afraid and most headed for Cabramatta in Sydney to rebuild their lives. It taught me to leave being a 'do-gooder' to the generous souls who had more skill and experience in those matters than ones like me. At any rate business and family commitment was more a priority than humanitarian causes for me at the time, but I did have a go at it for a short while. besides I was more interested in playing football, chasing personal goals of a material kind and relaxing in the glow of my alcoholic self indulgence. The one collective notion that' seemed to work for the benefit of a community was my latter days on a business committee to help town growth.

I had proposed an idea of a one day business carnival to encourage local and other towns to participate in the event promotion. It has now expanded into an annual three day carnival. I had sold my business and left town before the first day of the annual event became a happening. At any rate it was not my idea as it originated as the brain child of my father, and I just resurrected it after he died.

Many an opportunity erupted that I had thrown my cause behind, but to be fair, I was more interested in how I could gain a beneficial interest for my own cause, and that of my family in the provision of service to others. This applied right up to the dramatic calamity that enveloped me in my loss of family, home and business which brought me to a pit of hell and awakened me to a new dawning in the arms of AA and the God of my own understanding. To great degree the slow work of the Master of all and my journey of acceptance came at a price to my mental and physical health and my capacities to be of service with some semblance of generosity of spirit. I am still struggling as a non drinker with that generosity, but have faith that I am but a servant to the cause and thus must do whatever transpires not in my own time but his methods which are timeless. This being 'not of my will but of thine be done.' In this my awakening came, as it did on my many adventure's of lone tramps on the Camino in Spain, In Ireland and to some degree in New Zealand. These adventures I hope to continue doing long after the border restrictions of Covid -19 no longer apply. I am slowly recognising the limitation on my body, mind and spirit in achieving as much in truth as I did in the past, for my days are sure numbered as I head toward the end of this decade my seventies.

Still, I will continue to strive to the best fo my ability for the cause and benefit of those for who I am concerned, as it is my nature and my will to fulfil. My enlightenment to knowing God comes in slow progressive stages and not as a sudden clarity of being, as was the case of Bill Wilson co-founder of AA. Mine to a great degree came in my recognition of being an alcoholic and following the steps of the AA programme. However, Wilson came as a visionary enlightening moment, as did the influences of Carl Jung. The great man's clarity of being came as lifting of a fog in his mind at age eleven and his belief that followed resulted in his lifetime of work as a psychologist, Psychotherapist, Philosopher, Scientist, psychoanalyst of consciousness and essayist in the cause to follow his professional skills for the benefit of patients and students universally, and ultimately for the benefit of fellowship of AA and this alcoholic.

But what of James Baxter and his connection to AA, his new found belief as a Catholic and ultimately his journey to the street to help the hapless drunkard and drug addict? Did he have a sudden enlightening experience or was it the slow work of God in his life, devotion to Mary and the depth of a well read understanding of a intelligent mind delving into the all of Bill Wilson, who seem to be God inspired in his many books on the subject matter of alcoholism and spiritual soundness? To explore this a little more deeply we have to go back to the Oxford Group's influence on Bill Wilson and the part Carl Jung played in the foundation of AA.

Back in the early 1930s a man by the name of Roland H(the last name of an alcoholic is forever held within the faith of the fellowship of AA to protect one's anonymity). So Roland H, a well bred young man of means, who has long since passed away, had made his way to Zurich to seek help from the celebrated psychiatrist Dr. Jung for his helpless and hopeless addiction to alcohol. Roland had exhausted other means of recovery to alcoholism to no avail. So in 1931 he became a patient of Dr.Jung. A year of rehabilitation and guidance of Carl Jung saw Roland's return to USA having now considered that he was cured of his addiction. However, it was not long before he was intoxicated again and soon considered that Jung was his 'court of last resort.' He returned to the guidance and theory of consciousness which thus followed a chain of events that led to the founding of AA. It was a conversation between Jung and Roland which to the latter's dismay that proved ultimately to be his only answer. Dr. Jung told him frankly that his case was hopeless and that any further treatment medically or any further psychiatric treatment would be to no avail. This candid and humble statement of Carl Jung was beyond doubt the first foundation stone of Alcoholics Anonymous. Coming from Jung this statement had an immense impact on Ronald H. He enquired " Is there no other way?"

Carl Jung contemplated for a time before answering : "There might be a way, provided that he become a subject of a spiritual or religious experience- in short a genuine conversion. He pointed out that such an experience might remotivate him when nothing else could. Jung did caution him that whilst such an experience had sometimes brought complete recovery to alcoholics, they were nevertheless very rare. He recommend that Roland place himself in a religious atmosphere and hope for the best. Shortly after this conversation Roland joined the Oxford Group, an evangelical movement at the height of success in Europe, and one with which Carl Jung was doubtlessly familiar. The good Doctor at that time could not promote the idea of a religious experience publicly as a method of treatment for those whose case would be considered hopeless by his profession. He would otherwise have lost his licence to practice back then.

The Oxford Group placed large emphasis on self survey, confession, restitution and the giving of oneself in service to others. It was the receipt that Roland H needed and he did find a conversation that released him from the bonds of his compulsion to drink. Returning to New York, he became very active in the Oxford Group, then led by the Episcopal clergyman Dr. Samuel Shoemaker a local founder of that movement. He was a powerful personality that carried immense sincerity and conviction in his authority. At the time the Oxford Group had already sobered a number of alcoholics and Roland considered himself one of them, for he could surely identify with the sufferers and thus address himself to the service of others. One of these came to be an old school friend of Roland and Bill Wilson, his name was Edwin T, 'Ebby' for short. He had been committed to an institution for his alcoholism, but Roland and another ex alcoholic member of the Oxford Group secured his release. In the meantime, Bill Wilson had run his course of alcoholism and had been threatened with being committed to an institution too. It was fortunate that he was being treated by a physician- Dr. William D. Silkworth, who had a wonderful capacity to understand alcoholics. His old friend 'Ebby' T arrived at his bedside one evening with a message of his having got the 'religious' means to stay sober a day at a time. Bill would have nothing of it for he did not believe in religion and had lost his faith in God many moons ago.

"Ebby" T, knowing Bill's ability to research and wonder, furnished him with a copy of Henry James's "*Verity of religious Experiences.*' Bill concluded from his in-depth analyse of the book that most conversions came with a common denominator of ego collapse. James had indicated the individual faced an impossible dilemma as in Wilson's case, a compulsion of not being able to stop drinking, a deep feeling of hopelessness which had been vastly deepened by Dr Silkworth's consultations. It was deepened still by Ebby's visit when he acquainted Bill with the verdict of hopelessness with respect to Roland H, who returned to the drink despite counselling. This was at a time when Roland H was still finding his way into the six step programme of the Oxford Group.

In the reading of Henry James's masterpiece Bill W awakened to a vision of a society of alcoholics each identifying with, and transmitting his experience, strength and hope to fellow suffering alcoholics who in turn could maintain sobriety through. like him some spiritual transformation. To remain sober a least a day at a time was Bill's catch cry as he embedded the philosophy of the six steps of the Oxford group into those alcoholic of which he encountered. It was a vision that Bill W and Dr Bob lay wide open for every newcomer to a transforming spiritual experience. The work of Dr Carl Jung on spiritual consciousness played a great part in the AA movement as it still does and the twelve steps, tradition and promises afforded to AA members, one may well believe as God inspired in the hand of his ' spiritual vessel' Bill Wilson. Bill did , in a letter to Dr Jung indicate his deep person gratitude to Dr.Shoemaker, of the Oxford Groups, to William James and his own Dr. Silkworth for their guidance and most importantly to Dr. Jung himself for his insight into spiritual consciousness which Bill W continued to carry his every day duty to the programme of AA as all alcoholics with whom he encountered .

Mine was not so much an enlightening vision of the kind experienced by Bill Wilson. It was more a gradual getting over that state of mind of a compulsive alcoholic and replacing it with slow constant conditioning to a new way of life within the programme of AA. For in the end I had nowhere else to go in the depths of depression except through the doors of AA. My 'conversion' so to speak came as a result of listening to another alcoholic tell his story at a meeting. If there was any enlightenment, it came as he spoke, for it suddenly resonated with me that I was alcoholic. I knew then I was in the right place for my condition for there and then I had a recall, call it a vision if you will, of a pattern of drinking over decades that was totally uncontrolled and rendered me lost, bewildered and verging on suicide.

I could have easily blamed the catastrophic events that surrounded my life in the space of one year- divorce, suicide of a friend, suicide of a son, forced closure of my business interests, loss of material possession of home and it seemed the love of my family too. For sure, once I had recovered from my debilitative depression I immediately went on a bender again only to return back to rehabilitation. The wake up call had me back in AA and sober for the next decade. However, I drifted from the way of the programme for a time and it was not long before I drank again.

The shock of my fall from grace had me re-doing the steps of AA. again, recognising that I was powerless over alcohol, that my life had become once again unmanageable and only God could get me back on track and that I had to put myself into his guidance and care, follow the steps, clean house so to speak , learn to listen to the guidance of fellow alcoholics and do some service for others.

My travels around the world had a desired effect, for it led me to the Camino again and back to writing. More importantly though they led me back into the fellowship of AA. It has been five years now since I had that one night slip back into the drink, but I am glad of it in some way, for it got me back on track and more committed than ever to a spiritual way of life with God in control and not Doug and his various agenda.

James Baxter did ultimately gain sobriety coming not so much as an enlightened spiritual experience in a flash of reality but a vision of what was reality. Rather it was more a self searching such as he might do in poetry or in preparation of a class for his students. It was James's regular attendance at AA meetings, his work counselling other suffering alcoholics and the vagrant alcoholics and drug addicts of the streets of Wellington in the cause of the steps of AA where he came his own. In his search for meaning he opened up the change in himself into a new visions of action and grace to bare upon the dark and negative side of his own nature.

James had come to the development of a kind of humility that made it possible for him to receive God's help in his own life. This allowed him to circumnavigate the usual bounds of those in the depth of alcoholism. Those who had not yet got the message of God in their own lives. He used the AA steps in his own way, in his new found faith as a Catholic; for the initial six steps were not unlike those of the Catholic new testament; prayer, contritions, and eucharistic acceptance of the sacrifice made by Christ on his Cross for the retribution of humanities defects of character. James believed that through his reconciliation as a penitent man through his own efforts in sobriety he could help another poor suffering soul and thus relieve the sadness and suffering of his own. James Baxter was discarding the old ways of his former life and embracing a new life that worked in all conditions that befell him to the day of his death. He had AA steps now to use as a "Bible of his intent" to help others and in the image of the glory of the Son of God to whom he gave great praise, of which he lavished on the mother; for the the more he honoured her, the greater his glory of her Son.

Baxter had become to some a saint and in the words of a knowledgeable priest, a mystic. If it be so then to me he was more like a Rasputin mystic than the likes of a St. Anthony of the desert. Many Catholic's reaction to his verbose utterances and the way he went about proclaiming christian virtue, as an imposter and a hypocrite of the highest order. He would no-doubt disturb the minds of any black and white Catholic who were living in a world of fixed values and not the rational but radical mind of one who was suffering so deeply for his own 'sin' in the privacy of his soul. Such minds were closed to an ecumenical view of Christendom which become of age long after Baxter turned to dust. James Baxter was ahead of his time as a practical theologian for the man in the street and an oracle for the Maori people. In truth, Baxter's way now is to be well discarded by those who use cheque book generosity and philanthropic action to fulfil their christian duty and thus gain a tax deduction for their actions. If they are not rewarded in heaven for charitable works, then at least they are in this world.

James Baxter's style and grace theology was more of a simple kind that reflected the value systems of an old fashioned kind that predates changes of the Vatican Council of 1962. He was a radical in the public eye but at heart he was a natural conservative in the matters of faith and moral. His Catholic belief was the same as the one I was educated too as child of God. It was not open to the new developments of open confession, laymen and women serving in the role of the priest as distributors of the Holy Communion and certainly not for the marriage of priest or, God forbid, women as priests. However, in the areas of sexual morality he had a more open view than the doctrine of the Church of his time. JKBs own sexual difficulties led him to contest the restraints of the Church. However, he helped many a young Catholic in their acceptance of the code laid down in doctrine, but tended to place too much emphasis on sexual matters Baxter stuck within the strains of tradition religion but expressed his belief in his own way. His was a vision beyond the confines of Catholicism and a spiritually insightfulness force which was more of universal truth. He was not interested in converting others to his belief but to bring to the world human values for its betterment.

CHAPTER 11.

A VISION FOR JUNKIES

Baxter continued to write more plays and poetry and produce articles on faith within the Catholic press at the bequest of Bishop Kavanagh for which he had a one year paid contract. In between he counselled youth of the street. On the corner of King and Howe streets in Dunedin was a doss house flat above a bottle shop that a lot of young people struggling with life drifted to. It was where Baxter spent hours advising the young men, helping those shaking with DTs or desperate for a jab from a needle to ease their pain. They trusted him and his gentle way of advising them to deal with life's difficulties. Those who questioned the value of living admired that this older man of letters and a successful member of the local community shared their rejection. He had the same hang ups as they did and similar attitudes. He went to great lengths to fight for their freedom when in trouble with the law. Meanwhile he himself was struggling with life and family responsibility.

Whilst Jacquie and the children where great supporters of whatever cause he found himself fighting for, the life he led with his family was coming undone by the Spring of 1968. Daughter Hillary was having mental issues and wanted to leave home to have her own independence. Both parents felt inadequate to deal with her rebellion. John , on the other hand wanted to leave school and drift like his Father had done for a time in his own youth. To come to some agreement with him, they settled for a private tutor but when he expressed an interest to attend Art school, Baxter took him to Auckland to talk it over with an artist friend there. John was talked out of it and returned to the tutor studies.

Baxter during this time as a result of his Burns Fellowship at Otago University had taken a more radical view of education and become even more anti-academic. He felt exhausted mentally and physically. The demands on him from religious duty, people at the University, the Catholic press and others from the general community were taking its toll, not to mention the family difficulties he seemed to have that were never ending in his mind. Baxter found it hard to say no and his output from the Dunedin years was extraordinary- a mass of plays, poems, essays and religious material on baptism, confirmation and eucharistic practice, and public addresses were affecting his health. He was also worried about his parents' health. Baxter was beginning to feel burnt out, and had lost his belief in his ability as husband and father. The one year contract he had with Bishop Kavanagh was coming to an end and he didn't know what fate awaited him. It was not long after the work ended that an experience, not unlike that of Bill Wilson's spiritual awakening, took a hold on him. It was somewhat off kilter in that he saw a vision of Jerusalem from the banks of the Wanganui River and heard a voice communicating to him in a tongue that he took to be Maori.

He had written to a friend in April 1968 of being awakened to the sound of a voice calling 'Jerusalem' and saw the Maori mission on the banks of the Wanganui River. It came at a time of great difficulty, as such apparitions seem to do. His brother Terence's marriage had just broken up without any apparent fault on either side but with the fact that the good life of which one comes to accept as normal had within it the seeds of destruction. It was enough to drive Baxter to despair and cry to God in prayer for help in his own desperate marital situation.

Then he fell asleep and awoke to the vision and the voice which seemed to him like a command for action that immediately after he likened to a thought that entered into his consciousness that he should go to Jerusalem without money or books to start a new way of life. The voice had indicated to him that he should call on a man who may be called 'Matiu,' which is after the name of an island in Wellington harbour, and then with God's will, he might slowly form the nucleus of a community where the people both Maori and Pakeha (white) would try to live without money or books, but in worship of God by working the land.

How much of this visionary idea was from the imagination of Baxter and not the reality of a vision we will never know, but the central idea of a St. Francis like community appealed to him. He spoke of the vision later as being a genuine experience as if the Lord himself had spoken to him. He had indicated that there were two faces on the one coin so to speak. One had the face of a Maori whose face had been mangled and hurt by white civilisation of his country and that The Lord had desired him to labour and wash the Maori face clean in contrition. Baxter as much likened it to Veronica wiping the face of Jesus as he laboured his way up Calvary hill for the remission of sinful man. The other face to him was his own representation of a white man in retribution for his treatment of the native race. It was a picture of the face of the *Portrait of Dorian Grey* like Oscar Wilde's story of a man who revelled in his defect of character at the expense of the native mans suffering, only to become the face of the evil one itself. He saw his task then to right the wrong so that both sides of the coin of his imaginings could be purified in Godly acts of contrition and dutiful retribution pointing to redemption. He was told in his vision that he was to make haste to Jerusalem to learn the Maori language, and assume as far as possible a Maori identity. In such a place with his elder brothers in poverty he may suffer their closeness and thus the way of the Lord.

Baxter had interpreted the visionary event as being him becoming temporarily unhinged or that maybe God had given him a revelation for a change in his own behaviour. He realised the he may construe it as a deception, but felt he was being more invigorated and hopeful than he had been prior to the vision. He considered that a temporary reprieve from his wife and family may lead to some final reconciliation; for to him the current pattern of their lives was more likely to rot away and they would ultimately drift apart anyway. He felt that Jacquie, being of native blood would be more likely to be taken from him by the current white way of life then by him adopting the Maori way. In that, he deceived himself into thinking his path to a better reconciliation would be forthcoming. He had it in mind he must kill off the old James Baxter in-order to be the new man of faith and action. It may well have been a delusion of grandeur that seems to be the fate of those of us who long suffer from alcoholism or it may have been a genuine belief that a move to a new location would serve him much better spiritually than to continue with his present circumstances. It could have been a last ditch effort to escape from the servitude of his domestic responsibilities too. What is certain from his discussion with others and in particular in his weekly letter to priest and friend John Weir, he was now certain of the authenticity of his vision and that it was imperative that he must act on its directive.

An event which delayed his going to Jerusalem was the pregnancy of Hillary his daughter. This news was glad tidings to his viewpoint as the need for all living things being given life in preference to extension was always a part of his nature and viewpoint. For Hillary had admitted that she preferred to have the baby in preference to an abortion. It was a relief to James to see that his daughter had taken to the duties of preparing for the baby's arrival in preference to her former rebellious nature of wanting to escape to some sort of unknown freedom. It must have crossed his mind that what may have just been an imagining of a troubled mind he was planning to become his reality was not unlike his own daughter's former desires to escape reality. He waited for the birth of baby Stephanie, a lovely baby born in the spring of September and Baxter adored her.

I resonated with Baxter's work load, the causes that led to total exhaustion in his quest to satisfy the muses that drove him, in his unwavering devotion to family and those to whom he served. It was well apparent to those who knew him that this driven alcoholic personality, although long since sober was, never the less in need of some kind of new fulfilment to a better future, and his all consuming passion for spirituality would inevitably lead to a calamity at some point in the future. His came with not quite a breakdown but an all inspiring vision. Mine came with a rush of catastrophic events that brought me totally undone; landing me in a deep depression and a rehabilitation to regain some last clutch onto something verging on change of direction. For sure I had stopped drinking, found work and entered into the steps off AA, but the faith that I once had been my guiding light in my Catholic upbringing had vanished and I was left spiritually deprived. The steps of AA gave me a track to run with on a daily basis of sobriety whilst I regained my strength of body, minding a path way to the spirit that I can only express as God's will not mine. It was after seven years of hell but still sober that I ventured forth to walk the way of St. James on the Santiago de Compostela. Tramping daily in meditative way on the French route from St. Jean, at the base of the Pyrenees to the end of the journey on that first occasion, the Cathedral of Santiago where the bones of St. James reportedly lay. I didn't pay much attention to prayer on that walk but I did learn to let go a lot of my past life and a new Doug began to emerge like Phoenix rising form the ashes. What emerged was a lotus flower of creative ideas resulting in a book of poems and an album of songs on my return home. The faith of my fathers had left me but I felt free in my new spiritual understanding which was all consuming.

Baxter had gained a faith in his new catholicism and no longer considered the need for books nor writing when he ventured forth for his vision. I, on the other hand, lost my Catholic faith, gained a new spiritual way of viewing the world and began to write. It would have been fine if I had yet turned with a new freshness of spirit and mindfulness to duty only and just got on with the job at hand, living the twelve steps of AA and following the path of the founders in trusting in the slow work of God, examining my conscience to further overcoming my defects of character and administering the AA message to still suffering alcoholics, but at the time I saw no need for that cause much to my later dismay.

I had completed a property renovation prior to leaving for the Camino. I sold it during my travels but upon returning home quickly arranged bank finance and purchased another to be then occupied with its renovations. This would have been fine if that was all I had taken on, but a died in the wool now sober alcoholic had renewed energy and was bursting with enthusiasm to do even more. In the space of months I completed the renovation whilst trading the stock market in the cut and trust of derivate trading. It seemed I didn't need a lot of sleep and commenced to write a novel at night * and in the midst of it all I found time for another romance. All the while I was still holding down my contract work in Business Development. which was growing at a rapid rate. A friend in AA had warned me of over-exuberant efforts to multi-tasking and that I would crash sooner or later. Well, I didn't listen for I had also taken to writing and recording my songs with professional musicians and was enjoying the world of the dreamer, earning my loot and finding my new found boat of personality which was meant to sail on placid waters suddenly hit rapids and was fast sinking. I finished the year with bank balance of profit but no capital gains tax on my property sales, for the capital appreciation on the sales was offset by the capital losses on my stock market trades. All I really got at the time for my efforts was the value of a new car after trading in the old one.

The crunch came before I had the chance to complete my first novel. I was in a state of exhaustion again and it triggered another depressive episode that had me crawling back underneath the covers to hide myself from the world. I had not yet learnt the lesson of letting go and just trusting in whatever comes up. So after another rehabilitation and this time loads of shock treatment, I came out off it all. A year as a dull headed but well medicated part human, now content to just complete my book and learn lessons of relaxation and subdued work effort. I completed the book, did many a mountain tramp in New Zealand, wrote more poetry and was in my own opinion ready for another Camino in the late Spring of 2015. It was just two years and one rehab after my first walk of the way in 2013.

This time the journey was in the hope of more creative inspiration I had told myself, but in truth I just wanted to get into the cot again with some foreign beauty, hopefully without any later consequences. This all came to pass as my previous romance had faded into the blue and I was now in the arms of a new lover. The Camino journey of the spirit I advocated to others in my writings proved to be a false aspiration in this new Portuguese Way of the Camino. I was far too interested in the lady than the journey of good intent, but I did have a template in mind for a new book which ultimately come to completion after my third Camino in 2017. The romance on the Portuguese way proved to be a disastrous arrangement and the outcome provided much disappointment for my new found lover as she returned home. I too returned, but with a dreadful viral illness that rendered me bed ridden for weeks on end. I tried my best to do my job but it was not happening as I had hoped it would. My employer was in the main happy enough with the efforts I attempted but I was sadly embarrassed by my efforts in comparison to my former achievement.

Ultimately I returned for yet another rehabilitation for this time I did not know who I was. I had entered a fog and came out the other side in fear and in- trepidation of what I had become.. It was like I was a different person and as it turned out ultimately I was. For God had the " 'I' of 'me' in a new kind of spiritual happening and Doug was a shadow of himself running for   shelter. The heavy doses of shock treatment I put a stop to, but I kept on taking the multitude of pills to level the serotonin to the brain for a time. It's a cruel but sometimes   necessary treatment in extreme cases. I fought the psychiatrists with their diagnosis of my condition and took to the study of the meds and the long term effects on the brain, the damage to organs that ultimately followed in the consumption of large doses of their 'poison' for a sustained period of time.

As it was I don't recall much of my work effort for the year 2016 nor anything much except to say that I did write another book and commenced to see a variety of medical so called experts in my hunt for an answer to what was happening within me. Ultimately, in early 2017, I decided to once more walk the Camino and this time I returned once more to the French route to do it without any agenda to speak of. I went cold turkey off the meds in the first days of my tramping the Pyrenees and I would not recommend to any person to follow such a course of action without medical advise in doing so. I came out the other side of that dreadful experience after a week and walking near twelve hundred kilometres through Spain, the Aran Irelands, mountain paths of Ireland, and over a six weeks period of tramping from daylight till dark finally returning home. I had toughed out the cold, the continual rain and sleet, living in wet clothing and boots for weeks on end before returning home to nurse my weary body weakened by another viral condition. I emerged from this all to write more books and complete another album of my songs. It is not all over yet, my creative efforts still beckons me to write and not to let go and let God completely just yet.

Spiritual Life in the city of Dunedin for Baxter was not as for other men. He did not belong to the Catholic religion as those who were born to the faith, nor did he belong to the Catholic Men's Club or any other sect within the Catholic community, for he was a lost unknown except for the contribution of his writings in *The Tablet*. he was not a part of the parish ordinates. He was more known with young Catholic students of the University, for the older priests and parishioners frowned down on him as an imposter and infidel. JKB was more at home with the young with whom he could associate. Baxter's devotion was to the young Catholic lost souls on campus as well as the youth off the street. With them he found he was at ease to discuss difficulties of economic conditions and the almost impossible likelihood of early marriage; one of the many subject matters he could lend an ear to and give advise on. Whilst he expressed such matters in his poetry, he knew his new directional vision was to change this associations in the capacity to which they and he were accustomed.

When Baxter did leave Dunedin in 1969 he just faded into the mist and was not sighted by friends for months and sometimes years. It seemed he had no concept of time and he reappeared like he had been a way for just a few days. He could arrive at a friends door or a lecture room at any hour and just disappear and reappear suddenly without the slightest warning. His way was very disconcerting to those who lived by a routine but that did not trouble Baxter in any way, shape or form.

James had always been a writer of constant myth making and for his reappearance at Dunedin he made light of it as part of his mystique, and returned to tell stories to the delight of the young at heart and the sorrow of the old. When he finally left Dunedin for good, he returned to Auckland and there he wrote another letter to Fr. John Weir expressing the difficulties he felt in his marriage. He spoke of quarrels he had with New Zealand society and their focus on materialism and also his dissatisfaction with the education system. He was much burdened with anxiety, felt he had lost touch with his children now in their late teens and it seems with the now younger generation at large. He hinted at a kind of temporary marital separation from Jacquie. He finally left Auckland to visit Jerusalem on his way back to Wellington. He made a final call on local curate of the parish Fr. Charles Cooper, who was well known to Jacquie's family, for he likewise had come from Palmerston North. James had expressed his intent to the priest that by living among the Maori people, the personal experience of their ways may help him in his marriage. He vowed he was not walking out on in his wife but was leaving for her sake too. He felt he needed to know more of the origin of her people but was unsure that he should go. The priest enquired as to what would happen if his vision and plans did not work out he replied that he would return home again. To his mind his explanation seemed plausible enough as he had a great desire to please his audience, he found justification in his voiced opinion. It was naivety on his part to think that Jacquie would follow him to a land of another tribe; for she was of the Taranaki tribe and the Maori of Jerusalem were of a different time and culture. Some twenty years after Baxter had left for Jerusalem, Jacquie really did not know what was going on in his mind. It appears to a great degree that she felt Baxter himself was not at all sure either.

"There goes Jim Baxter , carrying his casket as always, with a vision to the grave were he may lay it down," it was said by a poetic friend on his travels. Baxter set off for Jerusalem in January 1969, after his stay in Auckland and evening confession with Fr. Cooper. He had travelled by train to the city after leaving Dunedin behind him a quagmire of negative images of the city which he expressed in a poem' Valediction.' The journey to Auckland was more to discuss his intentions on a change of direction in his life and to solicit the options of Fr. Cooper and long standing friends for their thoughts on the matter. In reality, he was more verbal in telling them than listening to what their considered opinions might be. It appeared to all intents that he had already made up his mind, but was somewhat hesitant about making the move to Jerusalem. For he realised the dangers of self deception and that his intended journey was a way of rejecting his responsibilities for a time to live the dream of the vision he had encountered and he was hesitant to proceed for months now had passed. James had spent the majority of 1968 helping addicts on the street, living as they did for a time . Now he was on his way to Jerusalem in late January in the absurd hope that Jacquie would ultimately pack up her belongings, leave the family to their own devices and come and join him there. He walked bare footed in the guise of what any God seeker might do on a pilgrimage. He was certainly dressed as such, and stood out conspicuously with a small nap sack over his shoulder; and minimal possessions that belong to one of dubious appearance. He was dressed in a ragged shirt with well worn long coat over his baggy trousers and rosary beads around his neck with a rather larger crucifix than usual attached. Near Wanganui he headed on foot to the rough shingled road high above the Wanganui River on his way to Jerusalem .

He walked his pilgrimage passing the small Maori settlements named by the famous nineteenth century missionary, Richard Taylor. First the settlement of Atene for Athens, then Koriniti for Corinth, Ranana for London and at last the settlement of Hiruhrama, known as Jerusalem. He was just taking a short visit there to gauge the hospitality of the local people. The little Maori settlement beside the Wanganui River comprising no more than a half dozen houses and a meeting room. Nearby a Catholic church, convent and Presbytery bordered the meeting room area. Baxter stayed but one night only in the presbytery with the Catholic priest and met some half dozen local families that made up the settlement. Maori elders Agnes and Wehi Walker were highly respected in the community and Baxter was well received by them. As a parting gift he was given a jar of jelly beans and the Walker's encouraged him to return there.

Baxter headed back along the track of the river intent on returning to Auckland and arrived at the home of Michael Illingwothy at Puhoi, near sixty five kilometres from the city. Appearing at the door of this acquaintance, he gave him the Maori gift of jelly beans. A different Baxter than Michael had known in Dunedin was present there. He remembered the once angelic face younger alcoholic when he himself was awarded the first Fellowship of the Francis Hodgkins award back in 1966. Baxter's hair had now grown long and he was sporting an equally untidy beard. Michael surmised that he had an agenda in calling on his old friend; for it was not just to renew his association from Dunedin University days. Baxter had known that Michael had lived in a Maori community at the Bay of Island.

For several years Michael Illingworth's home was shared with a Maori chief who looked upon him as a son. The local Maori had welcomed him as being one of his Maori family and community. James knew of this when he discussed his plan to move to Jerusalem with Illingworth. Baxter had asked the kindly Maori cultured Michael if it would be imposing on Maori hospitality to make such a move. Michael assured him that he would be received with love from the local Maori as he had been in his youth. Illingworth felt an admiration for Baxter's sensitivity to the Maori feelings and was happy to give him his opinion on the matter. Returning to Auckland Baxter stayed with Hone Tuwhare and his wife for a time. Hone arranged a job for him in the local Sugar Refinery where he worked as a cleaner for three weeks before being sacked. He wrote a poem of the events surrounding his suspension and arranged for a local printer to run some copies. The printer ceased the process after only six copies because upon reading the poem he feared a defamation suit might be brought against him for being involved. Baxter was hard put to extract the six copies from the printer. The printer reluctantly handed James the copies, but the poem was not printed until much later when it was included in Baxter's poetry collections. James had plenty of friends in Auckland but was still homeless when he met a Buddhist who invited him to share his one room with two mattress on the floor in Park Road, Grafton. Trixie, the Buddhist monk, burnt a small night lamp as a sign to anyone who needed help to call in. Both men had very long conversations on their religious convictions and duty to serve others. It was a great association, for the area provided a number of almost derelict houses which were rented out cheaply to university students.

Students then lived together in groups, as is still the case for communal pooling of food and finances to survive. Apart from the student groups who could afford food clothing and shelter, there were those who lived on the street with nothing to eat and when many had financial assistance they blew the lot on alcohol or illicit substances. Drug taking in New Zealand at the time in the 1960s had reached a peek and on the streets of Grafton and surrounds of the local campus, as well as the cheap digs, it was a common sight to see young people off their brain on drugs or perhaps in the early stages of the effect of excessive drinking. Many without help died on the street or were so heavily addicted that not much could be done but to take them in and clean them up to some semblance of sobriety, and encourage them to stay sober and clean by attending a 12 step programme. Baxter of course led many through the doors of the AA fellowship and others with the help of the Salvation Army had free rehabilitation to get them back on track again. Baxter sometimes got to the addicted persons before the police arrested them and arranged communal living in the established half way houses on Number 7 and Number 9 Boyle Crescent.

Baxter moved into No. 7 after Easter 1969 with his Buddhist friend. These communal shelters had a history as havens for hard drug addicts and those who associate with them. Baxter spent his time counselling addicts and giving them a place to stay. Not all living in No. 7 were on drugs, but some who stayed were heavily addicted and two young people, whilst Baxter was in residence, died of an overdose. Baxter was often confronted by Police but never took drugs of any kind and was always sober when Police checked him out. Baxter in residence meant that No.7 became a haven for the more well to do out of towner as a cheap place to stay. Most had an addiction of some kind or another and Baxter was their trusted guide and adviser. Boyle Crescent and its immediate surrounds became known for those with a hopeless background. Baxter knew them all including those who lived on the street and he often rounded them up and encouraged them to stay at No. 7. Sometimes he would have up to twenty people in a night though the premises were only suitable to ten people on a permanent basis. The place had limited bathroom facilities and many gave up trying to use the bathroom take a bath or use the toilet.

It was not just in New Zealand where such a communal life style was gaining a following. Internationally, in the mid 1960s a resurgence of communal living was gaining traction in Europe and the USA, India and even at home in Australia. The idea of a group of people living together, sharing living spaces, interests, values, beliefs, possessions, responsibilities and income seemed like a good idea at the time. The early communes were more like religious sects as their focus was on God, conversing with profound intensity and intermittent communication. The sharing from the heart with a common charity towards one another built up a mutual faith that resulted in even more such communities flourishing. The coming of the folk and rock culture to a large degree changed all that. I was not sure where the seed of Baxter's Commune ideal for his ultimate move to Jerusalem had its template manifest, but the experiences of No. 7 and No 9 Boyle Crescent in the suburbs of Grafton no doubt embedded in his mind the urgent need for action.

I was remembering the 1960s hippie culture of one size fits all communal member living. Some communes drifted deep into religious communities whilst still some remained secular. The communes worked well for a while but the free love movement, introduction of drugs to some communities and the occasional rise of an heir apparent Guru leader appearing to control the free lifestyle sits uncomfortably with me to this day.

In Baxter's Boyle Crescent community it had a flow of recovering alcoholic direct from mental hospitals, and junkies off the street without their needs or pills. He found his mentoring as full time counsellor, rent collector and doing his best to keep the house drugs free gave expression to his true feelings. JKB found it easy to encourage the inmates to sit with him, have a cup of coffee and talk of their suffering. It was real life that would appear to a casual observer's viewpoint, like a scene from a horror movie.

Baxter slept on a mattress on the floor in one room. He had a small wardrobe above the mattress were he placed a statue of 'Our lady of Perpetual Succour.' She was his guiding light exemplifying his belief in the 12 step program of AA. He burnt a candle all night as a symbol of his faith and to keep away the fear and terror that drug attacks seem to have in the dark. There was time a Maori addict, an ex con who had a drug induced notion that he was the Second Coming Of Jesus himself. Baxter had a hard time getting this damaged-brained man to stop the drugs and face reality. Equally with another user of amphetamines he managed to help her to remain clean. He felt all addicts were like children lost in the dark and in their helplessness he embraced them. Baxter had even managed to hide a young Maori girl from the Police until she remained sober again for a time and got a job. The pressure of the task in dealing with dyed in the wool alcoholics and more frequently young drug users was effecting him. He felt their fiery furnace, fear and agony as if it was his own. James was always up at night awaiting the squad car to come and take someone away. He had the clear mind of a sober man now and he thanked the Lord for his life and situation. JKB felt the tranquility of one who wakes without a hangover every morning; felt himself alike as a kind of elder brother guiding a younger sibling out of harm's way. He was not only amongst them, he was one of them. James wrote to his mother Millicent detailing his lifestyle in number 7 Boyle Crescent and expressed his confirmation to his mother that his father would have understood. It was just one month prior, the spring of 1970 when father Archie died. Archie Baxter know as the greatest conscientious objector of New Zealand in WW1 had refused to fight because of his pacifist beliefs. He suffered great punishment as a prisoner on the front line, but continued to be a stalwart for radical left views until the day of his death. James related to his mother that father Archie would have understood the greater good of emotionally disturbed people who lived not unlike his jail inmates in Number 7 Boyle Crescent.

JKB had great regard for the dignity of people he served, for he believed them to come to the half way house not so much in search for the drug of their choice but for love. Interviewed by Bernadette Noble, a local journalist he related his outward expression of his appearance, the home and the love: "They find something of it in the common house, the beard, the almost uniform clothes…." Despite his own inability to control his sexual desires he had great concern for the women who found no sense of companionship outside the four walls of their existence. "….only a big society of strangers. There is no village, no tribe. Women go mad in those places. And like the younger ones, when the pain is too great, they turn to drugs." Baxter knew this pain as an alcoholic, fear of death, fear of hallucination, fear of police , fear of fear self.

Initially Baxter welcomed the publicity that drew journalists to Boyle Crescent. It possibly renewed that sense of being someone of importance that he had so craved in the applause he was granted as poet, playwright and lecturer. Beneath this false premise he did knowingly believe that in what he was doing was for the greater good and naively thought that by drawing the country's attention to the problem he would enlist the public to provide for communal centres for those who wanted too get off drugs and find help. However, he came to realise that the curiosity and interest in the sexual nature of communal life both locally and internationally was more the intent of the press. Their mission was to highlight the viewpoint of those groups of people whose needs were not met instead of focusing on the problem at hand.

Those of us like Baxter of alcoholic nature long for shelter from the cold winds of indifference that we suffered in our childhood, the abandonment and lack of love that was seemingly fostered upon us only when we performed. It was a good feeling when we were encouraged to do just that and the nearest reward was the false premise of love and affection we received for the applause we received in doing so. Baxter wised up to it all and came to realise love as an expression of his true feelings in the sobriety of helping another poor suffering soul grace the realities of his own humanity. It was no longer in catering to worldly desire but to the world within his own soul that he was encountering. Bill Wilson got that message too, and expressed it by his efforts in providing a small miracle of steps and works to follow in his writings and his humanitarian efforts to see the growth of his work in the rooms of AA whilst he still lived.

I, after some fifteen years in the programme of AA stand in the wings still struggling with my own demons, but sober in the knowledge that my fault lay in the hardness of heart that such abandonment embedded in a poetic self. For it is only lately that I have realised it is in my heart of human kindness that counts in the long run. No amount of outward expressions voiced to the masses count for a cent in the scheme of things. It is through calamity, confusion and soul filled disillusion that the night comes and shines through the darkness and ones cry can be heard . It is then that comes the awakening to the knowledge of God and his love for us all. Jung, the great philosopher of conscious behaviour in an interview towards the end of his life when asked of his belief in God said: "No, I don't believe in God... I know God." It is in this knowledge and this alone that we reach that humanitarian stage of being that all we do think of is for another and that it is no longer about me, but about us.

CHAPTER 12.

THE GURU OF JERUSALEM

Baxter soon came to realise that Central Auckland was not the place to achieve his hopes and dreams. The ideal of his " Jerusalem" dream began to take place after some six months in Boyle Crescent and in the streets of the city attuning to drunks and addicts. If he could see his way clear to get some of the damaged humanity out of the city they might have a better chance of a normal way of life. Some of those who had lived in Boyle Crescent with Baxter were astonished with how much he achieved in such a short space of time. Others believed he was just an ego maniac who attracted unwelcome visits from the police. A prominent member of the medical fraternity considered that he had helped a good number of addicts and saved some lives to boot. In reality he was a radically active pioneer who had discovered that the best way to treat drug addicts was to bring them into a therapeutic environment. New Zealand was only coming to terms with the world and fellowship of AA but at the latter days of the 1960s and early 70s, they were not ready for a narcotics Anonymous programme of 12 steppers. Baxter twice made submissions to the Board of Health in 1969 an 1971 presenting concise but limited presentations on his work experience with his unusual acquaintance with drugs and drug users. He had developed in his short works a remarkable moderate ideal of religious meditation, detachment from material goods and the sense of importance of the freedom of people to help one another to sobriety and freedom from drug taking.

In his submissions he advocated a special Department of Justice as a bureau to receive and investigate complaints of violence by authority to that of the addict, total separation of hospital treatment and police action and the need for non-violent arrests except in matters of unavoidable self-defence. He presented his ideas of a communal organisations of drug-users, a Narcotics Anonymous of fellowship of live in and self help. He publicly and privately addressed one of the the most hideous social problems of his time. The value systems he had developed from his number 7 Boyle Crescent experiences under the most stressful circumstances were to be taken by him as a template for his commune in Jerusalem. He was a prodigy of his ancestral pacifism, a prodigal son of enormous output in word as in deed. A volume of poetry in a book called *The Rock of women* written and published in the same year he was living on the floor of a drug infested commune assisting those less fortunate than himself endorsed the brilliance of his unusual talent as both writer and poet. The work was too fortify and embed in reader's mind a full and empathetic overview of the poet. It did not get the recognition it deserved, for in the minds of the press at the time influenced by social norms of a more affluent kind it was estimated as considerably uneven in its approach. Poems from the book were better received in a posthumous selection of *Collected Poems* which was released in 1980. The Poetry collection included a a selection of poems from his *In Fires of No Return (1958)*, *Howrah Bridge (1961)* and his *Pig Island Letters (1966)*.

Out of the grim reality of his 1969 communal city experiences and the seeding of new ideas, an untidy bearded somewhat like of a new age Guru, set forth on the road to Jerusalem determined to establish a commune. It was for wayward lost souls and those in need of care for their addictive personalities. He had written of a Jerusalem of unshakable friendship with God to be established in the hearts of those who lived there, a commune of charity. Baxter had lost faith in the urban commune of isolation and the inadequate assistance of those who could have helped but didn't. He expressed as much in his path to the days of his poems, of the lack of compassion in *Ballad of the Junkies and the Fuzz* and later looked critically at Auckland life in *Ode to Auckland (1972)*.

Baxter was critical of the despair that the individual city dwellers presumes that he or she is the only sufferer. It was not so much a despair of the education of belief that society presented but the lack of the heart-felt soul searching need of the populous to help those in need that bothered him in the modern community. Heads were thus stuck in a hymn book of blindness and Police State corrections, whilst the reality of suffering souls was right outside their door. One only had (and still have) to go behind the false screen of the film set of city life to see desperation, addiction and hopelessness to understand that something is amiss in the whole concept of what life is all about. The education of the linear half brain of society, politics, business, religion and the educators need to take a longer hard 'educated' look at the realities of our modern culture. The facts are proven in our cities with rehabilitation hospitals full and burdened down with those lucky enough to get a bed. In my opinion, we need to put down the false sense of pride and look with a sense of kindness and concern upon those waiting on the sidewalks of life, fraught with anxiety and depression. There is still violence on the streets of Auckland as on our streets here in our Australian cities and indeed country towns . Alcoholism and drug addiction is still rife despite those small numbers who do their bit to help in the community. The number of suicides amoungst the young and old alike are not decreasing. I have first hand experience of that with the loss of one of my own through suicide. Being mindful now more than ever that something has to be done is an understatement. It must come from the elite, from the medical profession, business effort, and school education. More than that, a renewed clarity and indeed education of the majority of parents to be more intent on giving love and a listening ear to their kids who are being lost in quagmire of life of the me self importance that modern society advocates. Parents equally endorse such a meaningless self indulgence, turning a blind eye in their busy life of indifference to the spiritual needs of their own who they just tolerate.

The giving of education and material possessions does not make up for lack of love. I am only now learning to express these feelings of kindness and more openly to those who I now count as those I love, and wish that I did more fully in my former married years. For my now family leads me by their example in overlooking my defects of character. They sow love and concern and are and have been there at my lowest ebb of depression and anxiety, and are with me in my heart as I do sky best to emulate their example in my everyday life too.

It was similar for Baxter with a helping hand from those who loved and cared for him on his pathway. The fact that he arrived at the doors of AA as a desperate alcoholic, realised that he was powerless over alcohol, and found a God of his own understanding, attended to the Steps of AA which led him to a guiding light of a Mother image in 'Our Lady of Perpetual Succour,' was a miracle in itself. Baxter personified the man of Godliness and gave ever random acts of kindness to the lives of fellow Alcoholics and those in drug dependancy. He put aside his shame and weak will in sexual activity for the greater good and exemplified that in the main in his devotion at his Jerusalem commune. JKB was far from perfect and no saint but a man of many complexities who did his very best to overcome his own defects and focus his help, care and talent upon those he cared for more than his own gratifications. During his counselling and concern for those who drifted in and out of his commune, he gradually came to believe that New Zealanders had much to learn from the Maori race and in fact considered it a duty for all New Zealand teachers as far as possible, to soak themselves in Maori culture. He advocated the difference between Maori and Pakeha (white) and the breakdown of community because of the great divide between the two cultures since the first settlement with indigenous culture. Whites had done their every best to break down the Maori culture as we have here in Australia over the centuries.

Baxter did his very best to make amends in his advocation of the belief of Maori communal life being preserved and nurture for the benefit of both races. He had a view that the Maori were the elder brother whom we should embrace and learn from in preference to Pakeha values being imposed. When he arrived back in Jerusalem to settle, he was bare footed, ragged clothed and carrying a long stick cut from a tree- from a man of the appearance of John the Baptist emerging from the desert. In fact he wore the name ' John the Baptist' coined by the younger generation who attended at the Jerusalem commune. He initially did his best to follow the traditions of the native race in spiritual rituals, for they seemed far in a way more preserving of values of the spirit of Gods than that of the middle class educated European to which he was born. He moved into a room of the cottage of the Sisters of Compassion- two rooms, a stove and a range and with joy in his heart because it had a bath. So with a plot of land beside the cottage he began to cultivate the land for food growth. In order to be given permission for an extended stay at the cottage he had to seek the approval of the Mother general of the Congregation and this meant a trip to Wellington, where he stayed with estranged his wife Jacquie who was working win the local Public Library. He stayed and cared for Hillary's baby, Stephanie for a time with the help of John, his son. The Mother General extended his use of the cottage for the commune ideal and he then returned to Jerusalem.

Baxter's return to Jerusalem left him feeling lonely and afraid after his visit to his family He wrote to his mother of his desire to be reunited in Jerusalem with his wife and hoped that one day it would be so. The hope that he had in that regard was an illusion for Jacquie had no intention of embarking to another isolated location with her wayward husband who always seem to be in the process of fulfilling what she saw as an unrealistic dream of irresponsibility.

Jacquie had similar spiritual values but she felt they had drifted far apart in lifestyle. Baxter had no real reason now to set up a place in Jerusalem but he felt he had to do it anyway. A return to Auckland saw him return with two of the first of his illuminated residents. A young man and a sixteen year old girl lived with him in the cottage and when they left there was talk among the people of what went on there. It was soon silenced. Baxter expressed his feeling later in poems in his *Jerusalem Sonnets* which he sent to the two young people. It was not done for publication purpose, but more for their insights and to pass amongst friends they considered might need them.

Baxter expressed his poetic preoccupation with prayer in a sense of being a two sided coin of a spiritual journey of understanding in a mystical sense were myth existed to a greater degree on the one side and the opposite of the understanding of human behaviour prayerfully expressed in the first six steps of the AA doctrine of faith to follow in the workings of the consciousness that Carl Jung had expressed in his understating of spirituality. Baxter was ahead of the poetic pack of his day, his faith of pray in devotion to the mother of God that he drew upon on the one hand and his knowledge of and devotion that he drew upon in the AA steps on the other   James Baxter like me expressed in his jottings and poetic expression the meaning of his journey. He like me was a wanderer in search of love, a sick man trying to get well. The Spiritual character of this Baxter was of a heart looking for something beyond his imagination and that of this world. Prayer sustained him as did the AA spiritual programme; as it did in the character of his poetry of imaginings. At the centre and soul of his Jerusalem sonnets was mythical writings in part a meditation and yet another just a mysticism of poetic expression.

Baxter had no illusion about the handwork he would find in the prospects of a garden of Eden at Jerusalem. He dreaded the reality of what lay ahead for him. It was one thing to have a dream and yet another to found a tribe- a community life for one who did not quite fit the image of it all. He had visualised the group living and collective warmth of a tribe with a common purpose and the natural rhythm of divine charity. I could almost hear him say aloud 'Trust in the slow work of God' as he went about his task to establish the commune. Baxter did his best to encourage the isolated urban dwellers, frustrated with the barren world of existence in a society of strangers. Young people in particular were disconnected in a modern secular society that disregarded human worth and the dignity of humans being as secondary to making it big in the material world. It was also a time of experimentation in an attempt to create better relationships. A time when free love, drug taking and revolt out of old ways that appealed to some as their way of freedom to take a road less travelled. It seemed to have some logic to change the way of life in a new age that took precedence over discipline and regimentation to get ahead in a world that emulated the stomping of the downtrodden for the benefit of the few.

The wreckage of lost souls of addiction to alcohol and drugs with no place to call their own could now find love, hope and understanding. Hope for the future; there seemed no way out of it all until Baxter set up his Jerusalem commune. Society was dislocated at all levels, parents unable to account for their own anxieties were ill-equipped to cope with their children growing up and away from the old rule of authority.The grab for possessions over the emergent need for counselling and unity became the norm for many. The world of the family unit was fast crumbling as the 1960s wound down and the new age of the 1970s emerged. The education system, once of logic and reason, was in fact in fast decline as both young and old dropped out and tuned into an age of experimentation and questioning of values. Those who chose to stay with the status quo looked through the rational logical lens and saw nothing worthwhile or sacred in the new age thinkers and their radical ideals. The education system was ostensibly concerned with the rationality of quality and conformity, as each student of the times continued to be branded and churned out like the little boxes that Peter Seeger sang about A mass production of little boxes of different colour, all made out of 'ticky tacky' and all looking and being just the same. Variety was spontaneity and was lost as the young were forced like cattle to the life of undesirable education and conservative, one side of the brain fits all life, ahead. It was little wonder that the streets were littered with the dislocated, disillusioned lost souls.

Baxter himself a victim to this old world lifestyle and education system That was until Jerusalem came along. He initially felt the need to prepare a place for the reuniting of his family and had many times expressed his own need for a place where certain values could be lived and communicated; a place among the Maori where a new age community could live.

James Baxter continued through his initial establishment of a commune to practice prayerful meditation. He had thought a lot about founding a collective culture much like the ascetic group love he envisaged of the Maori tribes that he sought to emulate. The warmth of collective communication. a tribal love naturally based on divine charity. In Baxter the ways of earth and the ways of heaven were to be the way of this Jerusalem communal experiment. It did not take long for the numbers of people, in some sort of need to hear about the place and join in the communal life of Jerusalem. By mid 1971 there were some forty new members in the community. Some came on foot, other by cycle and often there was a traffic jam of cars around the place. It was not unusual to have up to eighty people seated around the dinner table. It became a floating population of folk which made it all the more difficult for the quality of consistency to ensure the objectives for a community to be maintained. By Baxter's reckoning up to one thousand people a year came to stay in the community. Most of those that stayed were of late teens to mid-twenties. He aways got consent from parents for anyone who was under age. He didn't needed the law coming down on him.

    James K Baxter was to some young people more like a father figure than a Guru or indeed an Ascetic saint, as he was once described. He was a great intellectual, a source of good counsel and mostly kind hearted man of a peculiar type of fascination and playful guidance. James was content to devote his energies to the young as he believed they were the ones who were sensitive to society's social consciousness. They seemed to speak more truth, they were the residue of a 1960s culture who were dispensing with institutional authority in preference to seeking out a new way of diversified alternatives. Baxter was their champion in his ability to express in his poems what they themselves thought and he was the spokesperson to express their hunger for freedom. The communal way of life at the time seemed to be the right choice. Amongst the young, James was not the chief of the tribe nor was he their instructor. For he wanted everyone to move about according to their own dictates and ethical standards, not his own. He took a prenatal role only to respond to their needs not their demands. He had taken that same stance in treating his own children as they grew up; he had stood back and encouraged them to make their own decisions, as to a great degree his parents had done with him. He made suggestions to help them but never demands. His approach they thought was magical and he won their confidence. JKB used the Steps of AA in his dealings with those who were addicts and were genuinely trying to get free of their drug of choice. The community had no authority for it lay in a group consciousness much like in the AA programme. The values Baxter hoped to install in the members was an ethic free from anxiety but projecting a communion of a home. He did not mind if his ideas were challenged, it was after all an experiment that he believed could be judged from a traditional standard to see if it resulted in bearing good fruit.

Jesus, in the parable of the sower, expresses the moral of a spiritual kind in that some of the sower's seed fell on good soil and produced good fruit, whilst some that fell on rough ground or by the wayside produced naught. Baxter was a sower of great spiritual tidings and he knew how to act out tidings of great joy in his kindness and friendship to the young residents. Equally he had a defect of character that made him a monster of the worst kind. For Jim Baxter, to his discredit if it were today, would probably be in jail as a serial rapist, for that is in part what he was to the all seeing eye. The difference of his time is that back in the era of his parents coming out of the depression and having experienced world war and the atrocities therein, such matters of a personal nature were hidden under the carpet so to speak, confessed to a priest behind a curtain, kept secreted as part of church doctrine never to be revealed or for the sake of family and community keeping up appearance was not spoken about nor ever saw the light of day. This was the atmosphere and understanding that lay at the heart of James's own introduction to the secret encounters he was attracted too.

    The difference in James Baxter was that he openly talked about this defect of character and wrote about his sexual indecent habits. In fact all his expressions of wanting to be loved and the urgency of sexual satisfaction had a rather cold hearted nonchalant approach even in his writings.

For such a man of diverse character this was his one most previous fault if one can be judge. After all he is no longer here to face any chargers or to give a defensive view of his actions. We do have his letters and they tell a tale of a sexually confused damaged youth that matured into a full blown rapist. We can only evaluate by the facts as written in his own words and those who survives who may endorse his 'sins.' For Baxter used the word 'rape' lightly in describing forced penetration of vagina or anus of another against their will or consent. Therein lay the rub, for there is a fine line as to a forced sexual act without consent that even in today's law is being reexamined. There is no doubt in my mind that the then age of communal free love, sexual perversion and letting it all hang out was part and parcel of the problem at hand .i.e. where did one draw the line in such matter as rape as it applied back then. Well Baxter and those of most of his communal victims have long since passed this earth, so we can only go by what we have, the letters and survivors.

The poet's candour, and corresponding openness may or may not damage his reputation, but to date it hasn't been considered important to the masses. For it is those editors, critics of his works and readers of Baxter's great insight into his brilliance that prefer to steer clear of comment in his 'confession' or of anything that may be considered abnormal sexual behaviour on his part. Far better for them to continue to sweep it all under the carpet in the interest of maintaining the mystique of his poetic genius.

James often corresponded with his mother Millicent, of whom both seemed to have a clammy and somewhat disconcerting relationship that plainly had its pains on both sides. As a young adult it seemed like his approach to her in matters of a sexual confession bordered on comedy: " Though I'm quite capable of infatuation, I think I could do without women. Except you and one or two others, they do not attract me as persons though I am over my earlier shyness. And it is intolerably humiliating to be attracted by someone you don't like…" Baxter was nineteen at the time. He later tied to explain away in publishing of the poem 'At Serrie`res,' on masturbation and Voyeurism, to his parents: "I can hardly be sorry… But I'm sorry I let it be published. And I ask your pardon for hurt or offence it gave to you. To clinch that, say 3 Hail Mary's quietly for me. that I may be of clearer mind and heart.. and I will say 3 for you."

Baxter, in the literary times of the 1950s and 1960s was the younger generation's champion, even though he was hardly interested in corresponding with his immediate cohorts of that age. He did however have one selected group of contemporaries who he engaged with intimately and at length. They were three of the most accomplished female writers of their generation, Fleur Adcock the poet, Phil Ferrabee writer of short fiction who submitted work for Baxter to edit or comment. Grace Adams as an aspiring poet, often sent him verse to critique, and Baxter replied in one of his correspondence a confession: " Neither of us are poem writing machines. You are a women (married)' I am a man (married). We will get friendly; have already begun to get friendly. Without some carrying wave of friendship, I don't see how we could make sense of one another. But I know, or should know, my own subconscious mind by now- it will want to make you number 19 of women with whom I have committed adultery."

Then he goes on to some honest admission of his dark defect of character. "My conscious intention is to be of help to you as a writer and fellow creature. But remember I am an old bag of shit, a psychopathic ex- drunk and don't think too well of your own subconscious either." A open confession of how deep down he acknowledged his feelings about himself, but at the same time to intellectualise a judgement of the woman.

Baxter seemed to be excited about correspondence with women but at the same time they yield a vivid account of his psych- sexual landscape. More unsettling is his insightful candour provided in his letters to wife Jacquie who appears as a task- mistress and above all a partner who refuses him sex. He was but six months into his marriage when he wrote to Millicent, his mother: " I use to think that marriage had a lot to do with sex, but find it has practically nothing to do with it." To Grace Adams in another letter: "Maybe I should't say anything of how things are for me at home here; because one is inclined to adopt the whinging tone, which is in me alas a version of the mating call!" In a letter to writer Phyl Ferrabee, Baxter makes a most appealing disclosure.... "a very sober and perhaps considerate knowledge' that he has dealt with his sexual frustration by force:" Sex relations with wife resumed. At least gives some common ground to stand on to clear up difficulties. Achieved by rape. From a very clear knowledge no other way could break down J's reservations and that she was gradually shoving herself round the bend ..." Then came his justifications. " ... she seems ten times happier in herself, but it looks as if each new act will have to repeat the rape pattern." Who know if Baxter really understood the horror of what he had done. A betrayal of trust that the violence that had taken place would possibly have to be repeated!

Later it seemed Baxter had second thoughts in his awareness of women enmeshed in the social pattern of New Zealand life. However, his understanding is more of his own myth making than social conscience: "What happens is either meaningless to me, or else it is mythology," he openly admits. Who really knows much about the masculine sexuality of men of Baxter's time. Where can one turn to discover how men privately thought about women, sex and relationships? Like the generation before Baxter, writers in New Zealand at least were by and large a stoical inexpressive bunch. There were not many who wrote or loved poetry the likes of this man. Baxter in virtue show a willingness to expresses feelings and self scrutinise. He was before his time in his familiarity with psychotherapy, he acknowledged the unconscious in a Carl Jung sort of fashion and seemed to want to accurately describe his own desires, his own flaws and the shadow places they took him. His letters provoke a textual insight into being available; self involved deeply flawed but unafraid of his own feelings and willing to share them for all the world to see. Baxter's commune not only attracted the suffering souls of addicts and those seeking to find clarity of direction, but the hippies of idealistic sincerity. Those who gravitated to the poet, are of similar bent and and were critical of mainstay society and its academic value system of education. The parents of these wandering souls had suffered through depression and war and were keen to gain for their children what they desired for themselves. They valued higher education and the need to make money in order to maintain stability of relationships to be secure. The youth of Baxter's commune were all together different , in that they saw themselves in different light, as of free spirits with robes, bell bottoms and bracelets dangling from their corporeal bodies, open to the mantra of the Beatles: " All you need is love."

Baxter's hopes were to realise a commune modelled on the values of a Maori community and to privilege their world view honoured in collective community rather than the soul destroying values of the white race which personified individualism, materialism and capitalism. In his commune their were many hugs and kisses, love, affection and sympathy; the love of the many brought with it much listening to each others conversations about life and the meaning off it all. They were a messy, chaotic lot of wounded souls who knew the healing power of love and connection. Baxter saw many people pass through his Jerusalem house for healing. Young men and women, old, gay, straight, drag queens, priest and clergy, lonely people and divorced married, transgendered single, depressed, lawyers, doctors, tradies and the unemployed. They learnt to cook the Maori way, ate, danced together and sometimes slept with one another. There was much hugging when in tears, laughter when the days seemed so sweet and there was always an embrace or a kind word from Baxter to call upon. When approached by an outside of what it was he really had to offer them , he simply answered: " I give them friendship and in return they give me theirs." More than anything the love and acceptance without judgment brought healing to many, but to some dreaded memories.

A telling of what happened with Baxter dispassionately dismissing with a relationship with a young girl of the commune was expressed by him in a letter to his wife Jacquie: " My love, the girl from Auckland who was carrying a child of mine has lost it. She was very melancholy, and I did my best to cheer her up. But I've decided from the bottom of my mind to keep my fly buttoned. For one thing, I've got too much to do… but it is probably necessary to know one is being celibate out of fear and impotence." Baxter's cold dispassionate objectifying of the 'girl' and at the same time mentioning of the need to keep his fly buttoned up as if he was doing something noble, is beyond belief. She was one of a number of young women acquainted with Baxters's attitude and actions towards women who had been sexually abused by the would be Guru. He did on one occasion appeal to a young girl that he wished to give her a special treat. She was granted the opportunity to watch him self abuse. With his charismatic, articulate soft spoken voice and status, in their minds at least, of a Guru showing concern for the lost souls adrift in the cities, alienated by capitalism, Baxter did a lot of good, but equally he exploited the female 'fatherless ones' for his own physical benefit. Baxter had described himself as a 'flawed' man and we are all flawed but it is no excuse for his exploitation of those young women who were vulnerable at the time.

In truth Baxter, for all his flaws did his utmost to make up for his lack of care and urgent need for sexual gratification. Baxter when considered with a wider lens than his deviate behaviour, was neither a Chief guru, nor ethical instructor. He wanted everyone to be free to move with gentle grace and learn from mistakes as he himself was trying to do. He was trying to respond to needs without being demanding. Though he was not experienced nor an expert at Christian mysticism he did his bit to encourage such principles. The night life of the soul was more to his liking. It was Baxter's practice to attend daily Mass at the local Catholic church and often preached the Sunday service homily. He so often said his rosary, but he never preached his way of faith as being the right way for those living in the commune. There were many diverse beliefs, religious differences or those with no belief at all. Baxter practised a kind of enlightened ecumenical approach to those in residence.

He spoke as a Buddhist as if one was a Buddhist and equally as a Jew if one was a Jew. JKB advocated that God we see as one of love, as all are members of an essence of religion. He emphasised the point in describing the Holy Spirit as 'blowing like the wind in a thousand paddocks, blowing where it takes itself to blow.' James knew something of the great age of mystics and he knew the actions of the Holy Spirit was more than confined to a religious philosophy. He had the insight of the spirit as a mystic and the practicality of a Zen Buddhist as he wrote in his Jerusalem day book. "Through a theology of kenosis Buddhist and Catholic stand on the same ground." In reality Catholic underlining spiritual commitment is quite different than that advocated by Baxter. For all Orthodox Christian mysticism is centred on the mystery of Christ, the scriptures and the Eucharist.

Baxter's devotion to Our Lady of Perpetual Succour (help) sustained him through his darkest hours. This Mother of God image that held so much significance for a man who discovered her beauty, purity and grace was his cathartic link to Christ her son. She was his unwavering link to the conversion of faith as a recently baptised Catholic. It was the way of his faith in her, the perfect women, the Virgin mother. Something about that icon of her image captured in his heart a bond that was unbreakable, to give this imaginative man the strength to overcome temptation, to turn to when he once more fell to the depth of despair or indeed to wash away his sin of sexual passions he found almost impossible to bear and to control. Who knows where or how her image came to him. Perhaps it was his Samaritan priest friend that had suggested devotion to her, that awakened in him that need of a true mother image; perhaps it was a fulfilment in the heart of his prayer, of his longing for emotional care that had been lacking in his own mother Millicent's apparent abandonment to his inner most needs as a child. Much may have been in the mind of the young James Baxter as he sat on his father's knee as a child and listen to his reading to him, his closeness and kindness, as opposed to his mother who sat reading alone, reading with apparent aloofness in her instructive methodology of advice and in her own lack of emotion he felt he was abandoned from the nurturing of what he needed from a mother. James the man had come across a mother icon that had a miraculous history for centuries.She was his guiding light, his inspiration of love to be as a pure man, purging himself , though prayer and devotion to her. free from what he had formerly been in his sexually defective way.

In my own childhood the iconic image of Our Lady of Perpetual Succour was displayed in our local Catholic Church in the form of a framed painting. I recall the Sisters of (No) Mercy 'encouraging' us primary school children to show devotion to the Mother of her son Jesus by lighting a candle placed before her and parting the rosary or at least a prayer of personal requests as occasion might dictate. It seems now that I spent many an hour engrossed in prayer before that icon for some kind of miraculous guidance in me passing the entrance to high school examinations and making the Rugby league football team. I did make the grade a little above the average academically and kept the pain of the cane away as punishment for failure of the lack of attention in class . I did also make the football team but the cane did follow in that regard, when inadvertently I was punished for bad sportsmanship as was the rest of the team.

CHAPTER 13.

THE DYING OF THE LIGHT

The devotion to Jesus by way of the intercession of the Mother stayed with me throughout my senior school education too. Unlike Baxter, I found the way through the Virgin mother's intercessions as a child, but drifted away from her guiding light in my adult life. She never much seemed to give me the answers I was looking for with my own sexual struggles anyway, but I did persevere for a time. That is until the delight of sexual encounters with my own bodily contact with the opposite sex became more enticing to me than lighting a candle to the Mother of my Saviour.

In the early stages of the Jerusalem community, it was financially held together by donations from those who could afford to pay to stay there. There were many who just lived off the rest who could pay and the hangers on who contributed naught; not even their labour. Some communal members in group conscious meetings complained to. Baxter to get rid of the bludgers but he insisted that the 'bludgers' and parasites are God's gift to us, our sacred guests, jewels hidden in the mud.' In this way he was much like St. Francis of Assisi approaching communal life. Someone with a realistic business sence was needed if the commune was to survive in the longterm. Francis in his absence on a journey to Rome to visit the Pope was usurped by a group of his brothers and an Order was founded. Francis was disturbed by this on his return, but if it had not happened then the Franciscan Order would not have come into being and would have faded out on Francis's death bed. Of course it is not a fair comparison, but the life blood of the Jerusalem community ultimately failed when Baxter lost interest. JKB had no real regard for money and donated all his commissions from his poetry and lectures to the upkeep and survival of the commune, whilst he held an interest there. Some members earned a little money doing casual work for farmers and visitors sometimes bying gifts of groceries. But financially the community was no better off than the days at number 7 Boyle Crescent, Grafton. It was the hippy type idealists who did all the work and the drones just continued to freeload.

Baxter had written in the early days of the commune that ' ... the way of life he led for years and that many around him had led was hollow, burdensome in the wrong way, far to analytical and too dominated by money and words.' He now felt the calling to live like St. Francis in a life of poverty and belief' for without a spirit of poverty communal life was impossible. It was the way of the ascetic monks and mystics of byegone days, but not really understood in a 20th century commune of the type that Baxter had envisaged. For most it suggested a lack of material resources needed for living a full life. In the religion of the spirit it meant detachment that is expressed in sharing of the material and letting go of the ideal of mental possession in any fashion. Baxter described the spirit of poverty as the light of communal non possession and that would bring peace and freedom. He did his best to practice what he preached and once told students at a graduation service in Christchurch Cathedral that he had chosen to live as far as possible without money and books which had brought him to the fringe of a new universe of great beauty and powerful involvement in the lives of others. He had described it as making him a little more chaste, wise and humble.

In Reality he was having a "lend" of himself, but Baxter saw it as a beginning, an open road towards others. He saw poverty as an emptying of self. To my mind I likened it to what I experienced walking the daily grind of a Camino and understood the privilege of being wet for days, sick with influenza with feet sorely blistered and little to eat or drink along The Way. There were nothing of possessions except what I carried in my knapsack. There had been something emptying and yet illuminating about that experience. but right now I care not to repeat it for I lay sick for three months after my last near 1200 km journey out of the darkness. It may have been a brief encounter with the mystics of the past but it just does not wash with me now. Still I yearn for the open road, the road less travelled, which in the comfort of my discontent still is calling me. It is the mysticism of void at the centre of the soul that I seek to fulfil. It is what every man sees if he or she but stops to ponder. It was there before I was created, perhaps before creation itself. But in the noise and confusion of a weary world we cling to attachments of the material like our life depended upon it all. Somewhere deep within we await the appointed hour to be turned into or perhaps return to the centre of our darkness where the light of the spirit shines; the light the disciples reportedly saw on the mountain at the Transfiguration of Christ's ascent into the heavenly kingdom.

I for one, through all my sham, drudgery and broken dreams still tramp the lonely path in search of such a salvation. When asked about pending death or the suggestion, that like most of the aged I will end up in a nursing home awaiting the master of my fate, I then fortuitously smile my reply: "I wish only to die climbing a mountain or maybe mounting a woman." The core of the thing runs much deeper than that, for I want, like all decrepit hapless souls to be a new creature of humanity, but I cant let go... and so I write and I write, like some kid who creates a castle on a beach in the sand. I, in my childlike way see strangers walk by observing with a kindly eye the extent of my creation. Others hardly notice in their dull heads that a child is creating and all he asks is a kind word of love, but they do not see; they are too far gone too see, too busy in their own misery to appreciate a child's gift of love in his creation. They are my friends, my family, those I look up to in offering the gift of my imagination in shifting sands. So it is that the child watches as the tide comes in and washes away his castle of love. It is then he turns once more to observe the ocean and returns to his task as the tide recedes, to create another castle, an expression of his yearning for the love, but it is no transfiguration.

The love Francis of Assisi attributed to poverty, a love of peace and harmonic symphony of soul were pieced into Baxter's writings of the vision of his new Jerusalem; but the reality of the place he so wanted to create in his dream was not possible. He had assumed the Maori would embrace the culture there in his communal ideal, but save for a few desperate Maori souls off the streets of Auckland, the majority of those who came to live there were from the moral and desert landscape of shattered white man's ways.

Baxter's ideal of learning from Maori culture did not work out because the members who did live there were not ready for it. The Maori who did live nearby only gradually came to stay but they were like small droplets of water from a tap and not a fast flowing river like the nearby Wanganui River he had reckoned for. The Jerusalem commune could not succeed without the approval of the local people- the Maori, the adjacent land hold farmers, the Sisters of the Compassionate Order and of course the law. Locals took some interest in the houses of the community more out of curiosity of how the members were faring than wanting to be a part of the movement. Some of the commune members objected to their roaming in and out at will and the demands of the Maori representatives, as they saw things from the view point that didn't seem to differ much from the authority of a world in which they were escaping and revolting against anyway. There were problems of hygiene and sanitation which brought conflict with the local Wanganui County Council, as well as representatives of authority who lived along the Wanganui River and kept a keen eye on the comings and goings of hitch-hikers. Attention of authorities regarding hygiene and sanitation ultimately brought the media and under the lights of TV cameras Baxter promised the Council that he would make extensive improvements to the facilities to satisfy the Council for the commune members to remain there. JKB welcomed the demands placed upon them for it gave the community a common goal but he insisted: 'The state of people inside themselves is more important than if we have two toilets or one.'

The effect of trial by media, public opinion on such a rebellious lot and the now ever present seeing eye of authority harmed the community. In time the commune gained acceptance locally, but further bad blood evolved when landowners at a special meeting asked Baxter and his followers to leave. Their reasoning was that they wanted Jerusalem cleaned up to attract more Maori back there. Baxter wholeheartedly embraced the ideal and welcomed the plan as the old Maori settlement provided a much better community life than any Pakeha (white man) could offer. By early September 1971 the first phase of Baxter's ideal enterprise had ceased. It was a grand vision that he had and it failed, not because of his ideal but more to the point, he could not realise it. The commune members were disorganised and lacked organised rules. So much was left to too few individuals to do and in the majority of cases they too were suffering depression and other mental issues. It has been proven historically that any religion or cult of religious or of a spiritual nature required a consensus and ability for a community to live happily with good training in the goals and aspiration of the whole group. Discipline was not something Baxter aspired to personally and indeed in within the communal life of Jerusalem was almost frowned upon with the members adhering too much to their ways of living.

The open handed approach of Baxter and his fellow members of the commune to all newcomers in a hand to mouth existence, the rapid turnover of a floating population of members and the lack of a shared vision other than building a second toilet block, led to instability, frustrations and poor relationships with members and the community at large. Baxter well knew that his personal religious and social views were at odds with those he commonly preached. Many members rejected the ways of formal religion whilst Baxter embraced his with the utmost intensity and emulated the virtues of such belief. He was himself to much indoctrinated to the ways of the 20th century to ever be able to put into practice the St Francis like doctrine of religious faith and morality to a rebellious group of misfits. The faith he so richly embraced did but little to save him from anxiety and suffering, nor the pain of falling so far short of his lofty goal for the Jerusalem community.

He was a poetic miracle of imaginative output in words but not so much in his ability to see through and carry out a collective mission of deeds. Baxter like Bill Wilson the co-founder of Alcoholics Anonymous could write the ideal and practice what he preached, using to a great degree the moral of the AA steps and the ' Big book' written by Wilson as his guide. It is one thing to encourage addictive personalities to give up their drug of choice and change their beliefs and habits to lead a better life by reading the material provided and listening to fellow members at meetings, but it is a horse of a different colour to actually live with them under the same roof on a day in day out basis. Baxter had no misguidance in himself of living with the mystery of his belief and the complexity of counselling suffering souls, but his own intensity in such matters brought him into conflict. This community of his own making was a statement towards an alternative to modern society. Being foot-loose and fancy-free of the restraints of society affirmed his ascetic values of stern beliefs. The statement of old clothing, long dirty hair, beard and bare feet together with the ever present rosary and crucifix around his neck, branded him a symbol of being poor and disadvantaged.

In his belief and mantra of faith in prayer and meditation he believed he was living in accord to the dictates of his God consciousness. To many he was a broken symbol of novelty and he aroused an indignation to the conservative nature of society. James K Baxter exemplified his awareness of this message that challenged people: 'He turns this man into an old coat and a broken stick, he makes him the nun's devil and a bad smell in the noses of good churchgoing people. It is not a pleasant vocation.' The second faze of the Jerusalem commune was coming as Baxter's own disillusion of having been led by his head brought it all undone. It was time to move on, but the commune and Maori people were still in his heart. In his own eyes now his spiritual journey lay in a different direction he had deduced it was an absurdity to follow such vision in the first place. To him he had completely failed and to pick up the pieces and resurrect the dream was simply too much trouble. In point of fact the commune failed not because his vision was not defective but because he did not have the ability to realise it. By September there were only four permanent members in the commune and it was then that Baxters enterprise ended. He simply could not fulfil his Maori settlement commune style of living the way of the native tribe with their deep attachment for the spirits and nature. As a poet he could express it but living it in reality was another matter.

Baxter returned to his family in Ngaio late in September 1971. He embraced the love of his family once more and felt the pangs of wanting to settle with them again. There was much love in him and he expressed this in his *the book of Jerusalem;* " The possibility of peace tugs at my soul. The old wooden bridge across the creek at the bottom of our bush section needs mending. There is wood to be chopped. I tuck my granddaughter down at night, as she shouts and plays a game of raising her feet in the air. Charity begins at home."

Baxter agonised over leaving his family once again for he could not let go the vision to do something worthwhile for those less fortunate and he, due to his former life in Jerusalem, was hatching up a new plan of attack. He learnt of a disused house at No. 26 MacDonald Crescent, off the Terrace in Wellington. As soon as he moved in the makings of a commune began again, but it only lasted six weeks. There were a number of similar houses lying empty for a long time in Wellington, so Baxter enlisted the help of friends and they set to work repairing the plumbing and fitting toilet facilities. He at least had people in authority that he knew would support his cause. Baxter had much difficulty keeping the idea and the people living out of the public eye. The newspaper *Truth* journalist and editor did not much like Baxter and reported on 14th December 71 that the house which his followers had been squatting in illegally for two months without paying rates, had been declared 'unfit for human inhabitation' by the Wellington City Council. Baxter had been told to immediately vacate much to his disaffection. After a brief period living in Mt.Victoria, Baxter decided to return to Jerusalem with an entirely different plan of making a commune work there. By February 72 he was once again in residence with the approval of the then owners of the property used by the first community. He assured the Maori owners that the old Jerusalem community had definitely closed and would not be reopened. The second commune was more cohesive and he had decided on a smaller community of ten members, but it grew to fifteen before the old ways revisited; They had limited money and the disorganised lack of a central purpose remained. Jerusalem had been changed by Baxter, but it had changed him too. The change saw in Baxter a renewed burst of creative energy, a new book *Autumn Testament* came out of this phase of the Jerusalem community partly because the divine presence of God seemed to be with him more now.

The introduction of Meditation at the commune allowed Baxter to recover some of his former beliefs in New Zealand's loss of spiritual values. He ascertained that the practice of poverty and meditation 'moved the river spirit back into the water. *'A way only a poet of Baxter's expression could thus write of God who can return from hidden places ... a sacramental approach that so commonly works for even the least of us with poetic expression.* Baxter's poetry in this new Jerusalem period gave him personal stability and solidarity in his poems. The words to Baxter in all the poems of this period were sacramental. The perception of prayer played a vital part in enhancing Baxters's life long ability to move as naturally through the ageless configurations of myth as through a city street. It was prayer that Baxter encountered the mystery of God For a merely intellectual road to God could never have satisfied him. As Frank McKay observed : 'The most lasting fruit of Baxter's dark pilgrimages to and from Jerusalem is his poetry and prose. The ' dark vocation now summoned him to undertake the last dark phase of his pilgrimage.' Quote, unquote.

* Extract- from Two Jerusalem's - Life of James K Baxter -Frank McKay 1990.

Baxter, for all his education and psychological knowledge lacked the leadership styles used in successful undertakings. He did not know how to apply an autocratic authoritative way of a leader, lacked the ability to delegate responsibly and whilst somewhat amiable in his free- reign lassie-faire approach was inconsistent in his leadership in dealing with damaged people. Much less he lacked the leader style for the free loving hippie ways of a Jerusalem commune. Whilst he could be democratic and paternalistic he was too inconsistent in that regard. He preferred to let things run along without a plan or common purpose, nor even explaining to members his vision for the future of the community. Whilst he applied the A A ideas of a regular group consciousness he had no apparent idea of having a chairperson with the message of leadership ideals and apply those to the commune. Bill Wilson stated the role of leadership well in his writings: "No society can function well without able leadership at all its levels, and A A can be no exception. But we A A's sometimes cherish the thought that we can do without much personal leadership. We are apt to warp the traditional idea of ' principles before personalities' around to such a point that there would be no 'personality' in leadership whatsoever. This would imply rather faceless robots trying to please everybody. A leader in A A service is a man or women who can personally put principles, plans and policies into such dedicated and effective action that the rest of us naturally wants to back him up and help him with his job. When a leader power drives us badly, we rebel; but when he too meekly becomes an order taker and he exercises no judgement of his own- well, he really isn't a leader at all."

Baxter over time however did get the AA message for himself that the more we depend upon a Higher Power the more independent we actually become. He was certainly a poet of personal, social and religious relationships. Through interaction in that regard the poet and the man grew. He did have the ability to command the spirit of ancestors in his dealings with people who were suffering hardship, be it in counselling them or in incorporating in meeting a Maori spirit of the dead. However, he was often in conflict with his own values on personal terms and he became more aware of the gap between reality and his imagination in the real world, a battle that raged within his spirit in contrast to his ego. In his second commune phase his writings personified this sense of a raging battle within; of the darkness of his defects of character challenged by the light that he did his best to portray in his poetry and lectures. Baxter was like any man on the road of the inner spirit, not at inner peace with himself.

JKB may well have recalled in the AA programme that ' half measures avail us nothing,' that one must be as a whole in the 'Yin Yang' of the living. In a sense in the essence of that Ancient philosophy of dualism-dark and light, female and male, moon as to sun within. Carl Jung described it as the conscious and unconscious being and doing together as a whole. Jesus reportedly, in this own words described it as ' two in one flesh.' In is not any easy task, as any married couple may well attest too. Baxter was well on the way to such an acceptance of understanding but as far as one can assume, he struggled with his own egocentricity, for despite his devotion to the Virgin Mary and her Son, and his prayerful utterances as one well schooled in psychological understanding., he was much driven by the demons of sexand ego, which were always his undoing.

In my own restless state of mind I am fully aware of the fact of my inner defects of character being masked by outward appearance as being an enthusiastic driven personality of goodwill towards others. In reality. I used to consider myself a good leader of men, a caring businessman of service and exemplifying the Christian way of family responsibility in my everyday way of life. Now that I am a non drinker and attempt to strive to be a better man in all I see, say and do I more often than not mask the real me. The ego self of the dark side of my character which raises its ugly head into the seven deadly sins of my defects of character are often there to serve Doug and not the inner spiritual self of the "I" of me. I need not describe these defects, except to say that I am wholly mindful of them now more than ever before I found the AA programme. More often than not in my former life I lacked charity, not in the practical sense of a James Baxter type of giving good counsel and lecturing. For as equally as Baxter I lived the moral life of family, Christianity, business and community, but it was always masked by outward appearances, for it was not in my poetic expression, my songs or my books, nor indeed my own lectures on how to make it in an inner spiritual world that I now sprout. Rather it was my lack of kindness towards those I love that I now hold up to the light. I am wanting in so many ways, as the shadow self of the Baxter used as a template to my own deficiencies. I hear the words of Jesus now: " If I should contribute all my goods (talents) to feed the poor, if I should deliver my body to be burnt and have not charity, it profits me nothing."

Baxter, to be fair to him, exemplified the meaning of charity, for he generously and helpfully did his bit to help the needs of the suffering souls who came his way. He shared his bread with the hungry, to the poor he provide money and the homeless he tried to house. His weakness in his plan of action was the difficulty of giving of himself whole heartedly. For he was most like the majority of us, we are not saints in the doing. In what we do to free ourselves to overcome our defects of character to all intentions are overcome by them. I only wish I had the spirit to be willing to give of my all, but to date, alas I do not.

In early 1972 Baxter was invited by the union of the parish of Dunedin to take part in an event for young men and women, to hear from him first hand what was happening in New Zealand society and to share with young people outside a church community what was happening for those within. The event was called Impulse 72 and as he had been a great influence at a similar event the year before, when he was asked to be a guest speaker he agreed to attend again. This new event was to be a kind of festival, alive with rock n'roll bands and lot of lively guest speakers of which Baxter would be one. In April, after some fore-thought he wrote from Jerusalem that he would leave for Christchurch in July and would be in Dunedin on the 29th July in time for the festival. Baxter had proposed to read two of his poems for the speech: '*Junkies and the Fuzz,*' and the '*Ballad of the Stonegut Sugarworks*' but had spent the morning of Impulse 72 pre-speech engrossed in his bible. In his previous year's speech he had caught the imagination of his youthful audience when he spoke of the weakness in New Zealand society but this time he supposedly used his Bible reading on Jeremiah as his template. This year he disappointed the organisers with his speech.

Baxter did not read the two poems that he proposed but spoke dispassionately on suffering, especially that of the poor. To support his point of view he quoted from the Pentecostal Prayer book. It was an unexpected turn of events from his usually fiery utterances and the young people present were simply bewildered by his address. Baxter well knew the mind of students and his present audience. Despite the speech the students in the Concert Chamber surrounded him after the speech anxious to speak with him. For all appearance the life seemed to have gone out of him. He was not his usual self. On his way back to Jerusalem from Dunedin he stayed with his family in Wellington . Catching up with his old friend, Wehi, who had always been his most ardent supporter and understood him the best, he noticed how thin he had become and wondered if he had cancer. Baxter well realised that he no longer had the energy to administer to the community. The poor were still short of food at both Grafton and Jerusalem and the long journeys on foot that he had formerly taken for the variety of causes he had involved himself on their behalf had drained him. Far too many people had enlisted his help, drawn too much of his personal resources and he was burnt out and physically exhausted.

The sense of depression had over come him as a consequence but he was not bitter nor angered, but realistic about his overall health issue. He had insight, perhaps a little too late, that for a commune to be sustainable it had to be limited to a small number of permanents, all with stable incoming earning occupations of some capacity. The failing health was forcing him to accept the death of his ideal. On his return to Jerusalem he handled over the running of the commune to another core member and advised that he was leaving to set up something else. His advice was simply: 'Sit quietly in the space at the centre, don't be too heavy, and keep good relations with the pa. (pa- by that he no doubt meant the heavenly Father). Baxters's final words to Maori friend Wehi was ' Look after nag Mokai,' which may be interpreted as 'look after my dance or my community.'

Baxter returned to the commune in Carrick Place, Mount Eden, Auckland which was run by friend Kathy, who owned two adjoining houses number 5 and number 7. To him it was a sign as it reminded him of his number 7 Boyle Crescent commune. So from then on Carrick Place was to be his base. Kathy noticed a kind of panic or fear in his eyes as if he was calling for help. As his health deteriorated he felt the vulnerability of a person who had even more minimal of life's securities. He was full of self doubt, questioning and evaluating everything he had ever done. He was a defeated man in need of a new start in life. He felt the need to settle down again, receive the love and care he had given others and in which he was now wanting. Thought of re-marrying crossed his mind in those latter days and he was bound by a lonely wish to be loved that never left him for all of his remaining days on earth. The melancholy mood never left him. He enlisted the help of a psychiatrist for several weeks. He so much wanted to go back to his childhood experiences and work things out. The obsession he had for his mother's love which he believed he had not received from her was ever present. As a last ditch effort he set off on a speaking tour of schools. He struggled to attend his appointed sessions and likened his counselling visits as 'going to the cleaners.' The love of his Faith, and attendance and assisting the priest at Mass every day continued. Kathy assisted him in smarting himself up a little. He trimmed his beard, cleaned his clothing and gained himself a small job assembling electrical components, but he had long been absent from work routine, so he soon lost the job. Baxter's most memorable poems were about the past and his writing in the present put the pressure of the past there. Baxter knew his chosen way of life had damaged his health irreparably, and that he was to die without accomplishing his aims.

In his absence   back in Auckland, Kathy began to worry about him. She rang the Karamu High Schools he was to attend and he sounded exhausted to her and promised to return soon. On the Friday 13th October he visited Father George McHardy at the Whangarei Presbytery who had instructed him into the Catholic faith. The priest had remarked that he looked tired and miserable. Despite this Baxter spoke to the primary school children at St Joseph's convent school. He was invited that night to attend a parish youth group catechetical weekend at Marsden Bay and was welcomed by the youth. He had no problem fitting in and gave a couple of talks and participated in learning activities. He strolled the beach with the youth and found the energy to piggy back a young rather plump girl, running in and out of the waves. In the evening he played five hundred card games and with utter seriousness discussed each hand after it had been played. In the course of the evening he impromptu recited '*Lament for Barney Flanagan*' in a flat tine voice. At about 4.30 a.m. in the final morning, he brought a cup of coffee into the bedroom of one of the young priests in charge of the camp and announced: I am going to rave for a couple of hours, so you will just have to listen." He spoke negatively of his mother and her relationship with his father, drawing an analogy of the pagans of the first Christians:"See how they love each other." He added: "Wouldn't it be wonderful if they had said: "see how they love us".' When he returned to the presbytery in Whangarei, Fr. Began, a long term friend persuaded James to write to the Sisters of Compassion to make peace for they were disappointed with his administration of the Jerusalem community. He wrote to them with a kind of admission that in some respects he had been wrong. More generally, he seemed to come for final reconciliation.

In the last week of his life Baxter was driven to Puhoi to spend some final time with Michael and Dene Illingworth who were renting a house there. He lay down most of the time, occasionally raising himself up to write. He seemed to have become old and slow. When he climbed into bed with them he was noticeably cold and had difficulty getting warm. He kept talking and they no doubt knew he was dying. The Jerusalem community was finished. He had done all he could do, so now the members would have to look after themselves. Yet, even though he was utterly drained, he kept arguing for the need for a new approach, structural change in society to become just. He proposed a structural revolution. He wanted to take his proposal to Auckland street kids a blend of Marxist and Christianity. Many he knew were Maori and he hoped to persuade them to return to found communities with a more radical understanding of duty and faith he himself seemed to be working towards. He still had the DNA of his father Archie, and expected to turn up a hornet's nest among civic and government authorities with his new ideal.

On his final Wednesday on earth, Baxter and Illingworth drove up Tunnel Road to a high ground commanding magnificent view over the Kaipara. They walked the final few hundred yards to the top with Baxter stopping frequently to regain his breath. He talked frequently that day about death and asked Michael to arrange a jazz band to play at his funeral and to put a stone on his grave. When they came to a huge kauri tree, he stood and hugged it for a long time. That night the two men talked until dawn, but this was not unusual for Baxter; all his life he only managed two or three hours sleep. Thursday morning, Illingworth and Baxter left Puhoi by car and went to Auckland, stopping at a coffee bar at Barry Lett gallery, an old stamping ground. After a couple of hours they said their r good-byes and Baxter went on to an appointment.

Back in Carrick Place, his friend thought he looked exhausted but he went on to dinner on the Thursday night with friends in Grafton. They all knew he was ill but they responded well to his company. He insisted on walking home with them together, a couple of kilometres down the road. Baxter had many frequent stops to regain his breath along the way. On the Friday night he went out to visit prisoners at Paremoremo prison, a practice that had long been part of his life. On the Saturday morning 21st October, Baxter went to Jean Tuwhare's place in Birkdale and asked if he could stay a few days. In the afternoon he helped in the garden, hoeing out onion weed with a mattock. The Sunday morning he complained of pains in his chest and she rang a doctor and made an appointment. The doctor who was familiar with Baxter and his poetry said he would open the surgery especially for him at 7.30 p.m. In the meantime, both Jean and Baxter went off to a sauna at Tskakapuna with a Maori women friend. Baxter was unusually quiet in the sauna but when the Maori friend asked him why he had left his wife, he replied that he loved her and wanted to be buried with her, but justified his wanderings on the basis that one with his creative gift is required to move around. On the way back from the sauna, the two women insisted they stop at a chemist to get him some tablets thinking that he may have a stomach ulcer. Baxter didn't not bother to explain that he had been mindful for some time that he had a bad heart.

That Sunday evening Jean drove him to the doctor's surgery in Glenfield Road. As they came to Eskdale Street, Baxter took his last glimpse of the sea. He was cracking jokes when she left him at the doctor's surgery. Jean believed that the doctor would talk to him for some time. She had planned to come and get him when he rang. The doctor wanted to arrange a check up, but Baxter insisted he was too busy. He did not appear to be in any immediate danger, so the doctor left for another appointment. Baxter soon after had a violent heart attack outside his surgery. He managed to cross the road and knock on the door of no.544 Glenfield Road. The residents were reluctant to admit this wild eyed shaggy dressed stranger. They immediately rang Jean Tuwhare , then rang another doctor who thought it better to wait for his own doctor who had just examined him. In considerable pain, Baxter was lying on a lounge at the back of the house when Jean arrived. She remembered him saying: " I have a wife and children in Wellington." The doctor arrived and applied heart massage but it was too late. Baxter died that night 22nd October 1972 in the house of a stranger, he was only forty six years old.

Baxter's death was recorded in the Evening Post billboard, in simple terms, it read : "James K Baxter, Friend 1926-72." The funeral attracted around 800 people, who came to pay tribute to the country's greatest poet. Bruce Mason, playwright, actor, critic and fiction writer wrote. " No death I have ever known has so swept the county in a huge wave of grief." Like the death of John F Kennedy, many people recalled years later what they were doing when they heard of James Baxter's death. When Jacquie heard of his death from the police, she rang a mutual friend Colin Durning and they both flew up to Auckland together on the Monday . The body was still under the coroner's jurisdiction but Jacquie insisted on permission to view it in the presence of two policeman. When all the family arrived to view the body, some of the members of the local communes Baxter had befriended were already there. It was apparent he was ready for the occasion, for they noticed Baxter had trimmed his beard.

CHAPTER 14.

POETS OF A COMMON DENOMINATOR

If I had not taken that fateful journey to Jerusalem with my Kiwi tramping companions Tony and Lorraine Freeman in the spring of 2018, I may never have know of James Baxter. By the chance reading of the old manuscript of his life's work I planted a seed of this poet in my head. It was not until a bleak day in the passing Autumn of this year, 2021, that the idea came into my head of a need for a template of self evaluation. It was to reevaluate my life, the steps of AA and where I may take things from here. It was thus that I recalled James K Baxter's poems I had glossed over in my brief encounter with his work in 2018. I had been told by Tony Freeman at the time of his fame as a poet, his work with the less fortunate, his establishment of a commune at Jerusalem and of his derelict lifestyle. I recalled reading at the time of Baxter's alcoholism, of his new found faith and rejection of anything he wrote in days he sat at a bar in Wellington sprouting his latest poetic creation.

It was then the thought struck me that James K baxter would be as good a vehicle as any with which to compare my life, my work, my alcoholism and my poetic creations as a shadow of a master full of defects of character like my own. I could in truth have picked anyone of a number of men of genius whose works I had studied but this poet somehow stuck in my craw. So it was that I set to work researching the man and reading noble works of great men of letters, critics of verse and story telling who had written on the life of Baxter, so to compare for the sake of checking out the inventory of my life, the love and curse I carry for creative expression, and the need to feed the wild beast of mythical and real story telling that lay within my own Irish nature.

But this story I have written as much for my own letting go of the past as to gain the effects of a faith of willingness to be of service to others as Baxter attempted to do. Not so much as to be thinking of ones own ego-centrical wants and needs but to learn by another's God given gifts of fortune and the consequences he suffered as the misfortunes of his own actions. I had fortunately walked the Camino de Santiago three times on my own journey of soul discovery, before Baxter's life and creative works came to be at my disposal. These Camino journeys instilled creativity and a litany of poems, songs and books of my adventures and imaginings to benefit my letting go, my past life of loss, of the pain of regrets, and more importantly the booze that was killing me.

It was St. James himself that ventured out on his own Camino in the first century after the death of Christ some two thousand years ago in a spirit of letting go his own nature to preach a message of faith and to do God's bidding to those of no faith in Spain. He reportedly preached a message of faith: "Grant me strength that I go out from here to do thy bidding, despite my own defects of character." Actually it was Bill Wilson of AA who preached that. St. James actually stated that we need to be men and women of action for " faith without works is dead."

So it is that I use the analogies of two men of action in this book, but still I am in search of the holy grail of a willingness to let go. I have shared with you the thoughts, words and actions of James K Baxter and my own in this little book. However, not once have I enlisted the help of a poem of Baxter, nor my own in the tale within these pages. So, I feel it is high time that I did just that and trust dear reader that you gain some benefit from the words of a genius poet, James K Baxter and some compromise in this one who is cast in his shadow.

Baxter's life runs parallel with that of Bill Wilson in that they both had a way with words in getting their message across. Baxter in his poetry, and in his lectures for an improved more balanced society, in leading alcoholics to sobriety, and in his own setting up of a model for of a community which at the time didn't work but ultimately has been emulated for improvement by various charities since his death. Wilson in writings of the Big Book, the twelve steps the traditions and the many books and promises that will come the way of any alcoholic who follows the (God) inspired steps to recovery from alcoholism.

Bill's commune turned out to be regular world wide meetings for Alcoholics and James in his teaching held out a hand to the street peoples he encountered and helped. It is from such as them that my true worth life potentially lay. That is to utilise my talent in service to my fellow man. Meanwhile it is more in anxious words and not deeds that I attempt to do this. It may be out of fear of not getting to put down on paper what I fear in my heart I will not finish before my appointed day to meet my maker that drives me. Whatever it is, it is helping a spiritually poor man to get well, that I may sooner rather than later put down my pen to do in deed what I profess in words.

Baxter had the genius of understanding the great Masters of the written word even before his teens. He could express more deeply than most his inner most feelings and had no shame in letting it all hang out on paper for the world to see. He wrote of his country, his fellows and faith and the political nature that disturbed him to the core of his being. I myself, was much less well read than he, but I enjoyed the classics through my high school education, discovered the ballads and sonnets of the poets of the middle ages in the Albatross book of verse. later the poetry of Percy B Shelley, Lord Byron and the spat of Shakespeare and Oscar Wilde were more to my liking. The influence of Dylan Thomas of Baxter's era parallel my fascination with death poems, particularly after loosing those close to me at an early age. later it was more the Australian poetic works and stories of Henry Lawson and that of Adam Lindsay Gordon that were more to my liking. So dear reader, in the poems of Baxter and myself here, I trust you gain some benefit.

Baxter like myself wrote much of his feelings of youth, maturity and of old age, of which alas the latter days he did not have the opportunity to enjoy, for as the biblical words state: "only the good die young that they may avoid corruption. The old live long that they may repent." JKB did his fair share of suffering and chanced a lot for his betterment with regular confessions as part and parcel of the mode of his life. He would no doubt have enlightened us with much more of his own creations if he had but lived longer. There are so many of his writings, as there are of mine, that I could share here. But save for fear of boring you with too much detail on poetry, for with rhythm and rhyme are not always of the taste for the majority of people, except to read but maybe once and then cast aside. I have therefore taken but a few that draw some parallel of Baxter and myself which you the reader may enjoy and hopefully gain benefit from.

The River Spirit.

Far up in the wild, cold moorlands
My rushing stream has birth.
And I tumble down past vale and town
To join the rock Firth-
I fall from a ledge to marshy sedge,
Wind through a rusty glen,
Then forth I sally down the valley
On to the haunts of men.
Past cobbled streets I softy flow
And bubble under bridges,
Then onward rush past bank and bush,
To tumble o'er the ridges-
Through all the smoke of busy towns,
By sewer, wall and quay,
I reach the sandy river-mouth
and plunge into the sea.

Then on his occasion to say goodbye to his old school Sidford he wrote:

Farewell to Sidford

Farewell to all the beauty,
That round old Sidford lies,
The daily round of duty,
The play 'neath sun and skies.

God give me strength and courage
To shape my destiny,
On Christ, the perfect image,
Of pure simplicity.

The spirit verse of my river analogy of life seemed to start in my mind where Baxter had left off or maybe it is just the way that I see it now. It was a call from 'The river and the ocean.'

There's a track to mission mountain
on the pathway of the mind,
in a valley of the spirit,
we're flows a gentle stream.

It trickles over cobble stones
in an ever constant theme,
murmurs a hushed lullaby
to the birth of its own dream.

Where its silence can be broken,
distracted by the glow,
as dark rolls back nights curtain
to reveal a constant flow.

It's flowing gently onward
through the valley of the wind,
skimming across the ripple flow
hastened to a world beyond.

In the deep wall of water flowing,
headlong to the valley floor below,
the spirit river meanders on,
in its mystic constant glow.

There's a child upon the waters,
cast out to natures way,
he trims his sail to glory
paddling his own canoe.

Now the water flows are plenty
as the river journeys on,
headlong to the valley floor
the spirit stream it glows.

The rivers constant spirit journey
meets the ocean of the blue,
flowing ever onward
in eternal rhythm theme.

The oceans source is restless
tide to the will of the moon,
in waves of constant motion,
from the deep of dynamic scene.

The oceans rise and swelling
in the dark mysterious depth,
attuned to nature's orchestra
and the power of conductor's whim!

There is a vision splendid
beyond the great divide,
on a source of Godly purpose,
to the river and ocean wide!

There's a child upon the waters,
cast out to nature's way
he trims his sail to glory,
paddling his own canoe!

Whilst Baxter's early teenage poetry built on the New Zealand landscape of his harsh childhood world of books and dreams, he at that time wrote of his own future vision of a reality that had come to pass for him. It was as a sixteen year old he wrote the following poem. It was then he felt Millicent, his mother ,threatenhis independence.

I will go to the coastline and mingle with men.
These mountain buttresses build beyond the horizon.
They call. But he whom they their spell upon
Leaves home, leaves kindred. The range of the telescope's eye
Is well, if the brain follows not to the outermost fields of vision.
I shall drown myself in humanity. Better to lie
Dumb in the city then under the mountainous wavering sky.

Baxter s younger years were despairing of life and drawn much to reading the works of poets focused on death more than life. JKB expressed this in the nature of his poem on the 'Death of a Swan.' It also demonstrates the unique variety of form in his verse.

Fell the wild swan: from haven-less crags of sky
Fell to no cool lagoon of summer flocks
But bruising river-ice: she fell to die
Beside a winter shore and wolfish rocks.
Fell the wild swan to ice and lay thus weakly:
The tower- shadows hung compassionate;
Night like the river flowed till day came bleakly…
Hooded and frozen, her webs spread full: of late
The piteous bill moved, clogged as snow sank.
Vaulting pinions, then immense heavens cloven
To blades of sunlight, where now? She had and dank,
And one with ice, snow-down to feel, wind-woven.
No baptismal save sleet; no Erin, priest- word repeating;
:Lost Child of Air, heart frozen and faint beating.

My own poetry differed to Baxter's context of death verse being more simplistic in style and expression, but taking in a broad extroverted approach to emerging images of life beyond the dark place of the mind. it was set in world view of my slant on the reality in which I was experiencing when I wrote it. It was perhaps a bit too cynical view of the reality of the personal and dark universal view of what lay beyond. I had only just ceased drinking.

The life reminder.

There is a life reminder
awaking in my womb
it is a strange reflection
within a harvest moon.

There is a soul of black light
piercing the impenetrable dark,
it is a strange reflection
the pain within my heart.

Oh! there is a joy of living
within the darkest hour
the power of my candle light
to germinate your flower.

No it's not here in the morning glow,
nor in the evening light,
its a view of some strange reflection
on the other side of midnight.

Here we are on the other side,
the other side of midnight,
here we are on the other side,
the other side of midnight.

Oh! the light maybe burning bright tonight,
as you view the universe,
your soul be struggling for some peace,
whilst the head is full of verse.

Maybe you're seeing fatted calf,
that feed the chosen few,
or you glimpse the starving millions,
through the eyes of a film crew.

Do you see the warring leaders,
the bodies dead and burnt,
do you see the learned gentry sing,
the chant of some beggars tune.

No it's not there in the morning glow,
nor in the evening light,
it's a view of some strange reflection
on the others side of midnight.

Here we are on the other side,
 the other side of midnight,
 here we are on the other side,
 the other side of midnight.

Do you cry out in the darkest hour,
whilst planes are dropping bombs,
shaking fear in your emotions,
as you die here in my arms.

Is it the fear of the bewitched,
before the morning glow?
do you hear the children crying?
or is it some old black crow?

Oh! I know not when I lost the dream,
maybe it was when my brain did scream,
for a little bit of peace within,
to let go of this ghastly scene.

For I saw the four horsemen riding
towards the end of the universe,
spreading fire, disease and pestilence,
to the peoples of this earth.

It was whilst I was entwined,
in the flesh of my lover's charms ,
riding my wild women,
lightning flashed fear in her demands.

Here we are in the glowing light,
its the hour before the dawn,
holding on in our nakedness
she is so soft and warm.

Now maybe the end is sooner
than a man can scarcely blink,
it can be a very scary dreaming
when you first give up the drink.

So I'm calling out to God now,
alone here in the dead of night
writing this poem, afraid to sleep,
please don't turn out the light.

Here I am on the other side,
the other side of midnight,
here I am on the other side,
the other side of midnight.

Baxter's journey from the first moment he gained sobriety seemed to be focused on doing twelve step work. " Having had a spiritual awakening as a result of these steps, we tried to carry this message to alcoholics, and to practise these principles in all our affairs." Initially it was counselling those struggling to beat the booze, then it was those on the street, alcoholics and drug addicts sleeping rough. It was in his Grafton half way house that he struck difficulties with authority and especially the police. He was himself not far removed from those he cared for and administered to. A barefooted guru, shabbily dressed, long hair and untidy beard; the poet of renown, the atheist turned spiritualist, the pacifist and alcoholic. He wanted to let the world know what it was like being outside society.

In the rickety streets of Grafton, where many gather
In a single house. sharing the kai, sharing the pain
    sharing the drug perhaps, sharing the
        paranoia;
Bearded, barefoot or sandalled, coming our crippled
    from the bin or the clink.
(The windows painted black; yet the black paint was
    scraped off again)-
In order that the junkie rock may crack and flown with
    water
And the rainbow of aroma shine on each one's face
Because love is in the look, stronger than lush, and
    truth is in the mouth, better than kai-

How strange, man, to see those spruce and angry ghosts
Suddenly materialise
In an old house in the middle of the morning
When several are eating soup, one is playing the
    guitar, two are talking about nasturtium leaves,
And the others are snoring after an all night party-
Suddenly you see them in the centre of the room,
The servants of the Zombie King-
Skorbul the football player with his brown moustache,
Krubble, who has habit of crushing fingers in doors,
Drooble, who is glad to bang girls' head on walls,
And one or two clean cut eager beagles
Young poltergeists squaring their shoulders, imitating
    the TV hero, hoping for a punch-up -
The fuzz are in the house.

It was necessary of course to invent the fuzz
to fence off the area of civilised coma
From the forces of revolt and lamentation
That rise around it, male and female
Ikons weeping tears of blood.

But every light on the ceiling of the room
In the light of a squad car
And every noise of stopping and acceleration
Grinding on the metal of the road outside
Means for him the fuzz are at there door -
To break the locks, brother,
To tear down the wallpaper,
To empty the cupboards on to the carpet,
Looking for a single roach.

I had been listening and watching Archie Roach singing on NITV when the poem came to me. The shadow of a childhood of my times with my Aboriginal black brothers. It was a painful recall of the good, the bad and the ugly times which seemed to me back then as a small boy to be a normal life, but in hindsight it wasn't.

Listening to Archie Roach

Who can explain
the strain on your face,
knowing the burden
you carry for race,
its like some itching
underneath the skin.

We were just kids back then,
we didn't understand
nature's link to the native man;
learning to throw a boomerang!

Being skilled killing with a spear,
using the woomera!
sending out messages overland
bull roarers singing in the air!

How could we understand
we stood in separate classes,
life was a prism back then,
coloured in rose coloured glasses.

We sat together in class,
there was no black or white
only shades of grey,
we took a caning from the nuns
bound by a code of rugby league.

We were the champion team,
white boy players were the pigs,
black boys had lightning speed,
we won the games and went back to our races.

We kissed the girls in the back row
oblivious to our heroes
on their movie screen,
popcorn and ice cream at interval:

The black boys ate the Jaffas
we rolled to them in the front row,
it was the only place they were allowed to sit,
a little too close to the screen.

It was Slim Dusty who sang on the radio
Dave Sands was the champ of the fighting team,
Jimmy Sharman was beating his boxing drum
and the kids at Burnt Bridge were a stolen generation.

Jimmy Little, like Slim Dusty
was the pride of our nation,
and Archie Roach was...
just a young boy's dream.

We climbed trees for birds nesting
collected our batch,
learnt to blow them
before they could hatch.

We killed lizards for pleasure,
smoked cain when in leisure,
cut cork wood for money,
caught fish when in need.

We were the kids of the drinking,
the dancing of the mind,
the fights and the poverty,
it all just seemed right at the time.

We were just kids,
we didn't understand,
the pride of the working class,
nature's link to the native man.

Mapped lines upon our faces tell
of old folk dead and gone,
children carry on oblivious,
to the life that is now dust.

We no longer have Slim Dusty
singing his travelling songs,
Jimmy Sharman's gone to heaven too,
black boxing troupe tagging along.

Dave Sands just a memory,
Like so many etched in stone,
and those of Burnt Bridge are still crying,
old men not knowing their home.

And the sound of Jimmy little
no longer a glory tune,
and the sound of Jimmy little
no longer a glory tune.

Black eyes are still showing the strain,
tears rising up to as tune,
women are out there dancing
afraid to stay back in the room.

Who can explain
the strain on your face,
knowing the burdens
you carry for race,
its like some itch
underneath the skin,

Listening to Archie Roach
singing the country blues,
Listening to Archie Roach
singing the country blues.

    There was something about the Aboriginal link with the spirit world that I got at an early age. Baxter got it in nature and in an icon of the Virgin Mary, but I seem to get it in both.

Dreamtime.

Awakened to the Dreamtime
wonder in a daze,
called by the love sound cicada
and the far off kookaburra!

Dazed in the sunlight
of where it all began,
telling a dream time tale
of Universe and man.

Viewing the seep of silver sky,
coloured rainbow too,
caught in the serpents fire
and the distant sound of a bird.

Swimming with fish to feel their fear,
sliding with crocodile,
slithering and hissing like a snake,
watching the pale moon rising!

> Dreaming and ancient story
> tribesmen must respect,
> one man's painted dream
> imagined in the telling,
> or playing an instrument!
>
> Feeling the dry earth under my feet,
> hearing the drum in my heart,
> seeing through ancient eyes,
> beginning and end at the start!
>
> Yes! We are the music makers,
> we are the makers of dreams,
> wandering by lone sea breakers,
> sitting by desolate streams.
>
> World losers and world shakers,
> on whom the pale moon gleams,
> we are there movers and shakers
> of the world forever it seems,

Baxter's battle was with authority, secular and state. He did not like any collective that took a view above the status of respect for the the least in the social structure. It did not matter to him if it be priest, police nor educator; James Baxter was a mover and shaker and the son of Archie Baxter. Like his father he was a true pacifist, and did in words what he experienced in deed. He may not have had the leadership capabilities required to be ultimately effective in his cause, but he was a pioneer of getting kids off the street in New Zealand long before any charity or church ventured there. Though they may not have approved of him nor his style in doing so his poem here relates to a fall our with an elderly Catholic priest,

I trapped the great boar,
A Jansenist priest in his lair.
His tusks were longer than the Auckland Harbour Bridge,
his logic pure as the sea foam,
'All men are damned except myself.
The Christly do not have erections.'
The occasion of our dispute was a teen-age chick
To whom I had written a poem.
Though he booted me out of his presbytery
We parted civilly enough.
I asked him for a conditional blessing.

The next was Baxter's fight against the Anglican Church- their moral judgement of others as if humans had no emotions- he summed it all up as - 'Ritualism, fetichism, moralism, simplistic-ism, angel -ism and dualism.' Baxter saw Anglicism as contrary to the message of Jesus asleep in the stable or Mary the dutiful Mother carrying water from the village well. It was to him a course contrary view summing it up as: " when the stables were cleansed of such impurities as anglicism, what was left was one iron crucifix and a thin medal of Our Lady." *

* The Life of James K. Baxter- Frank McKay 1990.

James Baxter had his battle with the press too.

' all day I ploughed with savage oxen
That snorted and farted like runaway tractors.
That was the labour involving the printed rubbish
Plain men use at evening to wrap up fish and oysters.'

Baxter had a fascination with death and most of what he wrote related to local issues of prejudice. In this next poem he vents his anger once again with the law, in this case - a Catholic policeman.:

The bout of Death was a hard one.
He wore a black uniform.
'why don't you cut your hair? 'he asked me.
'Life is filth. I keep the world clean.'
He had come with a pure heart from morning Mass
 For a work-out at the police gymnasium
Before supervising the cleaning of a cell
 That had some blood and vomit on its wall.
We wrestled in a fog of greyness
Till the swastika pin fell out of his shirt.
I was glad when the boss man called off.

Baxter's last poem was written tongue in cheek, as an objection to those who portray the voice of the Pharisees. He voiced this opinion that you may well know them but you don't want to hang around with them or they may well kill you with their views. He was disillusioned with middle class uppity Christian attitudes, with the education system, the institutions and the city of Auckland's down the nose approach to those less fortunate. than themselves.

I said ' Excuse me a minute, there's a Maori friend of mine,
 If he doesn't get a place to crash tonight
The cops will pick him up for the four crimes
They dislike most in Auckland,
Not having a job,
Wearing old clothes,
Having long hair, above all, for being Maori.
When they shift him to the cells in the meat wagon
The last crime might earn him five punches in the gut.
Could any one of you give him a night's lodging?

The sound of the opening and shutting of bankbooks,
The thudding of refrigerator doors,
The ripsaw voices of Glen Eden mothers yelling at their children,
The chugging noise of masturbation from bedrooms of the bourgeoisie,
The voices of dead teachers droning in dead classrooms,
The TV voice of Mr Muldoon,
The farting noise of the trucks that grind their way down Queen Street
Has drowned forever the song of Tangaroa on a thousand beaches,
The sounds of the wind among the green volcanoes,
And the whisper of the human heart.

Boredom is the essence of your death,
I would take a trip to another town
Except that the other towns resemble you exactly.

How can I live in a country where the towns are made like coffins
And the rich are eating the flesh of the poor
without even knowing it?

    Baxter's view of his world was from the bottom up. He like St. Francis viewed the world that way and both did something about it. Francis was not the poet that Baxter was but they both suffered so much for their past folly and whilst Francis took on the image of Christ on the Cross as his icon of the reality of suffering humanity in which he emulated. Baxter, he breathed the Virgin Mary and did this best, despite his defects of character to suffer and to chance for the sake of the less fortunate men and women of his time who like him were plagued with 'unfulfilled desires. living with the burden of a soulful life of isms, living in the main on the street.
    The character of Baxter was as a suffering soul to his very end. Yet he continued to work for those whom he viewed as less fortunate than himself. He was after all an alcoholic and if one can but overlooking his defects as a human, he did his best to live and work as in the dedicated pray of the third step of AA. ' God, I offer myself to Thee- to build with me and do with me as thou wilt…'

    Whilst Baxter's " Ode to Auckland " is one of disillusionment with the middle class uppityness of local disregard for the poor and lost of the street, by contrast my " Assassins" is more a plea for consideration of those in power internationally on behalf of humanity.

The Assassins.

Do you hear the words of the poet,
the music in the stories he tells?
Do you see the signs in the sky now,
how the climate is changing as well?

Do you feel the vibrations of instruments,
the planes that are dropping your bombs?
can you see the mushroom cloud now,
the killing and maiming this done?

Do you listen to raw emotion,
the voice in the wilderness ride?
have you joined in the unit of legions,
feeding on flesh with the carrion crows?

Cease the bombing and killing of children,
in the name of the father of peace,
give up the lying and cheating,
call your Assassins home to rest.

Oh! Hash is the drug of deception
for the killers given the job,
to take out the home of sub culture,
the souls that oppose your mob!

You're moving the souls by the thousands
to the legions of the all seeing eye,
so please change your war of deception,
just let us people try.

Now the poet's run out of writing
his voice has turned to decay,
the words of his songs and his music
somehow they are fading away.

Presidents and Prime Ministers
contemplating the hole in the wall,
praying to the prince of darkness
whilst the elephants still in the room.

Cease the bombing and killing of children
in the name of the father of peace,
give up the lying and cheating
call your assassins home to rest.

Oh! Hash is the drug of deception
for the killers given the job,
to take out the home of sub-culture
the souls that oppose your mob!

DO you take the message of darkness
the neon light bright in your room,
the all seeing eye of providence,
the dollar bills that sing your tune.

Do you see in the eye of God's country
prosperity for the land of the free,
is the message still in the star filled banner,
for justice, freedom and liberty.

Yeah! You've killed Presidents in their efforts
to make a better life for most
and you've killed your fair share
of civil rights men,
Sweet Jesus, just give up their ghost!

Is it the all seeing eye Master,
the architect of the Universe,
who set the deal in motion,
is it the four horseman at work?

Cease the bombing and killing of children
in the name of the Father of peace,
give up the lying and cheating,
call your Assassins home to rest.

Oh! Hash is the drug of deception
for the killers given the job,
to take out the home of sub-culture,
the souls that oppose your mob!

It is my call here to write two closing poems with thoughts of Baxter and my own shadow self will and determination in writing as a template of him in my poetry, my defects of character and my view of life that differ to a large degree to that of the famous and infamous Baxter. AA teaches us to focus on the principles not the personalities of those within our fellowship and those we choose to be of service to. We live within the realm of the twelve steps and twelve tradition of the AA programme.

    Suffice to say in my defence though, that on my view as I have travelled this journey in the shadow self, I have learnt a little more about my own lack of kindness on odd occasions and the ever challenging and changing difficulty of handing over to the God of my own understanding. I trust that I take away from this little work some improvement of my God given talents to use in the service of others as set down in the AA steps and not as a short sighted view of the now for my own benefit. I trust that you dear reader can see your way clear to do likewise.

The Breath of life.

In the beginning was the breath of life
that formed the word of God,
expressing the universal dream
wherein was formed the earth.

It all began with an explosion,
the Word that was made flesh,
forming planetary motion,
cosmic stars of the Universe.

In the dream was formed
both day and night,
The Sun, the Moon, the stars
many planets and Almighty forces.

We understand here on earth,
The Solar System starts near the Sun,
working outward there's the rocky ones
Mercury, Venus, Earth and Mars.

Then comes the enormous outer
mostly filled with gas and core,
they are known as the terrestrial planets,
Jupiter, Saturn, Uranus and Neptune of course.

We could include another one
on a widely tilted course
for its a different orbital path
Pluto goes its own way.

Then if you count 'Planet X,'
right now it's a mathematical guess,
if and when it passes the planetary test,
including Pluto, that makes ten.

Our solar System is vast and wide,
From earth to the naked eye,
Sun, Moon and majestic stars,
by day an night its wonder
to humanity at large.

The earth is home to creatures
minute, large and small,
and the one that's most puzzling,
it's the human form , that's us.

Somewhere in the eons of ages,
God's plan included man,
like the stars we live, we die,
and that's what puzzles us.

The Stars that are once lived,
they are dead in the sky when we see them,
propelling towards earth for millions of years,
though dead they burn like they're living light.

So like the stars we burn for a time,
in the order of the Universe,
we too ultimately die,
but still we wonder why?

In the breath that was first breath
the child form is made in God's likeness,
we grow, we learn, we live and we die,
why the hell were we ever born?

Perhaps it's in God's first breath dream,
we are here to imitate,
use the talents that his Universe gives us
to learn and to create.

Our duty in the scheme of things
to carry on with the God plan ,
to nurture and grow the dream,
and love our fellowman.

In my letting go, I walked the Camino de Santiago for the third time. All that came of it was a book of poetry, and template of my journey overplayed with a sword that pierced my heart. So it was that I journeyed onto the land of my ancestors and once more I discovered things about myself That I never knew until I reached that level of despair, and desperation. I walked that journey near 1200 km in all, at last returning to my home land in Australia. However, before I climbed the last path of my Irish tramping I walked the Wicklow Way, and the thoughts of all that I had achieved in writing poetry-books and songs I lay down there and it was then I came upon the images of the ghost of those great poets and authors of my Irish ancestry.

The Wicklow Way.

It was on the Wicklow trail
I stopped to make a stand,
put down my backpack upon the track
took pen and paper in hand.

The morning t'was bright with sunshine
the air was crisp and clear,
I had no reason for my pensive mood
just let me make that clear.

So I sat on a rock
overlooking the valley below
Glendalough not far away
vacant thoughts began to flow.

My pack was too great a burden
the sun was getting hot,
I could see no reason for my way,
the road was hard enough.

It seemed I'd lost my mojo
had nothing to sing about
so I stopped at the "Wicklow Heather"
for breakfast and a tea.

It was at that place near Glendalough
upon the Wicklow Way,
I'd put down my backpack burden
weary and hungry.

The room was dark and ghost like
so I just ventured on in,
but not before I finished
my breakfast and that tea.

The room was lit with memories
many books there to see,
ghostly photos of past authors
and faded memories.

There was Wilde and Joyce
Kavanagh and Durcan,
O'Casey and Behan
herein their thoughts still rang.

There was Yeats and Synge'
Heaney and many more,
and over in a corner
George Bernard Shaw.

There were so many old books
dusty by the door,
photos of ghost from the past
where memories linger more.

So I stayed with them a while
their words were clinging to me,
but I had to leave regrettably
I was busting for a pee!

Once more on the Wicklow way
I climbed a nearby hill,
gazing down upon the lure
of Glendalaugh's past still.

There I sat upon a rock
dead poets in my mind,
wisdom is written by long gone authors
some to reason, some to rhyme.

Oh! I carry my books for insurance
Cds of songs that I wrote,
singing a line or two of my rhythm
if they fork some lightning.

If you see me tramping on some foreign shore
with a burden on my back
just stop and say "Buen Camino,"
and I'll shout "Buen Camino" right back!

Now I'm happy to sell you a book or a song
to relieve my aching back,
in fact you can have the blooming lot
for just a few Euro at that!

But I won't sell you my back pack,
it carries my sleeping sack
nor the food that I need for my journey ahead,
I won't be selling you that!

158.

CHAPTER 15.

ACKNOWLEDGMENTS.

From the very first mention of James K Baxter's name, by my tramping companions Lorraine and Tony Freeman of Wellington, I was drawn to find out more about him. It did not take long to delve into the man's poetic genius, lectures and plays. As for Baxter the man of many talents- he had been a gloomy youth of dysfunctional behaviour, a sex maniac, academic drop out, odd jobs man, teacher of young children, family man, divorced, uncontrolled alcoholic drop out who founded a community for the rejected of society, an habitual counsellor of alcoholics, a searcher of self perception, an extreme pacifist with an eye always towards truth and personal distinction, religiosity and death. My own life seemed to parallel his in so many ways. So it was after a great deal of soul searching of his life that I concluded to use his life's experience and draw from it a template to write of my own life in his shadow.

I had no intention of writing a book about Baxter, but it has just happened that way. I began with the end in mind so to speak and achieved my desired outcome. So, in my search I have to give due acknowledgment to those from whom I gained the information necessary to achieve my desired aim. In doing so, from the very cover, I thank the work of Joseph Alach, a Yugoslavian born dabbler of hand colouring photographs who came to New Zealand in his youth prior to the Great War. Little is know of Alach's painting type, except to say he was a prolific primitive painter of a naive in natural self taught unsophisticated colour and composition. The only record uncovered of an utterance from Alach is in the Elam Archives of a small typed catalogue from an exhibition at the Grotto Gallery on Queen street : "I think it is the nicest thing in one's life to create something beautiful. I know my pictures are not perfect in any way, but they give me pleasure to paint them, and I hope that they might please someone else." Alach's words I endorse wholeheartedly for I feel the same way in writing books and recording songs of my own making. None are perfect and until recently I never bothered much with editing, typo errors and the like, but rather frantically completed them in the hope that they would at least be done before the good Lord extinguished me. Until lately I have realised it was more out of fear of just leaving a headstone as proof of my existence. In self analysis I realise it as a fear of death without the opportunity of expressing the love and care of my own, my friends and the community. Still, I take some comfort in the lessons of AA and the statement of 'progress not perfection.'

There is no known record of how Alach come to paint a portrait of James Baxter. It is obvious from the nature of Baxter's appearance, long beard and untidy guru like appearance in the painting, that it was done in the painter's old age and the latter day sainthood of the poet. The Portrait of James Baxter as it appears on this book's cover is one of more than 1000 artworks in the University of Auckland's Art Collection. It was gifted presumably by the the artist Joseph Alach to the General Library of the University in 1975 and is now cared for as part of the Art Collection. The cover here is a photo copy of the original that is sometimes dusted and looked up by the staff in the archives of the Art Library.

From the very first Chapter of containing academic knowledge and extremity of research, to the last words of the book, full acknowledgment is given to the due diligence and dedicated works I have read on the Life of James K Baxter by the Fr. Frank McKay SM; John Newton, in his' The Double Rainbow: James K. Baxter, Ngati Hau and the Jerusalem Commune; Elizabeth Beattie's article on the following of the radical poet steps to the Whanganui River; Ros Lewis frank' assessment of Baxter as Rapist and her own youthful nightmare of having lived in the Baxter community. Whilst in truth I am not a great lover of Baxter's poetry, I never the less acknowledge all of his work produced by the Caxton Press from 1944-53 of which I gain much in my research of his works for this book. In truth, I have glossed over many of his poems from all the sources of studies in his writings and publications of Mermaid Press Wellington,1957, Oxford University Press 1958-1969 and the Biographical works, poems and prose of various authors up to and as late as 1982; many of which are uncovered by internet research and as outlined in the content page of this book from The National Library of Australian Catalogues - in publication data: references and quotations from the Autobiography of James K Baxter: Portrait W.H. Oliver 1987, Life of James K Baxter, Frank McKay. 1990. There are references from the Oxford History of New Zealand Literature, articles in Landfall (1960) and NZ Listener (1972) with references to J.E. Weir, Baxters, letters to his mother Millicent from Baxter and various Alcoholics Anonymous Fourth Edition, 2001 references; Twelve Steps and Twelve Traditions, first print 1953 & daily Reflections Alcoholics Anonymous, 1990.

It is from all of the above that I acknowledge as their own material and only used by me in the course of the writing of this book as a means of getting my story across. Where I have directly quoted and overlooked in my acknowledgement here in, please accept that it was unintentional on my part, for they have been used for fair dealing for the purpose of study and research criticism or viewpoint as permitted under copy write as indicated in my content page herein.

The subject matter of James K Baxter for the studies of his work, of self evaluation of his defects of character and honest self appraisal are worthy of follow up by any reader who cares to delve more deeply than I have here…In doing so I suggest the books of J.E. Weir. The Poetry of James K Baxter Wellington: Oxford University Press, 1970, Vincent O' Sullivan's James K Baxter, Wellington: Oxford University Press; 1976, Charles Doyle, James K Baxter. Boston. Twayne Publishers, 1976, Christopher Parr, Introducing James K Baxter. Auckland: Longman Paul, 1983 and WH. Oliver, James K Baxter: A Portrait: Wellington : Port Nicholson Press, 1983. There are no doubt various other authors, copies of interviews, volumes of his poetry and criticism of Baxter not detailed here which may be worthy of scanning for ones own particular bent on the life of a genius who provided much knowledge, suffered for his own defects and gave so much of himself on the way back to the arms of the Virgin Mother of his ultimate obsession. I for one am grateful for having researched his life and having been given the opportunity of writing it and learning something more about my own soulful journey in so doing.

About The Author.

Doug McPhillips, poet, singer, songwriter, author commenced his journey of discovery over a decade ago as a result of life changing experiences.

The many tracks he has treversed in Spain, Ireland, New Zealand and Australia has resulted in novels of myth, legends, folklore and self evaluation for the enjoyment of his readers.

Doug sings and has recorded many of his songs that came to him on his travels. He sings with majestic melody in true Australian style.

Doug has written three books on his Camino Way, a book on One World Government, two books of poetry, an autobiography, travel guide, and one book of Masterful viewpoints. This book is the first on a subject matter of biography.

Doug is an adventurer who divides his time between creative pursuit, love of family, friends & for those who may benefit the most from his efforts and experience.

For a synopsis of all books written by me and albums of my songs, refer to www.caminoway.com.au or purchase on line via international publication at IngramSpark or at your local bookstore.

Any paperback purchased by way of my website will be provided with a free CD of one of my albums. All ISBN numbers for self order are on the website too.

Happy Trails ,

Doug McPhillips

1/09/21 DJM

www.ingramcontent.com/pod-product-compliance
Lightning Source LLC
Chambersburg PA
CBHW070257010526
44107CB00056B/2492